"With frequent references to modern and classical literature, O'Donnell illustrates the ever-present problems and dilemmas of life that Ecclesiastes deals with. But his fresh and relevant style never strays from the biblical text that he so artfully expounds. And he never leaves the various parts of Ecclesiastes alone until he has explored how they testify to the Christ in whom all the riches of wisdom and knowledge are found."

—**Graeme Goldsworthy**, Former Lecturer in Old Testament and Biblical Theology, Moore Theological College, Sydney, Australia

"Douglas O'Donnell's new commentary is a delight to read. Although originally preached (in part) as sermons, this commentary is much more than a series of seventeen well-crafted sermons on the book of Ecclesiastes. These footnoted sermons are based on solid research and spiced with wonderful insights, good humor, striking metaphors, clarifying illustrations and quotations, smooth transitions to Jesus Christ in the New Testament, and relevant applications. This commentary will serve preachers well for one or more series of sermons on Ecclesiastes. It will provide them with many sermon ideas, solid exegesis and applications, illustrations, and quotations from numerous books, songs, and movies. Above all, this commentary, with its God-centered, redemptive-historical approach, clearly shows how one can preach Christ from Ecclesiastes."

—**Sidney Greidanus**, Professor Emeritus of Preaching, Calvin Theological Seminary

"This is a fine commentary because it represents the confluence of, first, a deft exegetical precision in dealing with the words and symmetries of wisdom literature, therefore providing the reader with an unusually rich, polychrome understanding of God's glory amid the dark realities of earthly existence. Second, the book exhibits a masterly tracing of the exalted, Christ-infused, intercanonical connections that will aid the reader in focusing on Christ Jesus, the only answer to an empty life. Third, the author's engaging style—packed with wide-ranging literary references (from the ancients to Woody Allen)—makes for superb reading as well as study. Certainly its resources will be a boon to all students. And fourth, the commentary's application of the grand theme of how believers ought to live the brief span of their lives 'under the sun' will harrow and elevate the heart of every serious reader. This book is a tonic for the soul. Doug O'Donnell's *Ecclesiastes* is a masterwork that will be read for generations to come. It deserves an honored place in the libraries of those who would preach and teach the Word."

—**R. Kent Hughes**, Senior Pastor Emeritus, College Church in Wheaton

"Ecclesiastes is a book for our time: its relentless examination of the source of meaning and relevance finds echoes in every facet of contemporary life and its restless pursuit of happiness. Douglas Sean O'Donnell's treatment of Ecclesiastes is both fresh and thorough. Resolutely committed to exposition, O'Donnell makes these sermons come to life and speak with clarity and conviction. Reading these chapters proves a rich and nourishing experience. A wise pastor and careful exegete takes you to the heart of the gospel in Ecclesiastes again and again. A wonderful achievement."

—**Derek W. H. Thomas**, Professor of Historical and Systematic Theology, Reformed Theological Seminary, Atlanta; Senior Minister, First Presbyterian Church, Columbia, South Carolina; Editorial Director, Alliance of Confessing Evangelicals

"O'Donnell is a gifted preacher and pastor who is passionate about Christ and the gospel. In this engaging exposition, he pastors us by introducing us to "Pastor Solomon" (the author of Ecclesiastes), and though him to Jesus Christ, the greatest pastor of all. He shows how the glorious gospel of Christ shines all the more brightly when set against the depressing backdrop of the book of Ecclesiastes."

—**Barry G. Webb**, Senior Research Fellow Emeritus in Old Testament, Moore College, Sydney, Australia

"Witty, insightful, and exceptionally well researched, Doug O'Donnell's new commentary is one that I enthusiastically recommend. If you're a preacher who is interested in communicating the truth of Ecclesiastes in a fresh way, this is a must-have volume for your library."

—**Scott A. Wenig**, Haddon Robinson Chair of Biblical Preaching, Denver Seminary

Ecclesiastes

Reformed Expository Commentary

A Series

Series Editors

Richard D. Phillips
Philip Graham Ryken

Testament Editors

Iain M. Duguid, Old Testament
Daniel M. Doriani, New Testament

Ecclesiastes

Douglas Sean O'Donnell

P&R PUBLISHING

P.O. BOX 817 • PHILLIPSBURG • NEW JERSEY 08865-0817

© 2014 by Douglas Sean O'Donnell

Unless otherwise indicated, all Scripture quotations are from the ESV® Bible (*The Holy Bible, English Standard Version*®), copyright © 2001 by Crossway, a publishing ministry of Good News Publishers. Used by permission. All rights reserved.

Portions of this commentary also appear in Douglas Sean O'Donnell's *The Beginning and End of Wisdom: Preaching Christ from the First and Last Chapters of Proverbs, Ecclesiastes, and Job* (Wheaton, IL: Crossway, 2011) and are used with the publisher's permission.

THE ORCHARD from Red Bird by Mary Oliver—Published by Beacon Press, Boston. Copyright © 2008 by Mary Oliver. Reprinted by permission of The Charlotte Sheedy Literary Agency Inc.

Italics within Scripture quotations indicate emphasis added.

ISBN: 978-1-59638-398-2 (cloth)
ISBN: 978-1-62995-021-1 (ePub)
ISBN: 978-1-62995-022-8 (Mobi)

Printed in the United States of America

Library of Congress Cataloging-in-Publication Data

O'Donnell, Douglas Sean, 1972-
 Ecclesiastes / Douglas Sean O'Donnell.
  pages cm. -- (Reformed expository commentary)
 Includes bibliographical references and index.
 ISBN 978-1-59638-398-2 (cloth)
 1. Bible. Ecclesiastes--Commentaries. I. Title.
 BS1475.53.O35 2014
 223'.8077--dc23
                              2013042610

To my three daughters—
Lily Ruth, Evelyn Grace, and Charlotte Elise.
May you always fear the Lord by enjoying his blessings.

CONTENTS

Series Introduction   ix

Preface   xiii

1. The *End* of Ecclesiastes: An Introduction (Ecclesiastes 1:1–2)   3

2. Why I Wake Early (Ecclesiastes 1:3–11)   15

3. A Crack in the Window of Wisdom (Ecclesiastes 1:12–18)   31

4. The Hollow House of Hedonism (Ecclesiastes 2:1–11)   42

5. Enjoyment East of Eden (Ecclesiastes 2:12–26)   55

6. The Terrific Truth about Time (Ecclesiastes 3:1–15)   68

7. Sights under the Sun (Ecclesiastes 3:16–22)   81

8. It Is Not Good for the Children of Man to Be Alone
   (Ecclesiastes 4:1–16)   93

9. Sandals Off, Mouth Shut (Ecclesiastes 5:1–7)   107

10. Grievous Evils, Great Joys (Ecclesiastes 5:8–6:9)   120

11. Instructions from the Grave (Ecclesiastes 6:10–7:14)   132

12. Finding the Fear of God in a Crooked World
    (Ecclesiastes 7:15–29)   145

13. Living within the Limits to the Limit (Ecclesiastes 8:1–15)   157

14. What to Know about Knowing Nothing
    (Ecclesiastes 8:16–9:12)   169

Contents

15. Dead Flies, a Serpent's Bite, and Twitter
    (Ecclesiastes 9:13–10:20)   182
16. Before the Evil Days Come (Ecclesiastes 11:1–12:8)   196
17. Repining Restlessness (Ecclesiastes 12:9–14)   210

Select Bibliography   223
Index of Scripture   227
Index of Subjects and Names   241

SERIES INTRODUCTION

In every generation there is a fresh need for the faithful exposition of God's Word in the church. At the same time, the church must constantly do the work of theology: reflecting on the teaching of Scripture, confessing its doctrines of the Christian faith, and applying them to contemporary culture. We believe that these two tasks—the expositional and the theological—are interdependent. Our doctrine must derive from the biblical text, and our understanding of any particular passage of Scripture must arise from the doctrine taught in Scripture as a whole.

We further believe that these interdependent tasks of biblical exposition and theological reflection are best undertaken in the church, and most specifically in the pulpits of the church. This is all the more true since the study of Scripture properly results in doxology and praxis—that is, in praise to God and practical application in the lives of believers. In pursuit of these ends, we are pleased to present the Reformed Expository Commentary as a fresh exposition of Scripture for our generation in the church. We hope and pray that pastors, teachers, Bible study leaders, and many others will find this series to be a faithful, inspiring, and useful resource for the study of God's infallible, inerrant Word.

The Reformed Expository Commentary has four fundamental commitments. First, these commentaries aim to be *biblical*, presenting a comprehensive exposition characterized by careful attention to the details of the text. They are not exegetical commentaries—commenting word by word or even verse by verse—but integrated expositions of whole passages of Scripture. Each commentary will thus present a sequential, systematic treatment of an entire book of the Bible, passage by passage. Second, these commentaries are unashamedly *doctrinal*. We are committed to the Westminster Confession of Faith and Catechisms as containing the system of doctrine taught in the Scriptures of the Old and New Testaments. Each volume will teach, promote, and defend the doctrines of the Reformed faith as they are found in the Bible. Third, these commentaries are *redemptive-historical* in their orientation. We believe in the unity of the Bible and its central message of salvation in Christ. We are thus committed to a Christ-centered view of the Old Testament, in which its characters, events, regulations, and institutions are properly understood as pointing us to Christ and his gospel, as well as giving us examples to follow in living by faith. Fourth, these commentaries are *practical*, applying the text of Scripture to contemporary challenges of life—both public and private—with appropriate illustrations.

The contributors to the Reformed Expository Commentary are all pastor-scholars. As pastor, each author will first present his expositions in the pulpit ministry of his church. This means that these commentaries are rooted in the teaching of Scripture to real people in the church. While aiming to be scholarly, these expositions are not academic. Our intent is to be faithful, clear, and helpful to Christians who possess various levels of biblical and theological training—as should be true in any effective pulpit ministry. Inevitably this means that some issues of academic interest will not be covered. Nevertheless, we aim to achieve a responsible level of scholarship, seeking to promote and model this for pastors and other teachers in the church. Significant exegetical and theological difficulties, along with such historical and cultural background as is relevant to the text, will be treated with care.

We strive for a high standard of enduring excellence. This begins with the selection of the authors, all of whom have proved to be outstanding communicators of God's Word. But this pursuit of excellence is also reflected in a disciplined editorial process. Each volume is edited by both a series editor and a testament editor. The testament editors, Iain Duguid for the Old Testament and Daniel Doriani for the New Testament, are accomplished pastors and respected scholars who have taught at the seminary level. Their job is to ensure that each volume is sufficiently conversant with up-to-date scholarship and is faithful and accurate in its exposition of the text. As series editors, we oversee each volume to ensure its overall quality—including excellence of writing, soundness of teaching, and usefulness in application. Working together as an editorial team, along with the publisher, we are devoted to ensuring that these are the best commentaries that our gifted authors can provide, so that the church will be served with trustworthy and exemplary expositions of God's Word.

It is our goal and prayer that the Reformed Expository Commentary will serve the church by renewing confidence in the clarity and power of Scripture and by upholding the great doctrinal heritage of the Reformed faith. We hope that pastors who read these commentaries will be encouraged in their own expository preaching ministry, which we believe to be the best and most biblical pattern for teaching God's Word in the church. We hope that lay teachers will find these commentaries among the most useful resources they rely on for understanding and presenting the text of the Bible. And we hope that the devotional quality of these studies of Scripture will instruct and inspire each Christian who reads them in joyful, obedient discipleship to Jesus Christ.

May the Lord bless all who read the Reformed Expository Commentary. We commit these volumes to the Lord Jesus Christ, praying that the Holy Spirit will use them for the instruction and edification of the church, with thanksgiving to God the Father for his unceasing faithfulness in building his church through the ministry of his Word.

Richard D. Phillips
Philip Graham Ryken
Series Editors

PREFACE

My original preface began: "My comments are slender and insignificant; but those who have nothing better or who, like me, were once led astray by false glosses can find here an opportunity in their wisdom to become better themselves and to find something better." I then realized that Martin Luther had said precisely the same thing 480 years ago.[1] Alas! There is nothing new under the sun.

On a more serious note, I am thankful to the many excellent commentators who have gone before me and upon whose shoulders I stand. In some sense, the footnotes will show you whose work I found most stable and uplifting; in another sense, if I put a footnote to every thought I have gleaned from another, there would be more footnotes than pages—or, to borrow a Solomonic metaphor, more silver than stone.

The book of Ecclesiastes gets you to think. Have you thought much about death, work, wisdom, time, joy, and fearing God? If not, you will.

These sermons were originally (and in part) preached at New Covenant Church in Naperville, Illinois. I am grateful to the elders for their hearty approval of yet another series on an Old Testament wisdom book and the congregation for their persistent eagerness to hear Christ preached from *all* the Scriptures. I am also grateful for my longtime colleague in the ministry: Pastor Andrew Fulton. Without his steady support, constant encouragement, and prayerful protection, I wouldn't be freed to study, pray, and preach. I am also grateful for my family. This book is dedicated to my three girls—Lily, Evelyn, and Charlotte. After dedicating books to my wife (Emily) and sons (Sean and Simeon), I have finally succumbed to my daughters' constant plea,

---

1. Martin Luther, "Notes on Ecclesiastes," in *Luther's Works*, trans. and ed. Jaroslav Pelikan, 56 vols. (St. Louis: Concordia, 1972), 15:5.

"Daddy, when are you going to dedicate a book to us?" (It was too hard to resist.) Yet this book, my three little ladies, is not merely dedicated to you out of feminine pressure or filial fairness. My sincere hope and prayer is that the sober and celebratory truths of Ecclesiastes would make you wise unto salvation through faith in Jesus Christ.

I also hope this new commentary will be an encouragement to other young preachers to take up, read, study, *and preach* the tough texts of Scripture for the good of the church and the glory of God. Or, as Luther put it:

> I hope that someone endowed with a more abundant spirit and more eminent gifts will come forward to expound and adorn this book as it deserves, to the praise of God and of His creatures. To Him be glory forever through Jesus Christ, our Lord. Amen.[2]

2. Ibid., 15:6.

~ *Ecclesiastes*

ENJOYMENT EAST OF EDEN

1

THE *END* OF ECCLESIASTES: AN INTRODUCTION

Ecclesiastes 1:1–2

The words of the Preacher, the son of David, king in Jerusalem.
Vanity of vanities, says the Preacher, vanity of vanities!
All is vanity. (Eccl. 1:1–2)

How do we read the book of Ecclesiastes?

The first day of my Introduction to Philosophy class at Wheaton College, my professor, Dr. Mark Talbot, nonchalantly declared, "None of you know how to read." The students, all of whom had scored well on exams in order to get into that college, had various expressions—from "how arrogant" to "I'm dropping this class"—written across their unimpressed faces. Yet most of us, by the end of the term, after we had read all the words, sentences, and paragraphs from classic books such as Plato's *Republic*, Hume's *An Inquiry Concerning Human Understanding*, and Augustine's *Confessions*, confessed our inability to *really* read.

Ecclesiastes is a tough read.[1] You know it's a tough read when books that are supposed to help you read it (commentaries) contain sentences such

---

1. It is certainly true of Ecclesiastes, as Westminster Confession of Faith (WCF) 1.8 has it, that "all things in Scripture are not alike plain in themselves, nor alike clear unto all."

as: "This book is one of the more difficult books in all of Scripture, one which no one has ever completely mastered,"[2] and "Two thousand years of interpretation . . . have utterly failed to solve the enigma,"[3] and (my favorite) "Ecclesiastes is a lot like an octopus: just when you think you have all the tentacles under control—that is, you have understood the book—there is one waving about in the air!"[4] And so while I could start this commentary on Ecclesiastes by saying something bold such as "None of you knows how to read it," instead I will start more modestly. I will safely assume that we all need some help, and thus begin at the beginning of wisdom: in awe of God and in need of his divine assistance.

As I have asked for God's wisdom and with a prayerful and long-suffering attitude studied the book, and as I now seek to guide you in our understanding and application of it, I believe the best way to read Ecclesiastes is as (1) God's wisdom literature (2) with a unified message (3) that makes better sense in light of the crucified, risen, and returning Christ.

GOD'S WISDOM LITERATURE

First, we must read Ecclesiastes as *God's wisdom literature*. Note that the first word in that short summary is *God's*. As Christians, we come to this book as believers who are convinced that Ecclesiastes, as peculiar and puzzling as it is at times, is rightly part of the canon of Scripture because it has been uniquely inspired by God.[5] While it shares similarities with other wisdom literature of the world, including Jewish writings (e.g., Sirach and Wisdom of Solomon), it is unique among the wisdom books of the world in that it has Yahweh's breath in and upon and around it. And because of this, it is living and active and can cut us to the core of who we are.

Second, it is wisdom literature. This is its genre. It is not an epistle (like Galatians), a lawbook (like Leviticus), or an apocalyptic revelation (like

---

2. Martin Luther, "Notes on Ecclesiastes," in *Luther's Works*, trans. and ed. Jaroslav Pelikan, 56 vols. (St. Louis: Concordia, 1972), 15:7.

3. R. N. Whybray, *Ecclesiastes*, Old Testament Guides (Sheffield, UK: JSOT Press, 1989), 12.

4. Craig G. Bartholomew, *Ecclesiastes*, Baker Commentary on the Old Testament Wisdom and Psalms (Grand Rapids: Baker Academic, 2009), 13, summarized in Craig G. Bartholomew and Ryan P. O'Dowd, *Old Testament Wisdom Literature: A Theological Introduction* (Downers Grove, IL: InterVarsity Press, 2011), 188. Gregory of Nyssa's analogy of "wrestling in the gymnasium" is good, too! *Gregory of Nyssa: Homilies on Ecclesiastes*, ed. S. G. Hall (Berlin: de Gruyter, 1993), 33.

5. See WCF 1.2 on the canon and 1.8 on inspiration.

Revelation). And as a book of wisdom, it shares characteristics found in Proverbs, Job, and the Song of Songs. There is a plethora of poetry. There are piles of parallelisms (synonymous, antithetic, synthetic, and inverted), as well as many metaphors, similes, hyperboles, alliterations, assonances, and other wonderful wordplays. There might even be onomatopoeia. There are proverbs. There are short narratives with pointed, parable-like endings. There are practical admonitions. There are rhythmic-quality refrains. There are rhetorical questions. There are shared key terms, such as *wisdom, folly,* and *my son.* There are shared concepts, such as *the fear of God.* And as is true of much other biblical wisdom literature, it was written by or about or by *and* about Solomon, the Old Testament's ultimate wisdom sage (1 Kings 4:29–34).[6]

In the Christian canon, the order of the wisdom books is Proverbs, Ecclesiastes, and the Song of Songs. Proverbs begins: "The proverbs of Solomon, son of David, king of Israel" (Prov. 1:1). Ecclesiastes is introduced with: "The words of the Preacher, the son of David, king in Jerusalem" (Eccl. 1:1) = Solomon? The Song starts out: "The Song of Songs, which is Solomon's" (Song 1:1). Regarding Ecclesiastes, because Solomon wrote wisdom literature and was literally a "son of David" as well as a "king in Jerusalem" (Eccl. 1:1; see also 1:12), commentators before the nineteenth century thought Solomon was the author. Yet for various reasons (many legitimate ones),[7] most scholars today shy away from Solomonic authorship.[8] They claim that Ecclesiastes might have been written about Solomon (a fictional autobiography)[9] or in the tradition of Solomon, but probably not by Solomon.

Whatever the truth (who can know for certain and who doesn't eventually get a headache arguing about authorship?), I will call "the Preacher" (as the ESV translates the Hebrew word *Qoheleth*) *Solomon.* I will call him

6. Cf. 1 Kings 3:12; 5:12; 1 Chron. 29:25; 2 Chron. 1:12.

7. For a helpful, short summary of the grounds for non-Solomonic authorship, see Michael V. Fox, *Ecclesiastes*, JPS Bible Commentary (Philadelphia: Jewish Publication Society, 2004), x.

8. What Brevard Childs wrote over three decades ago still well summarizes the situation today: "There is an almost universal consensus, shared by extremely conservative scholars, that Solomon was not the author." *Introduction to the Old Testament as Scripture* (Philadelphia: Fortress, 1979), 582. But a growing number of conservative scholars now think Solomonic authorship probable (e.g., Walter Kaiser, Duane Garrett, Daniel Fredericks, James Bollhagen, and possibly Richard Schultz).

9. It might be that Ecclesiastes is a "royal autobiography," that is, that "the person who calls himself Qoheleth pretends to be Solomon in order to argue that if Solomon cannot find satisfaction and meaning in life in these areas, no one can." Tremper Longman III, *The Book of Ecclesiastes*, New International Commentary on the Old Testament (Grand Rapids: Eerdmans, 1998), 7.

Solomon because I'm not completely convinced by the consensus of modern scholarship,[10] and also because I'm sentimental when it comes to the opinions of the ancient church. Plus, *Solomon* is simpler to say than *Qoheleth*.

In fact, simple, down-to-earth preacher that I am, I will call him not only *Solomon* but also *Pastor Solomon*. I add the title *Pastor* because of the book's pastoral tone, motive, and message and also because the word *Qoheleth* is the Qal feminine singular participle of the verb *qāhal*, which means "to assemble." This verb was used of Solomon when he assembled God's people together for the temple consecration ceremony in 1 Kings 8:1 (cf. 2 Chron. 5:2). The implied setting for Solomon's speech here—the body of the book of Ecclesiastes itself—is that of an assembly or a church (*ekklesia* is the New Testament word for *church*).[11] This is why Phil Ryken writes that Qoheleth or the Assembler is "not so much a teacher in a classroom but more like a pastor in a church. He is preaching wisdom to a gathering of the people of God."[12] Precisely. So *Pastor Solomon* it is. But whoever the original author was (Pastor Solomon, King Qoheleth, Simon the Sage, Ephraim the Editor, or whatever we want to call him)—and whenever he wrote it (tenth century or third century B.C.)—his timeless message is what matters most. We turn to that message next.

A Unified Message

The book of Ecclesiastes can be, and too often has been, read as a noninspired, postexilic Jewish wisdom book that is as unorthodox as it is disjointed. I hold that Ecclesiastes should not be read that way. I find it unlikely, as some estimate, that an editor got hold of the raw material of what we now call *Ecclesiastes* and tried to clean up the contradictions and clear up the

10. For a critique of the consensus, see Duane A. Garrett, *Proverbs, Ecclesiastes, Song of Songs*, New American Commentary 14 (Nashville: Broadman & Holman, 1993), 254–67; and Daniel C. Fredericks, "Ecclesiastes," in Daniel C. Fredericks and Daniel J. Estes, *Ecclesiastes and the Song of Songs*, Apollos Old Testament Commentary 16 (Downers Grove, IL: InterVarsity Press, 2010), 31–36.

11. The ancient Greek (LXX) rendering of *Qoheleth* is *ekklēsiastēs*, from which we get, via the Vulgate (*Liber Ecclesiastes*), the English word for *church* (*ekklesia*). As Jerome notes, "Now the name 'Ecclesiastes' in the Greek language means 'one who assembles the gathering' (that is, the church)." *Commentary on Ecclesiastes*, trans. Richard J. Goodrich and David J. D. Miller, Ancient Christian Writers 66 (New York: Newman, 2012), 33–34.

12. Philip Graham Ryken, *Ecclesiastes: Why Everything Matters*, ed. R. Kent Hughes, Preaching the Word (Wheaton, IL: Crossway, 2010), 16.

confusions by adding a corrective verse here and there as well as tacking on an appropriate theological addendum at the end, and still in the end botched the whole project (i.e., that the canonical book remains slightly unorthodox and disjointed). Rather, the best way to read Ecclesiastes is as God's wisdom literature *with a unified message*.[13] For as we will see in our study of the whole book, there is persistent literary intention and a consistent theological argument to Ecclesiastes.

With that claim and clarification made, it is nevertheless true that if you look at all the separate parts of Ecclesiastes, the book is an enigma. It is confusing. What is meant by saying "the race is not to the swift" (Eccl. 9:11) or by the image "the grinders cease because they are few" (12:3)? Ecclesiastes is also filled with seeming contradictions. How does the maxim "For who knows what is good for man while he lives the few days of his vain life, which he passes like a shadow?" (6:12) fit with the refrainlike call to eat, drink, and find satisfaction in our work? And how does the observation "He who loves money will not be satisfied with money" (5:10) blend with the claim that "money answers everything" (10:19)? Ecclesiastes is like a thousand- piece puzzle taken from the box, thrown on the floor, and kicked around by the kids. But if you discipline the children (sit them in time-out or lock them in some "box of shame," to quote from the marvelous movie *Despicable Me*), quiet the house and your heart, start to lift the scattered pieces from the ground, lay them on a clean table, and slowly, humbly, and prayerfully (as one should always approach God and his Word) piece the pieces together, a clear picture emerges.

The obvious edge pieces are all filled with the unmistakable and undesirable word *vanity*. In Hebrew it is the word *hebel*, which is the same Hebrew spelling as the name of the first man to die, Abel (Gen. 4:8), and it is an example of an onomatopoeic word! As Daniel Fredericks notes: "One must aspirate twice with the initial he-sound, then again with the soft bet, pronounced as '-vel'. So the speaker illustrates what the nature of a breath is simply by saying the word."[14] This word is found thirty-eight times throughout the book, most prominently at the bookends—"Vanity of vanities, says the Preacher, vanity of

---

13. Since we do not know the prehistory of the book, Michael V. Fox's proposal that we read Ecclesiastes as a literary whole makes good sense. "Frame-Narrative and Composition in the Book of Qohelet," *Hebrew Union College Annual* 48 (1977): 83–106. Moreover, I agree with Garrett that the book is "seamlessly joined" because of "literary technique," not later redactions. *Proverbs, Ecclesiastes, Song of Songs*, 263.

14. Fredericks, "Ecclesiastes," 68.

vanities! All is vanity" (Eccl. 1:2; cf. 12:8). This word is translated in various ways, including "temporary," "transitory," "meaningless," "senseless," "futile," "ephemeral," "contingent," "incomprehensible," "incongruous," "absurd," "empty," and more visually as "a striving after wind," "a bubble," "smoke that curls up into the air,"[15] "mist," or "breath"/"mere breath."[16]

Man is like a breath [*hebel*];
    his days are like a passing shadow. (Ps. 144:4)

Behold, you have made my days a few handbreadths,
    and my lifetime is as nothing before you.
Surely all mankind stands as a mere breath [*hebel*]! (Ps. 39:5)

However we are to translate *hebel* (in most contexts, I like "breath" best), listen to a short list of Solomon's long list of mist. What is like your hot breath on a cold day disappearing into the air?

Every effort	Eccl. 1:14; 2:11, 17, 19
Any fruit of our labors	2:15, 21, 26
Pleasure	2:1
Life	3:19; 6:4, 12; 7:15; 9:9
Youth	11:10
Success	4:4
Wealth	4:7–8; 5:10; 6:2
Desire	6:9
Frivolity	7:6
Popularity	4:16; 8:10
Injustice	8:14
All future events	11:8
Everything!	1:2; 12:8[17]

15. See William Ernest Henley, "Of the Nothingness of Things," in *Poems* (London: David Nutt, 1919), 94–97. Jerome suggested "smoky vapor." *Commentary on Ecclesiastes*, 36.

16. For example, Fredericks's translation is " 'Breath of breaths,' said Qoheleth, 'Breath of breaths. Everything is temporary!' " "Ecclesiastes," 65. Robert Alter's is "Merest breath . . . . All is mere breath." Robert Alter, *The Wisdom Books: Job, Proverbs, and Ecclesiastes: A Translation with Commentary* (New York: W. W. Norton & Co., 2010), 346.

17. Fredericks, "Ecclesiastes," 30–31.

Look again at Ecclesiastes 1:2, and let this ash-in-your-mouth, curse-filled concept fill your imagination. It reads, "Vanity of vanities, says the Preacher, vanity of vanities! All is vanity." In Hebrew, as in English, there is a nice wordplay on this superlative genitive: *vanity of vanities* (English) or *hăbēl hăbālîm* (Hebrew). As "the Song of Songs" is the best of all songs, "the God of gods" is the greatest or the only God, and "the heaven of heavens" is the highest heaven, so Solomon sounds this sad and sober message of "vanity of vanities"—everything is utterly futile. Put differently, because of God's curse on creation (the consequences of the fall recorded in Genesis 3:14–19 are assumed throughout),[18] in all our endeavors we cannot find *much* meaning or *sustainable* joy in this world or present age. It's vanity. Vanity. Vanity. Vanity. Vanity. It's all vanity.

These are dark pieces to the puzzle. They constitute the black border that connects to the dark gray pieces of death, injustice, and other bleak realities. And yet like a Rembrandt painting, in which darkness and light play off each other and blend together in seemingly inexplicable ways, those gray pieces of Ecclesiastes do eventually connect with God, who is at the center of the picture and is bright in all his incompressible glory and wisdom.

This God of glory and wisdom is touched, if you will stay with my puzzle analogy, only through the *fear of God*.[19] This is the central concept of biblical wisdom literature, and we will explore its meaning and significance in the chapters to come. For now, I'll summarize this central concept as *trembling trust*. Those who, in the midst of all the hard truths and awful troubles of this fallen world, come before the Lord with trembling trust are given by him the gift of grateful obedience, steady contentment, and surprising joy.[20] The puzzle of Ecclesiastes includes the black border, the seemingly random gray pieces, the white, bright center, *and* the multicolored blessings given to those who have given

18. As Barry G. Webb summarizes: Vanity "is not simply a brute fact, something which happens to be there without cause or explanation. It is a judgment, a condition, imposed on the world, and on human beings in particular, by God. It is a manifestation of the fall and, positively, of God's rule as creator and judge." *Five Festal Garments: Christian Reflections on the Song of Songs, Ruth, Lamentations, Ecclesiastes, and Esther*, New Studies in Biblical Theology 10 (Downers Grove, IL: InterVarsity Press, 2000), 104.

19. Eccl. 3:14; 5:7; 7:18; 8:12–13; 12:13.

20. Eccl. 2:24; 3:12–13, 22; 5:18; 8:15; 9:7–9; 11:9–12:7.

themselves to God. "The fear of God . . . is not only the beginning of wisdom; it is also the beginning of . . . purposeful life."[21]

In order to arrive at the picture above, I have taken key words—such as *vanity* (thirty-eight times), *wise/wisdom* (fifty-three times), *God* (forty times), *toil* (thirty-three times), *give/gives/given* (sixteen times), *death* (mentioned or alluded to twenty-one times), *sun*, as in "under the sun" (thirty-three times), and *joy* and derivatives such as *rejoice, enjoy, enjoys, enjoyed,* and *enjoyment* (seventeen times)—as well as key themes such as *God and man, futility and fleetingness, time and chance, gain and portion, work and toil, wealth and poverty, power and domination, wisdom and folly, justice and judgment, eating, drinking, and pleasure*[22]—and attempted to show you what Ecclesiastes looks like. It might be better, however, to simply state what the unified message is.

Three authors on Ecclesiastes have summarized the book as follows. (These are the three best I have found.) Michael Eaton claims that Ecclesiastes "defends the life of faith in a generous God by pointing to the grimness of the alternative."[23] Jeffrey Meyers says that "true wisdom" that Ecclesiastes offers us "is to fear God and keep his commandments, to receive and use the gifts of God with joy and gratitude."[24] And Sidney Greidanus writes this excellent summary admonition: "Fear God in order to turn a vain, empty life into a meaningful life which will enjoy God's gifts."[25]

Another way to get at the unified message is to answer the key questions raised by Pastor Solomon. The first key question is the one raised in Ecclesiastes 1:3, "What does man gain by all the toil at which he toils under the sun?" The implied answer is "nothing." Death makes all human work and wisdom and wealth and pleasure "vain." From a mere observation of this world and its workings, human work, wisdom, wealth, and pleasure appear to be of no eternal value or significance.

21. Michael A. Eaton, *Ecclesiastes: An Introduction and Commentary*, Tyndale Old Testament Commentaries 16 (Downers Grove, IL: InterVarsity Press, 1983), 48.

22. See Thomas Krüger, *Qoheleth*, ed. Klaus Baltzer, trans. O. C. Dean Jr., Hermeneia (Minneapolis: Fortress, 2004), 1–5. I added "justice and judgment."

23. Eaton, *Ecclesiastes*, 44.

24. Jeffrey Meyers, *A Table in the Mist: Meditations on Ecclesiastes*, Through New Eyes Bible Commentary (Monroe, LA: Athanasius Press, 2006), 17.

25. Sidney Greidanus, *Preaching Christ from Ecclesiastes: Foundations for Expository Sermons* (Grand Rapids: Eerdmans, 2010), 22.

The second key question follows that blunt and realistic reality: "In light of such vanity—the fact that our work and knowledge and pleasures and possessions are ultimately made futile by death—how, then, should we live this temporary life under the sun?" The answer to that riddle is simple. We are to live our earthly lives by abandoning human "illusions of self-importance" and "all pretense of pride" and by embracing divine wisdom.[26] This is done, according to Ecclesiastes, by trusting the Lord and doing what he says: "[This is] the end of the matter; all has been heard. Fear God and keep his commandments, for this is the whole duty of man" (Eccl. 12:13). Obedient trust—that is the *end* (or goal) of Ecclesiastes.

IN LIGHT OF THE CRUCIFIED, RISEN, AND RETURNING CHRIST

That might be the end of Ecclesiastes (its goal and its conclusion), but it is not the end (the conclusion) of God's story of salvation. When the last chapter of Ecclesiastes was completed, hundreds of chapters in God's inspired book were yet to be written. Soon Ezra and Jeremiah, as well as Peter and Paul and all the others, would pick up their pens and add their voices to the divine drama ultimately fulfilled in Jesus.

While Ecclesiastes contains no obvious messianic prophecy or promise, and while the New Testament rarely quotes from or alludes to the book, my ultimate concern as a Christian preacher is to preach the words of "the Preacher" in light of the words and works of the Word incarnate. This is not a concern or commission laid upon me by my local church or the denomination in which I am ordained, but by Jesus himself. Our Lord taught us to read our Old Testaments with him in mind—"everything written about *me* in the Law of Moses and the Prophets and the Psalms" (Luke 24:44). Even "the Psalms" (or "the Writings"), which includes Ecclesiastes, bear witness to him (John 5:39) and can "make [us] *wise* for salvation" (2 Tim. 3:15). So woe to me if I teach through Ecclesiastes as though Jesus had never touched his feet on this vain earth!

Derek Kidner writes that one way to read Ecclesiastes is to see "the shafts of light" (i.e., the call-to-joy refrain) and "the author's own position and

26. Garrett, *Proverbs, Ecclesiastes, Song of Songs*, 278.

conclusions" to get to the purpose of the book.[27] To that helpful reading strategy, we may add that if we read the book *through* the lens of Jesus Christ—the true embodiment of wisdom who has crushed the curse of death on the cross, brought hope through his resurrection, and will bring justice at his return—we actually understand the book better. Put simply, the best way to read Ecclesiastes, as we have noted, is as (1) God's wisdom literature (2) with a unified message (3) *that makes better (but not perfect) sense in light of the crucified, risen, and returning Christ.*

Earlier, I painted the picture of Ecclesiastes—with its black border, shades of gray, and white, bright center. There is another image of Ecclesiastes that I have found tremendously helpful in reading the whole book. It is the banner that Marge Gieser made for the original book jacket for Phil Ryken's commentary on Ecclesiastes, which is aptly and cleverly titled *Why Everything Matters.* The banner has three colors—black, gold, and red. In the black section, which takes up the bottom third of the banner, are words such as *meaningless, wearisome, twisted, toil, nothing, grievous, madness,* and *folly.* Those words are in gold. Above the black section is a red section, also with words, such as *pleasure, contentment, abundance,* and *joy.* Those are also written in gold. The black and red sections are divided by a slanted, slightly off-center gold cross that is faintly lifted above the rest of the fabric. About the design Gieser wrote:

> Words such as meaningless, wearisome, . . . folly, etc., cover the background of the banner, describing life as it really is. Life without God is futile. But for the believer, redeemed by the blood of Christ, life takes on meaning, and there is hope for all of life's tough questions.
>
> The colors included in the banner all have a meaning. Black symbolizes life lived in struggle and confusion with no hope; the gold of the cross that cuts through the entire design symbolizes the redeeming work of Christ, who intercedes for us at the right hand of the Father in Heaven; the red background at the top of the design stands for Christ's blood shed for us, offering us a hopeful and eternal worldview.[28]

Jesus Christ redeemed us from the vanity that Pastor Solomon so wrestled with and suffered under by subjecting himself to our temporary, meaningless,

---

27. Derek Kidner, *The Wisdom of Proverbs, Job and Ecclesiastes: An Introduction to Wisdom Literature* (Downers Grove, IL: InterVarsity Press, 1985), 93.

28. See "About the Book Jacket," in Ryken, *Ecclesiastes,* 319.

futile, incomprehensible, incongruous, absurd, smoke-curling-up-into-the-air, mere-breath, vain life. He was born under the sun. He toiled under the sun. He suffered under the sun. He died under the sun. But in his subjection to the curse of death by his own death on the cross, this Son of God "redeemed us from the curse" (Gal. 3:13). By his resurrection, he restored meaning to our toil. And by his return, he will exact every injustice and elucidate every absurdity as he ushers those who fear the Lord into the glorious presence of our all-wise, never-completely-comprehensible God.

LOVE AND DEATH . . . AND GOD!

In Woody Allen's comedy *Love and Death*, Allen's character, Boris, and Diane Keaton's character, Sonia, have the following exchange:

Boris: Sonia, what if there is no God?
Sonia: Boris Demitrovich, are you joking?
Boris: What if we're just a bunch of absurd people who are running around with no rhyme or reason.
Sonia: But if there is no God, then life has no meaning. Why go on living? Why not just commit suicide?
Boris: Well, let's not get hysterical; I could be wrong. I'd hate to blow my brains out and then read in the papers they'd found something.[29]

In the small book of Ecclesiastes we will discover (it's quite the finding!) a great God who brings rock-solid meaning to everything under the sun by means of his Son. We will discover that he brings meaning to our work, learning, possessions, and pleasures. We will discover that he will bring meaning even to the world's accidents, injustices, oppressions, absurdities, and evils.

And so our quest begins!

---

29. Woody Allen, quoted in Thomas V. Morris, *Making Sense of It All: Pascal and the Meaning of Life* (Grand Rapids: Eerdmans, 1993), 51.

2

WHY I WAKE EARLY[1]

Ecclesiastes 1:3—11

What does man gain by all the toil at which he toils
under the sun? (Eccl. 1:3)

I have something to confess. I am addicted to reading modern poetry. Pray for me. I will also admit that since doing the research for my book *The Beginning and End of Wisdom*, I have been obsessed with finding and collecting illustrations for Ecclesiastes sermons from modern poems. I will give you two now, and maybe forty later. The poet Billy Collins, in his poem "Forgetfulness," begins by bemoaning the frailty of the human memory as ironically illustrated by the longevity of a writer's work:

> The name of the author is the first to go
> followed obediently by the title, the plot,
> the heartbreaking conclusion, the entire novel
> which suddenly becomes one you have never read, never
>   even heard of . . . .[2]

The second example comes from the poet Mary Oliver. In her poem "The Orchard," she writes:

---

1. The chapter title is borrowed from the title of one of Mary Oliver's poems and books: *Why I Wake Early: New Poems* (Boston: Beacon, 2005).
2. Billy Collins, *Sailing around the Room: New and Selected Poems* (New York: Random House, 2001), 29.

I have dreamed
of accomplishment.
I have fed

ambition.
I have traded
nights of sleep

for a length of work.
Lo, and I have discovered
how soft bloom

turns to green fruit
which turns to sweet fruit.
Lo, and I have discovered

all winds blow cold
at last,
and the leaves,

so pretty, so many,
vanish
in the great, black

packet of time,
in the great, black
packet of ambition,

and the ripeness
of the apple
is its downfall.[3]

The book of Ecclesiastes is a God-inspired look into what Mary Oliver called "the great, black packet of time . . . [and] of ambition." It examines how "the ripeness of the apple is its downfall." That is, it shows us the futility of our work in this world, even our most fruitful work. Like an apple that

3. Mary Oliver, *Red Bird* (Boston: Beacon Press, 2008), 20–21.

16

ripens only to fall to the ground and decay, so our work eventually comes to nothing. This is what "the Preacher, the son of David, king in Jerusalem" (Eccl. 1:1)—whom I'm calling *Pastor Solomon*—saw many years ago, and what we will see now in our exploration of Ecclesiastes 1:3–11.

OUR WORK: ITS MAJOR VANITIES

We begin with Ecclesiastes 1:3. After the abrupt (and I imagine loud!) opening cry, "Vanity of vanities, . . . vanity of vanities! All is vanity" (1:2), we come to the key question, "What does man gain by all the toil at which he toils under the sun?" (1:3; cf. 3:9; 5:16; 6:8, 11).

Allow me three brief observations about this question. First, the word *man* is the word *adam* in Hebrew. Just as the word *vanity* (*hebel*) is the same word as *Abel* (*hebel*) in Hebrew, so the word *adam* leads us back to Genesis and reminds us that the fall of *Adam* is never far from Pastor Solomon's mind.

Second, the repetition of the word *toil*—"all the toil at which he toils"—reminds us of Adam's curse. God said to Adam:

Cursed is the ground because of you;
   in pain you shall eat of it all the days of your life;
thorns and thistles it shall bring forth for you;
   and you shall eat the plants of the field.
By the sweat of your face
   you shall eat bread,
till you return to the ground,
   for out of it you were taken;
for you are dust,
   and to dust you shall return. (Gen. 3:17b–19)

Third, the phrase "under the sun" (used twice in our text and twenty-eight times in the book, synonymous with the expressions "under the heavens" and "on earth") draws a geographical line between God, who is "in heaven," and man, who lives "on earth" (Eccl. 5:2; cf. Matt. 6:9), and also a theological one. This phrase designates not the secular life (life without reference to God) but the fallen world that both the secular and nonsecular share as sinners under God's curse—his faithful carrying out of his promised punishment to Adam. What is found on earth—the thorn and thistle-infested

17

ground, our sun-soaked sweaty toil of the ground, our bodies dying and returning to the ground—is not found with God in heaven. We are "under the sun"; he is above it.

So when Pastor Solomon asks his question ("What does man gain by all the toil at which he toils under the sun?" Eccl. 1:3), it is a curse-filled question, one that has already been answered by that sober superlative—"Vanity of vanities, . . . all is vanity!" (v. 2). It is also one that will be further answered pessimistically in verses 4–11,[4] to which we next turn.

Nothing New

Like an overcritical building inspector, in Ecclesiastes 1:4–11 Pastor Solomon shows us what is wrong with our work. Later, he will point out what I call "minor problems"—that our willingness to work often comes from impure motives such as envy (4:4); that our work, if profitable, often leads to sleepless nights (5:12; cf. 2:23); and that all the wealth from our work must be bequeathed to someone who doesn't deserve it and might foolishly squander it (2:18–19). The two major problems in our construct, however, he addresses in verses 4–11.

The first major problem is that our work adds *nothing new* to this world.

> What has been is what will be,
>   and what has been done is what will be done,
>   and there is nothing new under the sun.
> Is there a thing of which it is said,
>   "See, this is new"?
> It has been already
>   in the ages before us. (Eccl. 1:9–10)

We might balk at this strongly pessimistic view. In fact, we might instead boast of how "new and improved" everything is. This is the information age! The day of discovery! The time of technology! Yet I doubt that we would balk or boast if our perspective were appropriately shaped by Solomon's two important insights about our work.

---

4. Later, Pastor Solomon admits that there are some natural advantages and God-given rewards for working wisely and industriously (e.g., Eccl. 2:13; 3:13, 22; 5:18; 7:11–12; 10:10). In 1:3–11, the picture is only pessimistic.

The wisdom literature of the Bible most often deals with general realities. The book of Job is different, as is Psalm 73. Such texts speak of the exceptions to the rule. But in general, the wicked are punished and the righteous prosper. In general, sloth leads to poverty and adultery to discord. Thus, in general, most of our work is not new.

Think of it this way. Thousands of people today still labor with their hands, doing work similar to what was done thousands of years ago. There is not much difference between the guy who dug ditches in Jerusalem in 942 B.C. and the guy who digs them today for Shanghai's sewer and sanitation department. As for those who do not work with their hands, even if they are part of the new division of a new company selling a new product that was newly invented, what they actually do isn't so new: an owner is still an owner, a manufacturer is still a manufacturer, and a salesman is still a salesman. The computer salesman who sells the latest gadget follows in the same line of work as the Spanish merchant 550 years ago who sold the newest silk from the Far East. The newest is relative to the age in which we live. But when viewed against the backdrop of human history, the novelty fades.

In Ecclesiastes 1:4–8, Solomon describes this unoriginality and repetitiveness of our activities in comparison with the earth's circularity and in contrast with its stability:

A generation goes, and a generation comes,
　　but the earth remains forever.
The sun rises, and the sun goes down,
　　and hastens to the place where it rises.
The wind blows to the south
　　and goes around to the north;
around and around goes the wind,
　　and on its circuits the wind returns.
All streams run to the sea,
　　but the sea is not full;
to the place where the streams flow,
　　there they flow again.
All things are full of weariness;
　　a man cannot utter it;
the eye is not satisfied with seeing,
　　nor the ear filled with hearing.

Here Solomon illustrates the weariness of our work—what is uninspiring to the eye and humdrum to the ear, as well as too wearisome for words (Eccl. 1:8)—with the sun, the wind, and the streams. These hardworking forces all seem to be quite busy doing something *new* each and every day. But a closer look will show their motion-filled monotony.

First we have the sun. The sun rises and sets—over and over and over again, same old, same old. It never gets anywhere. It never does anything new. It is still a big old ball of hot gas seemingly doing perpetual somersaults around the earth. It is exhausting even to think about. Then we have the wind, the second example of "the dreary rhythm of ceaseless activity."[5] One day the wind blows south, and then the next day that same wind journeys north. What a lot of commotion for so little consequence. What a lot of hot air! It appears that this wind is getting somewhere, when in reality it is just moving in an endless circle.[6] Finally, we have the streams and rivers. How is it that the Mississippi River can flow into the Gulf of Mexico and then into the Atlantic Ocean, but that ocean never overflows or gets any deeper? The mighty Mississippi works exhaustively, pushing its waters south every second of every day. But what does it accomplish? What can we see? It does not even affect the ocean's water level. We know about the precipitation and evaporation process (as even the wisdom literature notes, Job 36:27–28), but to the naked eye, where does all the water go? It is especially amazing in Solomon's context; perhaps he is thinking of the Dead Sea. The Jordan River incessantly empties into the Dead Sea (from which no river flows out), and yet this sea is "not full" (Eccl. 1:7).

Do you see what the Preacher is saying? The work of the sun, wind, and waters is like our work on the earth. We think we are making such a difference, but the irony (the sad reality of the curse) is that the earth remains and we die: "A generation goes, and a generation comes, but the earth" sticks around forever, or so it seems (Eccl. 1:4). Jerome put it this way: "What is more a vanity of vanities than the fact that the earth endures, although it

<hr />

5. Walter C. Kaiser, *Ecclesiastes: Total Life*, Everyman's Bible Commentary (Chicago: Moody, 1979), 51.

6. Robert Alter's translation of Ecclesiastes 1:6 expresses this well: "It goes to the south and swings around to the north, round and round goes the wind, and on its rounds the wind returns." *The Wisdom Books: Job, Proverbs, and Ecclesiastes: A Translation with Commentary* (New York: W. W. Norton & Co., 2010), 346.

was made for the benefit of man, while man himself, the master of the earth, suddenly crumbles into dust?"[7]

Nothing Remembered

The first major problem with our work is that there is nothing significantly or substantially new. The second major problem is that our work will not be remembered. Nothing new, *nothing remembered*. Look at the last verse of our text: "There is no *remembrance* of former things, nor will there be any *remembrance* of later things yet to be among those who come after" (Eccl. 1:11).

Again we are dealing with generalizations. Daniel Fredericks summarizes the situation:

> History notes and respects the efforts of an infinitesimally small fraction of the earth's inhabitants, and the intensities of even these legacies are evanescent, fading with every passing year. Anyone who sees their eternal significance referred to in their journals and diaries or autobiographies has not sat at the feet of Qoheleth. Any artist, ruler, entrepreneur, hero, scientist or theologian who aspires to be read about in a "Who's Who" should understand that their innovations, awards, writings, or whatever feats that are honoured now, will be assessed in the new earth much more modestly compared to the pomp with which they were first celebrated.[8]

So while every generation might remember the work of David, Isaiah, or Paul, as well as Aristotle, Shakespeare, or Mozart, how will other famous people fare? For example, what about Elvis Presley, Muhammad Ali, John F. Kennedy, and Walt Disney? These men made a recent list of the top ten most famous people of all time. How well will they be remembered a century from now? Or consider John Lennon, who said that he and his band were "more popular than Jesus." In 1966, at the height of Beatlemania, Lennon made this prediction: "Christianity will go . . . . It will vanish and shrink. I needn't argue with that; I'm right and I will be proved right. We're

---

7. Jerome, *Commentary on Ecclesiastes*, trans. Richard J. Goodrich and David J. Miller, Ancient Christian Writers 66 (New York: Newman, 2012), 36.

8. Daniel C. Fredericks, "Ecclesiastes," in Daniel C. Fredericks and Daniel J. Estes, *Ecclesiastes and the Song of Songs*, Apollos Old Testament Commentary 16 (Downers Grove, IL: InterVarsity Press, 2010), 106.

more popular than Jesus now; I don't know which will go first—rock and roll or Christianity."[9]

Well, John, I can tell you which will go first. Imagine there's no Beatles; it's easy if you try! Just ask children today to name "the Fab Four." Just name them. With two of these superstars still alive and touring—coming to a city near you—there should be no excuse if our six-year-olds, twelve-year-olds, or eighteen-year-olds don't know the names of the Beatles. But they probably don't. Or if they do, just wait a few years—maybe 20 or 120—and soon the memory of even the Beatles will be as dead and buried as George and John. The black-and-white silhouettes of these four extraordinarily famous men will soon be relics in a time capsule buried deep in the Liverpool soil.

Today's celebrities are tomorrow's obituaries, and their names are as disposable as the morning paper in which their life stories will be printed. And if that is what becomes of our celebrities, what will become of us?

A few years ago, I went back to my high school to play in an alumni basketball game. I was "the star" back in the day. Yet when I returned to play in this game (a mere fifteen years after my graduation), almost nobody recognized my face or name. The alumni team I was on, which had players mostly ten years older or younger than I, didn't know me. I was so frustrated that I wanted to pull out the record book, point to my name, and say, "Hey, that's me." But then I looked at the record book and saw that my name had been relegated to the bottom of a few long lists. Someone had broken every glorious record that I had once held. How tragic! I had worked so hard back then, only to be forgotten now. What a waste. What vanity. My fame was as short (and embarrassing) as an air ball. To add irony to this tragedy, my high school was closed and then leveled shortly after the alumni game.

Have you ever had that kind of realistic look in the mirror? It is not a pleasant thing to do or see, for we all want to be remembered. This "need" makes us call our friends and relatives when our name or our picture makes the paper. It attracts us to social media, where our face and our story and even our deepest thoughts can be shared. It is also this need, so twisted and distorted, that makes people do the most banal things on the most banal reality TV shows. In part, it is also what makes a deranged teenager walk into his school and open fire on his own classmates—the need to be remembered.

9. From Lennon's famous interview with Maureen Cleave of the London *Evening Standard* on March 4, 1966.

But what does it all matter? That is what Pastor Solomon is getting us to think about. There is one problem with our need to be known and remembered. That problem is death.[10] "And therefore never send to know for whom the *bell* tolls; it tolls for *thee*."[11] Death stands, almost boastingly, at the end of the corridor of our lives. And death doesn't play favorites. It takes everyone's solid labors and vaporizes them.

Just think about it. Think seriously, soberly, and realistically about it. What good is work? What good is ambition? What good is fame? We must admit that the history of the world appears to be a mass of men and women living, working, and dying—punching in and punching out of this life. Each weekday, as the sun lifts its head over the horizon, we peek out over the bedsheets, hit the alarm, wash and feed our bodies, and then spend the remainder of our day working. But working for what? Will we ever be remembered?

> Naked a man comes from his mother's womb, and as he comes, so he departs. He takes nothing from his labor that he can carry in his hand. . . . As a man comes, so he departs, and what does he gain, since he toils for the wind? (Eccl. 5:15–16 NIV)

As the hourglass of human history is turned over, all our accomplishments are slowly buried by the sands of time. All our laborious labors—they are nothing new, nothing that will be remembered. Ah, the tragedy of time and death. Time and death. Time—and death. Time. And. Death.

OUR WORK: LABOR IN THE LORD IS *NOT* IN VAIN

What are we to do about the tick and tock of time over our heads and the trapdoor of death beneath our feet? Shall we try to escape? Give up? Party? These are three widespread ways in which people deal with this meaninglessness of which Solomon writes: escapism, nihilism, and hedonism. In later chapters, I will exegete texts related to these three themes—for example, Ecclesiastes 2:3; 4:5; 6:7. For now, I will merely illustrate them.

10. Death is named or alluded to twenty-one times in the book: 3:2, 19–22; 4:2–3; 6:3, 12; 7:1–2; 8:8, 10; 9:3–5, 10; cf. 1:4, 11; 2:14–18, 20–21; 4:16; 5:15–16, 20; 7:14; 8:13; 11:8; 12:1–7.

11. From Meditation 17 of John Donne's *Devotions upon Emergent Occasions*, ed. Anthony Raspa (New York: Oxford University Press, 1987), 87.

The Escapist

I have an open invitation to watch Notre Dame football at a neighbor's house. I enjoy college football, the Fighting Irish, and my neighbor and his friends. But I was struck the first time I attended by the fact that six sensible, well-educated, reasonably successful men could gather together and spend a whole afternoon watching and talking only about the game and the games—as we switched from channel to channel, from football to baseball to golf. The most interesting and probing question that anyone asked all afternoon was about Wake Forest's team name, Demon Deacons. "Is the school religiously affiliated?" someone asked. The answer—via cellphone technology—came quickly: "Yes, Baptist." The word *Baptist* was the closest we got to talking about the meaning of life.

Perhaps I should have taken that opportunity to grab the remote, hit MUTE, stand up, and ask, "So, guys, what kind of work do you do? And does it ever bother you that it won't last forever?" I had no such courage. But can you imagine if I had? Such unorthodox behavior might have started a good conversation—or, more likely, a barrage of secret text messages: "Who *is* this guy?" "Please don't invite him again." "Oh, and pass the chips."

Some people—normal "good" people (your neighbors and mine)—deal with the bleak reality that Ecclesiastes addresses through *escapism*—not through drugs or alcohol or sex (although some do that), but through watching the game, going to work, playing with the kids, loving the wife, taking the family vacation, and then watching the game, watching the game, watching the game. Escapism.

The Nihilist

Others are more philosophical about life. They have attempted a staredown with time and death, and lost; thus, they have come to the end of themselves. The esteemed Russian novelist Leo Tolstoy was one such person. Despite having written two of the world's greatest works, *War and Peace* and *Anna Karenina*, he considered his life to be a meaningless, regrettable failure. In his book *A Confession*, he wrote:

> My question—that which at the age of fifty brought me to the verge of suicide—was the simplest of questions, lying in the soul of every man . . . a question without an answer to which one cannot live. It was: "What will

come of what I am doing today or tomorrow? What will come of my whole life? Why should I live, why wish for anything, or do anything?" It can also be expressed thus: Is there any meaning in my life that the inevitable death awaiting me does not destroy?[12]

Tolstoy is asking the same question that Pastor Solomon asked, in updated form.

Listen also to Jean-Paul Sartre, the French existentialist philosopher. Sartre was also a novelist and far more depressing than Tolstoy. We might call him nihilistic (*nihil* in Latin means "nothing," as in *ex nihilo*, "out of nothing"). Nihilism teaches that life has no objective meaning or intrinsic value. This is the soil from which postmodern thinking has grown. In his novel *La Nausée* ("Nausea"—an uplifting title indeed!), Sartre writes:

> It was true, I had always realized it—I hadn't any "right" to exist at all. I had appeared by chance, I existed like a stone, a plant, a microbe. I could feel nothing to myself but an inconsequential buzzing. I was thinking . . . that here we are eating and drinking, to preserve our precious existence, and that there's nothing, nothing, absolutely no reason for existing.[13]

These are depressing, hopeless answers. But apart from God, they are also realistic answers. Why continue on if life is meaningless? Why bask in the summer sunlight if you're just a leaf that will soon fall from a tree, only to be raked up and burned?

The Hedonist

Most people are not honest enough to come to the nihilist position. This explains why the philosophy department will always be smaller than the business/economics department. It is also why, instead of becoming nihilistic, most people become hedonistic. They live for pleasure as the ultimate pursuit. Their slogan is "Let us eat and drink, for tomorrow we die" (Isa. 22:13; 1 Cor. 15:32). We know we are dying, so let's live life for all it's got. Peggy Lee's famous refrain about breaking out the booze and having a

---

12. Leo Tolstoy, quoted in Timothy Keller, *The Reason for God: Belief in an Age of Skepticism* (New York: Dutton, 2008), 201.

13. Jean-Paul Sartre, quoted in ibid., 127.

ball still resounds today.[14] Just pick up an issue of *People* magazine, as I did one day while waiting for an oil change, and you will see this lifestyle in living color. Or take an hour to read another French philosopher's short and witty novel—Voltaire's *Candide*—which I did after the oil change. Candide allegedly lives in the "best of all worlds," yet he experiences one senseless and random suffering after another until finally he abandons the view of his upbringing and embraces hedonism. He decides that since "we can't know the whys and wherefores of what happens in this world," we should just do our "very best to enjoy it while [we] can."[15]

We will examine hedonism further in Ecclesiastes 2:1–11. Stay tuned for that sorry show.

Gospel Glasses

Escapism, nihilism, and hedonism—these are three prevalent answers offered by our world to Ecclesiastes' questions. Thankfully, the Bible directs us to a vastly different resolution. While God's Word certainly shows us the circular nature of our existence, it also moves us forward in a linear, hopeful direction. Although our text does conclude that the answer to the question "What do we gain from all the toil at which we toil under the sun?" is "Nothing," it does not offer this same bleak conclusion to the question "In light of such vanity—that time and death makes all human work 'vain'—how, then, should we live this temporary life under the sun?" The answer to the second question is not "Nothing," but "Something," something very wonderful. In Pastor Solomon's sermon, this is the answer (and we will soon hear it): abandon human wisdom, embrace divine wisdom, and then receive all the good things of this life as a gift from God. In the words of Jesus, the greater Solomon, the answer is this: "Seek first the kingdom of God . . . , and all these things will be added" (Matt. 6:33).

Having contemplated what the tyranny of time does to our work—nothing new, nothing remembered—we turn now to "consider the work of God" (Eccl. 7:13; see also 8:17; 11:5), most notably the work of God in Jesus Christ.

---

14. Jerry Leiber and Mike Stoller, "Is That All There Is?," available on Peggy Lee, *All-Time Greatest Hits*, vol. 1, Curb Records D2–77379 (compact disc).

15. Voltaire's *Candide*, as summarized by Bart D. Ehrman, *God's Problem: How the Bible Fails to Answer Our Most Important Question—Why We Suffer* (New York: HarperOne, 2008), 11–12.

If we put on gospel glasses and look at Ecclesiastes 1:3–11 again, we see clearly how what we have in God's Son transforms a world shrouded in hopeless blackness into a garden of beautiful and brilliant light—or, to change the metaphor, how it changes a buried seed into a budding flower.

Why work? When we put on gospel glasses, we see that Jesus' work mattered. Our work—nothing new, nothing remembered. Jesus' work—it was and is *new*, and it has been and will be remembered. Therefore, the work that we do, as enabled by and through Christ, matters, too. We can put it this way: life *under the sun* is brief and bleak, but life *through the Son* is eternal and joyful.

The Work of Jesus

First, we have the work of Jesus. Here I am not referring to our Lord's work with Joseph as a carpenter (Mark 6:3), although that work mattered, too, because it was part of his humanity. Rather, I am referring to Jesus' work of redemption, which entails not only his death and resurrection but also every deed recorded for us in the Gospels: his obedience to and fulfillment of the law, his proclamation of the gospel of the kingdom, and his miracles. Jesus was about his Father's business (Luke 2:49).[16]

The Gospel of John, especially, emphasizes the work of Jesus. In John 4:34, Jesus says, "My food is to do the will of him who sent me and to accomplish his work." In 5:36, he speaks of the works that his Father has given him to accomplish, the very works he is doing. In 9:4, after healing the man blind from birth, he speaks of working "the works of him who sent me" (cf. 10:32ff.; 17:4). And when upon the cross he cried out, "It is finished" (19:30), his work of atonement was indeed finished. He had accomplished the work that the Father had sent him to do.

If we are viewing Ecclesiastes 1:3–11 through gospel glasses, we see the significance of Jesus' work. His work is *new*. Through our Lord's life, death, and resurrection, for the first and only time the fundamental problem of humanity's sin has been fixed. Jesus has done what no one before or after him could accomplish: the Son of God has reconciled the children of Adam to their Creator.

---

16. Every deed that Jesus did was *justifying* "wisdom" (Matt. 11:19). Wisdom's "deeds" (11:2) here allude to Jesus' deeds in 11:5 (cf. chaps. 8–9), which pave the way for the identification of Jesus as wisdom incarnate ("come to me" in 11:28–30).

Jesus' work is also *remembered*. At the Last Supper, Jesus established the new covenant, and through our perpetual celebration of his death in the sacrament of the Lord's Supper, we remember his work. Jesus' work is *new* and *remembered*—something that very few people can claim. More precisely, many people can claim it, but few can prove it. Yet for Jesus it continues to be proved two thousand years after the fact. We prove it every Sunday as we gather together in his name, singing and speaking of him and of what he has done. Jesus' work will never vanish into the "great, black packet of time."

A New Workforce

When we come to believe in Jesus—partaking of the new covenant that gives new birth, new life, and a new commandment—we enter into a new workforce.[17] Now what we do matters. Even the smallest, seemingly insignificant act, such as giving a cup of cold water to a disciple (Matt. 10:42), matters—if done in faith, for the sake of the gospel, and for the glory of God. Our labor is not in vain. "Vanity of vanities . . . ! All is vanity." True, unless we work "as to the Lord," as Paul puts it (Eph. 5:22; 6:7).

Allow me to illustrate. Think of the thief on the cross, who saw his sin for what it was, repented, and came to faith in Christ—all while hanging next to Jesus. While dying, he was brought to life; while suffocating, he breathed in the Holy Spirit. In his profession of faith, the penitent thief said to Jesus, "Jesus, *remember* me when you come into your kingdom." With kingly confidence, Jesus replied, "Truly, I say to you, today you will be with me in Paradise" (Luke 23:42–43). In other words, "Remember you? Of course I'll remember you!" We might think that Jesus would have had other more important things to do as he died and went into glory than to remember this criminal. But as Paul writes in 1 Corinthians 8:3, "If anyone loves God, he is known by God." Isn't that extraordinary? Do not take that verse for granted. "If anyone loves God, he is *known* by God."

It is not as though God doesn't know everything and everyone equally. But he especially knows—in a unique, fatherly way—what is going on in the lives of those who believe, who call out to him as sons and daughters

---

17. Duane A. Garrett, *Proverbs, Ecclesiastes, Songs of Songs*, New American Commentary 14 (Nashville: Broadman & Holman, 1993), 288.

through Christ, "Abba! Father!" (Gal. 4:6–9). And because he knows us, he knows our work. In Philippians 2:12, Paul echoes the wisdom literature by instructing believers to "work out your own salvation with fear and trembling." This kind of work is known to God and thus meaningful because, as Paul goes on to say, ultimately it is God's own work through us: "For it is God who works in you, both to will and to work for his good pleasure" (v. 13).

Think of what Jesus said in Matthew 25 about the righteous—those who cared for the hungry, the thirsty, the stranger, the naked, the sick, and the imprisoned. He stated, "Truly, I say to you, as you did it to one of the least of these my brothers, you did it to me" (v. 40). Or think of the example in Matthew 26 of what kind of work matters. A woman came to Jesus as he was reclining at table and poured on his head an alabaster flask's worth of expensive ointment (the equivalent of a whole year's wages). The disciples were indignant. "What a waste!" they said. But Jesus replied, marvelously:

Why do you trouble the woman? For she has done a beautiful thing to me. . . . In pouring this ointment on my body, she has done it to prepare me for burial. Truly, I say to you, wherever this gospel is proclaimed in the whole world, *what she has done* will also be told *in memory of her.* (Matt. 26:10–13)

The woman's little act of sacrificial love made it into the Bible, and to this day preachers are still talking about her and what she did. Jesus was right! This fascinating prophecy is fulfilled as we read it.

The woman's work for Jesus mattered, and so does ours. Paul gives an analogy in 1 Corinthians 3:9–14. God is building a kingdom. Jesus is the foundation. We are called to build on that foundation. If we work for ourselves and our own glory, it is like building our own foundation with wood or hay or straw. It will not last. But if we build for the sake of our God, it's like building a medieval cathedral: our names might be forgotten by man, but our names and our work will be remembered by God.

Our work under the sun: nothing new, nothing remembered. But our work in and through the Son: something very new. It is significant, substantial— something that will be remembered and even rewarded.

An Eternal Orchard

Perhaps you have dreamed of accomplishment, fed ambition, and traded nights of sleep for tomorrow's success. Yet perhaps you have discovered, as Pastor Solomon did, how as the seasons change and the leaves twist and tumble to the ground, our own work under the sun will vanish into that "great, black packet of time."

Yet through Christ our work can be substantial and lasting. Jesus brings life out of death. He takes decaying apples that have fallen to the ground and births from them a vast and beautiful and everlasting orchard, one full of fruit and life and joy.

3

A Crack in the Window
of Wisdom

Ecclesiastes 1:12—18

*And I applied my heart to know wisdom and to know madness
and folly. I perceived that this also is but a striving after wind.
For in much wisdom is much vexation, and he who increases
knowledge increases sorrow.* (Eccl. 1:17–18)

*O*n March 14, 2004, Daniel Tammet broke the European record
for reciting π (pi) from memory. Pi is the mathematical constant
that is the ratio of a circle's circumference to its diameter. For
five hours and nine minutes, he recited 22,514 digits (3.14 and the rest)
without error.

Tammet "suffers from" (if that is the appropriate phrase) Asperger syndrome. This condition allows him to be extraordinary in activities such as
memorizing numbers and learning languages. He learned Icelandic in a
week! Such brilliance, however, has its drawbacks. In his memoir, *Born on
a Blue Day: Inside the Extraordinary Mind of an Autistic Savant*, he recalls:

> I still remember vividly the experience I had as a teenager lying on the floor
> of my room staring up at the ceiling. I was trying to picture the universe in

my head, to have a concrete understanding of what "everything" was. In my mind I traveled to the edges of existence and looked over them, wondering what I would find. In that instant I felt really unwell and I could feel my heart beating hard inside me, because for the first time I had realized that thought and logic had limits and could only take a person so far. This realization frightened me and it took me a long time to come to terms with it.[1]

In Ecclesiastes 1:12–18, we witness the brilliant King Solomon flat on the floor staring up at the ceiling, unnerved by the frightening realization of the limits of human wisdom.

CONTEXT AND STRUCTURE

Before we gaze up with him, however, we should set the context and show the structure of our text. First, we have the context. Ecclesiastes 1:12–2:26 is a new textual unit. It contains a number of phrases that we have already seen in verses 1–11, such as "under heaven" (1:13; 2:3), "under the sun" (1:14; 2:11, 17, 18, 19, 20, 22), "all is vanity" (1:14; 2:1, 11, 17, 19; 2:1, 23), and "a striving after wind" (1:14; 2:11, 17, 26). We can be certain that the key question we examined in the previous study ("What does man gain by all the toil at which he toils under the sun?" 1:3) is still being answered because the Hebrew word for *toil* is repeated fifteen times in 1:12–2:26.[2] What is new, however, starting with verse 12, is the theme of wisdom through autobiographical reflection.

So for the first time in Ecclesiastes, we find the word *I*—as in "I the Preacher" (Eccl. 1:12) and "I applied my heart" (v. 13) and "I have seen" (v. 14) and "I said in my heart, 'I have acquired'" (v. 16) and "I applied my heart" (v. 17) and "I perceived" (v. 17).[3] Moreover, for the first time we see the words *wise* and *wisdom*. These words are used fifty-three times throughout Ecclesiastes and seventeen times in 1:12–2:26. If you add to those words synonymous or nearly synonymous words—such as *know*

---

1. Daniel Tammet, *Born on a Blue Day: Inside the Extraordinary Mind of an Autistic Savant* (New York: Free Press, 2006), 223–24.

2. I am indebted to Sidney Greidanus, *Preaching Christ from Ecclesiastes: Foundations for Expository Sermons* (Grand Rapids: Eerdmans, 2010), 50–51. Greidanus also notes that God is mentioned three times at the top (Eccl. 1:13) and tail (2:24, 26) of our text, "forming a possible inclusio for this literary unit" (51).

3. Note that from Ecclesiastes 1:12 on, the autobiographical *I* remains. I count forty-three occurrences, at least one in every chapter but chapter 11 (e.g., 3:10; 4:1; 5:13; 6:1; 7:15; 8:2; 9:1; 10:5; 12:1).

and *knowledge*—the count for this section rises to twenty-three. This is the highest concentration of wisdom words in the Bible! Undoubtedly this is a section about wisdom.

Second, we have the structure. The more you see various poetic structures, the easier it will be to read, understand, and apply this poem. As in most other Hebrew poetry, the structure is simple, or what I prefer to call "simply beautiful." After an introductory statement (Eccl. 1:12), there follow two reflections, each of which gives a statement about the vanity of pursuing wisdom, followed by a proverb that supports the statement. To express the poetic structure in outline form:

I. First Reflection—vv. 13–15
   A. Statement of the vanity of pursuing wisdom—vv. 13–14
   B. A proverb quoted in support—v. 15
II. Second Reflection—vv. 16–18
   A. Statement of the vanity of pursuing wisdom (and folly)—vv. 16–17
   B. A proverb quoted in support—v. 18[4]

From this simple structure, it is easy to find and summarize what Solomon discovered about wisdom. His first reflection is that wisdom cannot change reality; his second is that wisdom can increase sorrow.[5]

WHAT SOLOMON FOUND

Wisdom Cannot Change Reality

Look now at Ecclesiastes 1:12–15. Here we will reflect on how wisdom cannot change reality, starting with verses 12–13a: "I the Preacher have been king over Israel in Jerusalem. And I applied my heart to seek and to search out by wisdom all that is done under heaven." Here we are introduced to the speaker and the immense quest that he has set himself to accomplish, along with his position and some of the qualifications for such a task.

4. This outline comes from Roland E. Murphy, *Wisdom Literature*, Forms of the Old Testament Literature 13 (Grand Rapids: Eerdmans, 1981), 134.
5. David Hubbard, *Ecclesiastes, Song of Solomon*, Mastering the Old Testament 15B (Dallas: Word, 1991), 62, 65.

In a historical sense, only David and Solomon had been "king *over* [all of] *Israel* in Jerusalem" (Eccl. 1:12). This is one reason why some scholars believe that King Solomon was the author.[6] Yet the phrase *hayiti melekh*, translated "I . . . have been king," is confusing if it refers to Solomon because he reigned as king until his death. The best way to make sense of the perfect tense is as a personal reflection. That is, in his old age, Solomon is simply "looking back on his earlier experiences at some distance, reporting them, and evaluating them."[7] Thus, we might fairly add to "I . . . have been king" the phrase "for a long time now" or "up to the time I am writing this."

This reading also makes sense in light of Ecclesiastes 1:16: "I said in my heart, 'I have acquired great wisdom, surpassing all who were over Jerusalem before me, and my heart has had great experience of wisdom and knowledge.'" If this is Solomon (it sure sounds like him), he is not bragging, for his voice merely echoes what Scripture says. In 1 Kings 3:12, God said to Solomon, "Behold, I give you a wise and discerning mind, so that none like you has been before you and none like you shall arise after you." In 1 Kings 4:29–34, we read that "God gave Solomon wisdom and understanding beyond measure . . . , so that Solomon's wisdom surpassed the wisdom of all the people of the east and all the wisdom of Egypt. . . . And people of all nations came to hear the wisdom of Solomon, and from all the kings of the earth, who had heard of his wisdom." Finally, in 1 Kings 10:23–24, the summary comment is made: "Thus King Solomon excelled all the kings of the earth in riches and in wisdom. And the whole earth sought the presence of Solomon to hear his wisdom, which God had put into his mind." If anyone's résumé fit the job of exploring what the world had to offer with wisdom as his guide, it was King Solomon's.

6. Related to that is the argument that the audience of Ecclesiastes is a group of Israelites who were currently under a king. For example, for someone to write in the fourth century B.C.—a time when there was no king in Israel—statements such as "the word of the king is supreme" (Eccl. 8:4) and warnings such as "do not curse the king" (10:20) make no sense. (Although to be fair, the references to "the king" could refer to a foreign ruler, which completely undercuts this objection!)

7. Michael V. Fox, *Ecclesiastes*, JPS Bible Commentary (Philadelphia: Jewish Publication Society, 2004), 8. On the perfect tense of Ecclesiastes 1:12, Duane A. Garrett writes that it "may indicate that Ecclesiastes was written by an aged Solomon near the end of his life. Throughout the book, in fact, the perspective seems to be that of an older man, as in the description of old age in 12:1–5." *Proverbs, Ecclesiastes, Song of Songs*, New American Commentary 14 (Nashville: Broadman & Holman, 1993), 261.

Armed with such advantages and the ambition (he is ready to apply the whole of who he is—"my heart," Eccl. 1:13—to seek and search), consider what he found, and see what he "[has] seen" (v. 14):[8]

> It is an unhappy business that God has given to the children of man to be busy with. I have seen everything that is done under the sun [his version of "I've seen it all"], and behold, all is vanity and a striving after wind.
>
> What is crooked cannot be made straight,
> and what is lacking cannot be counted. (Eccl. 1:13b–15)

What Pastor Solomon found is what I have already stated. He found that even the highest human wisdom (his wisdom!) cannot change reality. That is what he says in two different ways (in prose and proverb form) in Ecclesiastes 1:14–15.

In both verses, images are used. In Ecclesiastes 1:14, it is the image of "striving after wind." Perhaps the image is of someone witnessing the wind rustle through some leaves and then attempting to chase that elusive and invisible force in the hope of grabbing it. Or perhaps the image is that of someone trying to corral the wind into a contained area. When I coached kindergarten girls' soccer and my wife asked how the practice went, I'd usually say, "It was like herding cats." Solomon found that making sense of earthly toil is like trying to herd the wind. Good luck with that! Whether the image is of running after or herding the wind, the image is one of impossibility.

The Cambridge astrophysicist Stephen Hawking famously said, "We are just an advanced breed of monkeys on a minor planet of a very average star. But we can understand the universe."[9] The Bible says nearly the opposite. While it does not claim that the earth is the only planet with life (which it is, as far as we know), it does claim that humanity is the height of God's created order. Yet the Bible also says that we understand little about how this universe works and can do almost nothing to change it.

---

8. The word *rāʾāh* is used over twenty times, often expressing observation, reflection, or careful examination.

9. Stephen Hawking, quoted in Philip Graham Ryken, *Ecclesiastes: Why Everything Matters*, ed. R. Kent Hughes, Preaching the Word (Wheaton, IL: Crossway, 2010), 39. Hawking elsewhere admits, "It would be very difficult to explain why the universe should have begun in just this way, except as the act of a God who intended to create beings like us." Stephen Hawking, *A Brief History in Time* (New York: Bantam, 1998), 144.

Listen again to the proverb of Ecclesiastes 1:15: "What is crooked cannot be made straight, and what is lacking cannot be counted." Here there are two images, which make the same point by stating it differently. Think of a steel bar that is bent as something that "is crooked [that] cannot be made straight." Another image—following the wind analogy of verse 14 and Daniel Fredericks's translation, "What has been twisted cannot be straightened" (v. 15)[10]—is that of a tornado. So think of trying to catch a tornado—to strive after *that* whimlike wind. Then suppose you actually do grab hold of it. Next, straighten it out. Again, best of luck with that! Such an achievement is impossible. It is like trying to take five blocks and four blocks and make them equal ten blocks. However you might count and however you might line up the blocks, they will never add up to ten. We cannot, with all the human wisdom in the world, change certain foundational realities.

But why? Why can't human wisdom straighten everything out or add everything up? Here is where the second part of Ecclesiastes 1:13 comes into play, giving theological grounding to Solomon's frustrating finding. We read, "It is an unhappy business that God has given to the children of man to be busy with."

Note that the Gift-Giver is "God." This is the first time God is mentioned in Ecclesiastes, but it won't be the last. The name used here and everywhere else in Ecclesiastes for *God* is *Elohim*. Why not *Yahweh*, the covenant name of God given to Israel? Likely it is *Elohim* because Ecclesiastes has an "apologetic goal to speak universally."[11] The book was written to appeal to all nations (not just Israel), so that all people everywhere might recognize and return to the one universal Creator God (Gen. 1:1; cf. Eccl. 12:1). More significant than the name of God, though, is the gift of God. What does God give? Grace? Peace? Mercy? Freedom? Happiness? No. Not here. Rather, God has given "the children of *man*" (literally, *adam*) "an unhappy business . . . to be busy with." Or this can be translated (and I prefer this translation) "a tragic affliction . . . to afflict"[12] the sons of Adam and daughters of Eve.

Why can't the highest human wisdom change reality? The answer is Adam's sin; God's curse (cf. Eccl. 7:13)! Because of Adam's sin, God has

---

10. Daniel C. Fredericks, "Ecclesiastes," in Daniel C. Fredericks and Daniel J. Estes, *Ecclesiastes and the Song of Songs*, Apollos Old Testament Commentary 16 (Downers Grove, IL: InterVarsity Press, 2010), 76.

11. Ibid., 81.

12. Ibid., 76.

cursed creation and the children of Adam. In Romans, Paul phrases it like this: "For the creation was subjected to futility [think about the motion-filled monotony of the sun, wind, and streams in Ecclesiastes 1:5–7], not willingly, but because of him [God!] who subjected it" (Rom. 8:20).

Thankfully, Paul concludes with a word of hope—that because of Jesus' resurrection and the Spirit's transforming power, "the creation itself will be set free from its bondage to corruption and obtain the freedom of the glory of the children [not of *adam* but] of [Elohim] God" (Rom. 8:21). This is our future hope in Ecclesiastes. Yet it is Genesis 3, not Romans 8 or Revelation 22, that is forcefully pressed upon us. Feel the crushing weight of Adam's curse.

When we witness life "under the sun" scarred by suffering, overflowing with oppression, infected with injustice, crawling with crime, traumatized by terrorists, polluted with impurity, we know that this is not just the way things are. People say, "It is what it is." On the contrary, it is not what it could have been. We all live east of Eden. And so when we see death (oh, accursed death!) knocking on the door of a child in the womb, a newborn baby girl, a five-year-old boy crossing the street on his bike, a group of teenagers driving home from the prom, a newlywed wife with brain cancer, a father of five leaping in front of a train, a ninety-year-old bachelor in a hospital bed, know that this is not just the way things are. There was a fall and, because of the fall, a curse. We are all punished in Adam for Adam's sin. That is the way things are *now*. And day after day after day after day, we all walk down the same sorry street.

Chapter 1 quoted a dialogue from a Woody Allen movie. Here I will insert another (and do not be surprised if this is not the last time I use Allen's material in our journey through Ecclesiastes). He is one of the few entertainers who take death seriously. Of course, he takes it seriously in a comical way. In his film *Annie Hall*, Allen's character, Alvy Singer, says to the title character (Diane Keaton), "I feel that life is divided into the horrible and the miserable. That's the two categories. The horrible are like, I don't know, terminal cases, you know, and blind people, crippled. I don't know how they get through life. It's amazing to me. And the miserable is everyone else. So you be thankful that you're miserable, because that's very lucky, to be miserable." It is hard not to laugh at that tragic punch line. We laugh because we all know there is so much truth to it.

Wisdom Increases Sorrow

Whether we like it or not, Pastor Solomon has busied himself with discovering tragic truths and uncovering them for us. After he discovers that human wisdom (even his own famous wisdom!) cannot undo the curse of a sovereign God on Adam's offspring (cf. Eccl. 7:29), his search continues. As we turn to Ecclesiastes 1:16–18, we should not expect a happy ending:

> I said in my heart, "I have acquired great wisdom, surpassing all who were over Jerusalem before me, and my heart has had great experience of wisdom and knowledge." And I applied my heart to know wisdom and to know madness and folly. I perceived that this also is but a striving after wind.
>
> For in much wisdom is much vexation,
>   and he who increases knowledge increases sorrow.

Before saying something negative about these negative verses, we should say something positive. While Solomon's findings are not what he hoped, nevertheless, his quest is commendable.

In one of Bill Watterson's classic comic strips, the curious boy Calvin asks Hobbes, his stuffed tiger who comes to life in his imagination, "Why do you suppose we're here?" They are both sitting on the ground, leaning against a large tree. Hobbes replies, "Because we walked here." "No, no," Calvin retorts; "I mean here on earth." Hobbes replies, "Because earth can support life." "No, I mean why are we anywhere? Why do we exist?" Again, Hobbes comments, "Because we were born." Frustrated, Calvin moves around to the other side of the tree, lowers his head, and says, "Forget it." Hobbes concludes, "I will, thank you."[13]

In the previous chapter we met the escapist, who, like Hobbes, avoids answering or even trying to answer Ecclesiastes' questions. Our world is filled with escapists. (You might even be one.) Sure, plenty of people take on the ancient sage's task of observing the world. We have our psychologists, sociologists, anthropologists, zoologists, botanists, astrophysicists, and other scientists who examine anything from black holes to brown moles. But so few—even from those professions—stop to observe, reflect on, or consider what we are

---

13. Bill Watterson, *Weirdos from Another Planet* (Kansas City, MO: Universal Press Syndicate, 1990), 21.

doing here on planet Earth. They are like Hobbes. They are masterly at avoiding life's larger-than-an-old-oak-tree questions.

Perhaps you have had the same experience I have had. You are talking with a neighbor. Once he learns that you are a Christian, he asks you a question or two about your faith. When you are finished proselytizing, he says politely, "That's nice." (He has no interest in Jesus.) Then, when you question him about his views on ultimate issues, he nonchalantly replies, "Well, I haven't given such things much thought." Now, that answer is normal enough. That is how people talk because that is how people think. What is not normal is why our culture thinks that such a reply is reasonable. I am not impressed (are you?) by an educated, middle-aged man who holds no ideas whatsoever on how we got here, why we are here, and where we are going after the doctor pulls the sheet over our dead bodies. People think and talk like that new neighbor, and other people let them. Some might even be impressed by their agnosticism! Well, I'm not. And I invite you to join me in my intellectual contempt.

Some people purposely avoid seeking out the answers to Ecclesiastes' questions. Others unwittingly anesthetize themselves to the implications of Adam's sin. Who hasn't watched the news while eating dinner, hearing about some brutal murder, and never once feeling uneasy or so sick to our stomach that we stop eating? In fact, we are so anesthetized that we hear the one-minute story on the brutal murder followed by a one-minute story on a shelter for stray dogs and we think nothing about the odd placement of the story of random violence next to an act of premeditated kindness.

Pastor Solomon should be commended for not being dulled by daily diversions and the commonalities of the curse, and also for seeking to find answers to life's tough questions. If only more people would share the tenacious intensity of his exploration!

To return to the text, the problem with Solomon's exploration was that he did not stop with wisdom. He also considered its opposite, what he calls "madness and folly" (Eccl. 1:17). Just as *wisdom* and *knowledge* are synonyms, so, too, are *madness* and *folly*, with the latter two meaning not the study of insanity but the pursuit of pleasures, immoral ones (in 9:3, "madness" [*holelot*] is equated with "evil").[14] As we will learn in 2:1–11, as Solomon

---

14. See Graham S. Ogden, *Qoheleth*, 2nd ed., Readings: A New Biblical Commentary (Sheffield, UK: Sheffield Phoenix Press, 2007), 47. Cf. Ecclesiastes 7:25, "the wickedness of folly and the foolishness that is madness."

stockpiled wisdom, he also amassed amusements. And with wisdom in one hand and folly in the other, he still couldn't grasp the meaning of life—"this also [was] but a striving after wind" (1:17). In fact, when he had finished trying wisdom and then trying folly, he found that tasting from the fruit of "the tree of the knowledge of good and evil" (Gen. 2:17) only increased sorrow (Eccl. 1:18). The ignorance of innocence is indeed bliss, but the awareness of evil is an awful vexation. As a professional musician is pained by hearing the first notes screeched out at her student's first violin lesson, so Solomon is pained by all that he has experienced under the sun. The more he has seen, the more he is pierced by the thorns and thistles of the fall.

WHAT ONLY GOD CAN GIVE

Once again (cf. Eccl. 1:11), with this text (1:12–18) we conclude with another bleak ending (v. 18). The last word is *sorrow* (in English). But if we remember that this is part of a fuller argument, one that ends in a call and ode to joy in 2:24–26, we can gather an ounce of hope even here. Ecclesiastes 1:12–18 can be called "What Solomon Found"; then Ecclesiastes 2:1–26—especially focusing on the end—can be called "What God Gives." Look especially at verse 26. Trapped as it were in a deep black box, Solomon has found all escape routes closed to him. Earthly wisdom cannot reach high enough to get him out. The glow of earthly pleasures cannot last long enough to even see a way out. Finally, Pastor Solomon finds divine wisdom the way it is always found in the Bible's wisdom literature: with God, and only as God's gift to those who fear him and obey his commandments. He states, "For to the one who pleases him *God has given* wisdom and knowledge" (2:26).

People too often think that the accumulation and implementation of information (human wisdom) will solve the world's problems. But we know enough history and have experienced enough life to know how foolish this proposition is. In Isaiah, God declared that he would "destroy the wisdom of the wise" (Isa. 29:14, quoted in 1 Cor. 1:19). Of course, in the coming of Christ we learn how on the one hand God destroyed the wisdom of the wise, and how on the other hand he offered true wisdom to those who cling to Jesus and his cross.

For the word of the cross is folly to those who are perishing, but to us who are being saved it is the power of God. For it is written,

"I will destroy the *wisdom* of the wise,
    and the discernment of the discerning I will thwart."

. . . Has not God made foolish the *wisdom* of the world? For since, in the *wisdom* of God, the world did not know God through *wisdom*, it pleased God through the folly of what we preach to save those who believe. For Jews demand signs and Greeks seek *wisdom*, but we preach Christ crucified, a stumbling block to Jews and folly to Gentiles, but to those who are called, both Jews and Greeks, Christ the power of God and the *wisdom* of God. (1 Cor. 1:18–24)

Christians are fools. That is Paul's argument in 1 Corinthians 1–2. In other words, those who trust that God, through the crucifixion, made Christ "wisdom from God, righteousness and sanctification and redemption" (1:30) appear foolish to the unwise—to the overly-wise-in-their-own-eyes—world. Yet he is no fool who abandons human pride and power to find the "secret and hidden wisdom of God" (2:7) now revealed in "Christ and him crucified" (2:2). The seeming folly of a crucified Creator is God's wisdom perfected.

While Pastor Solomon never witnessed divine wisdom's ultimate achievement, he leaned toward it. He wholeheartedly quested after it! We, however, are close enough to reach out and receive it. In Christ we are given wisdom that *can* change reality as well as increase our joy. Why not grab hold of it now?

4

The Hollow House
of Hedonism

Ecclesiastes 2:1—11

I said in my heart, "Come now, I will test you with pleasure;
enjoy yourself." But behold, this also was vanity. (Eccl. 2:1)

*I*n the 1950s, the journalist Malcolm Muggeridge was as popular in England as Katie Couric is today in America. If you have never heard of Muggeridge (or Couric, for that matter), it only reinforces Ecclesiastes' teaching on the fleetingness of fame. Yet he will be remembered by God for putting his faith in Jesus Christ, late but not too late in life. In his book *Jesus Rediscovered*, Muggeridge wrote:

I may, I suppose, regard myself, or pass for being, as a relatively success-ful man. People occasionally stare at me in the streets—that's fame. I can fairly easily earn enough to qualify for admission to the higher slopes of the Internal Revenue—that's success. Furnished with money and a little fame even the elderly, if they care to, may partake of trendy diversions—that's pleasure. It might happen once in a while that something I said or wrote was sufficiently heeded for me to persuade myself that it represented a serious impact on our time—that's fulfillment. Yet I say to you—and I beg you to believe me—multiply these tiny triumphs by a million, add them all together, and they are nothing—less than nothing, a positive impediment—measured against one draught of that living water Christ offers to the spiritually thirsty, irrespective of who or what they are.[1]

That is precisely the lesson we will learn in this chapter. In the language of the prophet Jeremiah, the lesson is to turn from drinking idolatry's "broken cisterns that can hold no water" to the Lord, "the fountain of living waters" (Jer. 2:13). Or in the language of our Savior himself, it is to drink from him, the water that quenches our thirst forever, a spring welling up to eternal life (John 4:13–14). But before we get to the living water that God in Christ offers, first we must walk through the waterless wilderness of Pastor Solomon's testing of pleasure.

My wife Emily and I enjoyed watching the BBC's superb rendition of Charles Dickens's *Little Dorrit*. Dickens had a gift for naming people and places in his stories. Think of the people. There is Jeremiah Flintwinch (*Little Dorrit*), Mr. M'Choakumchild (*Hard Times*), Philip Pirrip or Pip (*Great Expectations*), Mr. and Mrs. Spottletoe (*Martin Chuzzlewit*), Uriah Heap (*David Copperfield*), Canon Crisparkle (*The Mystery of Edwin Drood*), Volumnia Dedlock (*Bleak House*), and Ebenezer Scrooge (*A Christmas Carol*). Think of the places. There is the Curiosity Shop (*The Old Curiosity Shop*), the Circumlocution Office (*Little Dorrit*), Cloisterham Cathedral (*The Mystery of Edwin Drood*), Krook's Bottle Shop (*Bleak House*), Dotheboys Hall (*Nicholas Nickleby*), and Dr. Blimber's Academy (*Dombey and Son*). Here in our text, in almost Dickensian form, Pastor Solomon takes us to a place that we can name the *hollow house of hedonism*. Yes, the house is filled with wine and women, gardens and gold, songs and servants; but it is hollow when it comes to satisfying our deepest needs.

Within the house of hedonism there are many rooms. Solomon will show us four of them in Ecclesiastes 2:1–11: the private pub, the garden, the treasury, and the bedroom. Take my hand now and I'll show you. Be careful, though, for seeing what Solomon saw might tempt you to want what he had. And that is not what we should truly *desire*.

1. Malcolm Muggeridge, *Jesus Rediscovered* (Garden City, NY: Doubleday, 1969), 77. Note also his autobiography, which has a great title in and of itself for Ecclesiastes 2:1–11: *Chronicles of Wasted Time* (Vancouver, BC: Regent College Publishing, 2006).

THE PRIVATE PUB

First, we come to the private pub. The word *pub* stands for "public," and thus *private pub* is a seemingly contradictory phrase. But in naming a place in our society that offers in one place what Solomon tested, *pub* fits best. It is *private*, however, because it is located in the privacy of his house, seemingly for his sole entertainment. Look at Ecclesiastes 2:1–3, along with the middle of verse 8. It's helpful to reorder Solomon's ordering in this first room because in our culture these pleasures are often found in the same place (the pub)—the pleasures of laughter, alcohol, and music:

> I said in my heart, "Come now, I will test you with pleasure; enjoy yourself." But behold, this also was vanity. I said of laughter, "It is mad," and of pleasure, "What use is it?" I searched with my heart how to cheer my body with wine—my heart still guiding me with wisdom—and how to lay hold on folly, till I might see what was good for the children of man to do under heaven during the few days of their life. (Eccl. 2:1–3)

And then verse 8b reads, "I got singers, both men and women."

We will revisit the results of Solomon's pleasure experiment (the "but behold, this also was vanity" of Ecclesiastes 2:1 and the "What use is it?" of verse 2) after we have viewed all four rooms. For now, we observe that in his private pub, Solomon enjoyed laughter, alcohol, and music.

First, he had the best music of the day, seemingly daily. In Ecclesiastes 2:7, he begins to list his household possessions—"I bought male and female slaves"—and then in verse 8, his language is "I got singers." Did he buy them as he would the slaves, or did he hire them for special occasions? Based on the context, my sense is that they served in his house just as his servants and concubines did. Whatever the case, when he wanted music, he got it. This is the ancient version of the radio with only one station available. (I hope he liked choral music!) Unlike today's radio, however, the music here was live, expensive, and slightly exotic. I say *exotic* because unlike the temple choir, which comprised men only,[2] this choir had "both men and women." This rare musical pleasure in those days was not so rare for the pleasure preacher.

---

2. See the section "Female Choristers" in JewishEncyclopedia.com, s.v. "Choir," www.jewish encyclopedia.com/articles/4348-choir.

Along with the music came alcohol. With his "heart still guiding [him] with wisdom"—that is, with a certain amount of mindful self-control or objective indulgence—he tests wine to see whether it will cheer him enough to forget "the few *days* [not *years*!]" of earthly existence or to find some happiness in his own happy hour.

And with wine comes laughter, touched on in Ecclesiastes 2:2. Like the surroundings of a fool who laughs while he unwittingly plays with fire (e.g., Prov. 26:18–19), Solomon's private pub is alive with deadly frivolity. Another song is sung. Another round is served. Another joke is told.

We close the door. There is nothing more to see, hear, and smell but the blur of bodies lifting another glass, with perhaps the subtle sound of Johannes Brahms's *Vier ernste Gesänge* echoing in the air,[3] and the faint residue of doom wafting about the room. Onward and outward we move.

THE GARDEN

We come next to the garden. We open the cedar-framed French doors of the private pub and walk out into the most beautiful garden east of Eden. Consider Solomon's amazing architectural and agricultural accomplishments:

> I made great works. I built houses and planted vineyards for myself. I made myself gardens and parks, and planted in them all kinds of fruit trees. I made myself pools from which to water the forest of growing trees. [In order to maintain my masterpieces, I employed a massive workforce.] I bought male and female slaves, and had slaves who were born in my house. I had also great possessions of herds and flocks, more than any who had been before me in Jerusalem. (Eccl. 2:4–7)

Derek Kidner notes that Solomon here created "a secular Garden of Eden... with no forbidden fruits."[4] *Secular* is the right term because God and his command to man to cultivate creation is nowhere to be found. Solomon has

---

3. The first two songs of Brahms's "Four Serious Songs" are based on Ecclesiastes 3:19–22 and 4:1–3. In Eric S. Christianson's excellent book *Ecclesiastes through the Centuries*, Blackwell Bible Commentaries (Malden, MA: Blackwell, 2007), 77–83, 120–21, he discusses various musical pieces that were based on texts and themes from Ecclesiastes.

4. Derek Kidner, *The Message of Ecclesiastes: A Time to Mourn, and a Time to Dance*, The Bible Speaks Today (Downers Grove, IL: InterVarsity Press, 1976), 32.

done all that Adam was to do—the verbs "to plant," "to water," "to make" here are the same as those used in Genesis 2, as are the nouns "garden" and "all kinds of fruit trees."[5] Genesis is echoed here, but its nouns and verbs bounce off the proud preacher. I made great works. I built houses.[6] I planted vineyards. I made myself gardens and parks. I planted fruit trees. I made myself pools.

Along the Fox River in downtown Batavia, Illinois, is a bronze sculpture entitled *The Self-Made Man*. It depicts a muscular man chiseling himself out of a rock. Here in Ecclesiastes 2:4–7, we see the self-made man who has made so much more than himself. With godlike creativity and control,[7] he has created a little ideal world within the fallen world. This is *Lifestyles of the Rich and Famous* on steroids!

But we have no time to stop, gawk, and covet. We are being moved along because the photographer from *Better Homes and Gardens* has arrived. He wants to be certain to outdo the cover shot of last month's *Architectural Digest*. Solomon's servants take us back inside, down a narrow stairway, deep beneath the wine cellar, past the reporter from *Forbes* magazine, through the iron door into the treasury.

The Treasury

How can Solomon afford all this—the houses, vineyards, pools, parks, trees, servants, singers, liquor, cattle, sheep, goats, oxen, and more? The answer is found here: "I also gathered for myself silver and gold and the

5. See A. J. C. Verheij, "Paradise Retried: On Qohelet 2:4–6," *Journal for the Study of the Old Testament* 50 (1991): 113–15.

"To plant" (Eccl. 2:4) = Gen. 2:8
"Garden" (Eccl. 2:5) = Gen. 2:8–10, 15–16
"All kinds of fruit trees" (Eccl. 2:5) = Gen. 1:11–12, 29; 2:9, 16–17
"To water" (Eccl. 2:6) = Gen. 2:5–6
"to make" (Eccl. 2:5–6) = Gen. 1:7, 16, 25–26, 31; 2:2–4, 18

6. It took thirteen years to build Solomon's house (1 Kings 7:1), the first of many grand building projects. As Walter C. Kaiser comments: "Then he built 'the house of the forest of Lebanon' (1 Kings 10:17) and another house for his wife, pharaoh's daughter. He also built the cities of Hazor, Megiddo, Gezer, Beth-horon, Baalath, and Tadmor in the wilderness." *Ecclesiastes: Total Life*, Everyman's Bible Commentary (Chicago: Moody, 1979), 56. Note also, as many commentators do, that Solomon took only seven years to build the temple (cf. 1 Kings 7:1; 9:10). This smaller number suggests confused priorities.

7. Philip Graham Ryken, *Ecclesiastes: Why Everything Matters*, ed. R. Kent Hughes, Preaching the Word (Wheaton, IL: Crossway, 2010), 48.

treasure of kings and provinces" (Eccl. 2:8). This is the understatement of the day, for in 1 Kings 10:14–29 we read about Solomon's incredible wealth acquired through taxes, tributes, and trade. Notice how often *gold* is mentioned:

> Now the weight of *gold* that came to Solomon in one year was 666 talents of *gold*, besides that which came from the explorers and from the business of the merchants, and from all the kings of the west and from the governors of the land. King Solomon made 200 large shields of beaten *gold*; 600 shekels of *gold* went into each shield. And he made 300 shields of beaten *gold*; three minas of *gold* went into each shield. And the king put them in the House of the Forest of Lebanon. The king also made a great ivory throne and overlaid it with the finest *gold*. The throne had six steps, and at the back of the throne was a calf's head, and on each side of the seat were armrests and two lions standing beside the armrests, while twelve lions stood there, one on each end of a step on the six steps. The like of it was never made in any kingdom. All King Solomon's drinking vessels were of *gold*, and all the vessels of the House of the Forest of Lebanon were of pure *gold*. None were of silver; silver was not considered as anything in the days of Solomon. For the king had a fleet of ships of Tarshish at sea with the fleet of Hiram. Once every three years the fleet of ships of Tarshish used to come bringing *gold*, silver, ivory, apes, and peacocks.
>
> Thus King Solomon excelled all the kings of the earth in riches and in wisdom. And the whole earth sought the presence of Solomon to hear his wisdom, which God had put into his mind. Every one of them brought his present, articles of silver and *gold*, garments, myrrh, spices, horses, and mules, so much year by year.
>
> And Solomon gathered together chariots and horsemen. He had 1,400 chariots and 12,000 horsemen, whom he stationed in the chariot cities and with the king in Jerusalem. And the king made silver as common in Jerusalem as stone, and he made cedar as plentiful as the sycamore of the Shephelah. And Solomon's import of horses was from Egypt and Kue, and the king's traders received them from Kue at a price. A chariot could be imported from Egypt for 600 shekels of silver and a horse for 150, and so through the king's traders they were exported to all the kings of the Hittites and the kings of Syria. (Cf. 1 Kings 4:22–23; 1 Chron. 27:29–31; 2 Chron. 9:25–27)

Put differently and much more succinctly, money was no issue for Solomon. Whatever he wanted, he got. He had the chateau in Switzerland, the beach house in the Bahamas, and the penthouse in Paris. He was the primary stockholder for McDonald's and Ford. And he had that Donald Trump snap of the finger ("get me this; do it now, or you're fired"); that Steve Jobs business genius ("let's try this; let's try that . . . ah, see, it works!"); that spoiled-rich-teenager-at-the-shopping-mall disposition ("like I totally need those $500 jeans"). Like King Midas, everything Solomon touched turned to gold. (The word *gold* is repeated fourteen times in 1 Kings 10!)

But gold is cold. It can't touch you, embrace you, or make love to you. And so Solomon dialogued again with himself: "Might the pleasures of the human body be the answer? Let me see if women can quench this 'strange melancholy' not satiated by money and the stuff money can buy."[8]

THE BEDROOM

As the book of 1 Kings transitions from Solomon's wealth in chapter 10 to Solomon's women in chapter 11—"Now King Solomon loved many foreign women . . . . He had 700 wives, princesses, and 300 concubines" (vv. 1a, 3a)—so the first part of Ecclesiastes 2:8 transitions to the last part of that verse, where we read: "I also gathered for myself . . . many concubines, the delight of the children of man."[9] John Donne wrote of Solomon that "he hides none of his owne sins . . . . *Solomon* preaches himself . . . and poures out his owne soule in that Book [Ecclesiastes]."[10] True, but it is a tragic tale he tells. This compromise of the covenant is what led to his spiritual downfall and divided his kingdom, which perhaps explains why it is listed last among his pleasure experiments—for emphasis.

The Hebrew word here for "concubines" (*šiddāh*) is related to the word *shad*, which means "breast."[11] This is why some translators translate

8. As Timothy J. Keller notes: "In the 1830s, when Alexis de Tocqueville recorded his famous observations on America, he noted a 'strange melancholy that haunts the inhabitants . . . in the midst of abundance.' Americans believed that prosperity could quench their yearning for happiness, but such a hope was illusory, because, de Tocqueville added, 'the complete joys of this world will never satisfy [the human] heart.'" *Counterfeit Gods: The Empty Promises of Money, Sex, and Power, and the Only Hope That Matters* (New York: Dutton, 2009), x.

9. Thus far, I have taken the phrase "children of man" to represent all of fallen humanity. Given the context, however, it makes best sense to take this phrase in Ecclesiastes 2:8 to represent men literally.

10. John Donne, quoted in Christianson, *Ecclesiastes through the Centuries*, 97.

11. Along with the word *delight(s)*, it is used in Song of Songs 7:6–7: "How beautiful and pleasant you are, O loved one, with your *delights*! Your stature is like a palm tree, and your *breasts* are like its clusters."

"concubines" as "breasts" and "many concubines" as "abundant breasts."[12] However we translate the word, it is "a crude reference to women who are used for sexual pleasure only."[13] While the king might have married for political power and military stability, that is not the stress here. Sex is the stress. Sexual immorality is the stress. In rejecting the biblical standard of one man plus one woman for life, Solomon was anti-Genesis (see Gen. 2:23–25) and anti-Jesus (see Matt. 19:3–6).

But isn't our culture equally opposed to the biblical view of sexuality? Sadly, this bedroom scene isn't anything that we haven't seen before. While our sex-crazed culture gasped when basketball star Wilt Chamberlain bragged in his autobiography about sleeping with ten thousand women, it doesn't gasp about teenage promiscuity, best-selling books about erotic bondage (*Fifty Shades of Grey*), the $100 billion porn industry, easy divorce often arising from acceptable and inevitable adultery, and the now-overwhelming approval of homosexual behavior. Conventional morality has been shelved. The biblical ethic is labeled "outdated" or "expired" or "danger: poison." What Woody Allen said to the media about his sexual relationship with the adopted teenage daughter of his wife—"The heart wants what it wants"—is the slogan that more and more people are living by. We have listened to the seductive sounds of the Sirens (see *The Odyssey*). We have sacrificed our souls on the altar of sexual idolatry. For what Solomon gave only one line to, our culture needs five thousand libraries to fill. Solomon's private bedchamber is now open to public view, and no one blushes anymore.

Walking Away from Vanity Fair

But let us blush and then turn our eyes away, shall we? Let's leave it all behind: the private pub, the garden, the treasury, and the bedroom of the hollow house of hedonism. Let us run for our lives and not look back, lest, like a pillar of salt, we be swept away by the wilderness's wind (Gen. 19:17,

---

12. Daniel C. Fredericks, "Ecclesiastes," in Daniel C. Fredericks and Daniel J. Estes, *Ecclesiastes and the Song of Songs*, Apollos Old Testament Commentary 16 (Downers Grove, IL: InterVarsity Press, 2010), 89. He calls it "an indefinite but impressive plurality" (89).

13. Tremper Longman III, *The Book of Ecclesiastes*, New International Commentary on the Old Testament (Grand Rapids: Eerdmans, 1998), 92. Duane A. Garrett calls it "a colloquialism for a girl of pleasure." *Proverbs, Ecclesiastes, Song of Songs*, New American Commentary 14 (Nashville: Broadman & Holman, 1993), 292.

26). To toss some John Bunyan into the analogy mix: it is time to flee Vanity Fair. Take my hand again, and let us run over the Delectable Mountains through the Wicket Gate into the Celestial City.

Solomon's pleasure test was a failure, and he admits as much in Ecclesiastes 2:1–2 and 9–11. The key transition word to the test results is *behold*.

> I said in my heart, "Come now, I will test you with pleasure; enjoy yourself." But *behold*, this also was vanity. I said of laughter, "It is mad," and of pleasure, "What use is it?" (Eccl. 2:1–2)

Later, the same bitter disillusionment is put differently and in summary form:

> So I became great and surpassed all who were before me in Jerusalem. Also my wisdom remained with me. And whatever my eyes desired [outward delights] I did not keep from them. I kept my heart from no pleasure [inward delights], for my heart found pleasure in all my toil, and this was my reward for all my toil. Then I considered all that my hands had done and the toil I had expended in doing it, and *behold*, all was vanity and a striving after wind, and there was nothing to be gained under the sun. (Eccl. 2:9–11)

In the popular sitcom *The Simpsons* (a show that I neither endorse nor completely condemn), Homer Simpson says to his boss, Mr. Burns, "You're the richest man I know." To which Burns replies, "Yes, but I'd trade it all for more." That is *not* how Solomon feels the morning after his years-long pleasure party. Instead, we hear him humming Nine Inch Nails' song "Empire of Dirt." At the beginning and end of our text, Pastor Solomon stamps "empire of dirt" across everything in the middle—the wine and women, gardens and gold, songs and servants. He had it all, but all was not enough.

But why? What went wrong with the pleasure-and-possessions experiment, that he would pronounce it profitless? There are at least two explanations for the failure. Putting self first, ironically, fails to satisfy self and also, ironically, fails to give pleasure. The first failure deals with the sin of selfishness and the second with the sin of idolatry. The first failure breaks the second-greatest commandment ("You shall love your neighbor as yourself," Matt. 22:39), while the second failure breaks the greatest commandment ("You shall love the Lord your God with all your heart and with all your soul and with all your mind," v. 37).

THE SIN OF SELFISHNESS

Notice the issue of self. We have already noted in Ecclesiastes 2:4–7 how much Solomon spoke about himself. But further notice how self saturates this section of Scripture. The first word in verse 1 is *I*. Normally, this wouldn't raise an exegetical eyebrow. Psalm 18 begins, "I love you, O LORD." Here, however, the word *I*, along with *me*, *my*, and *myself*, is the dominant refrain. *I* is used eighteen times, *my* thirteen times, *me* four times, and *myself* four times. Even the word *yourself*—"Enjoy yourself" (Eccl. 2:1)—is intended to convey the idea of Solomon's talking to himself. That's a lot of self-focus!

It is not simply the language, but also the focus of the accomplishments. Solomon's list is self-serving. His works are not philanthropic. He doesn't mention any public parks he built to be enjoyed by the populace.[14] "*I* built houses and planted vineyards *for myself*" (Eccl. 2:4). This self-focus is all artistically intentional, written so that we can see what he saw. So let the reader understand: As Solomon boasts in his achievements and enjoyments, he underscores, ironically, their ultimate inadequacy.[15]

We all know that self-centeredness and self-indulgence never satisfy for long. Why? Because of common grace, and because of the way God designed us. We can call it the *pleasure paradox*. If we answer the first question of the Westminster Shorter Catechism (WSC), "What is the chief end of man?" by saying, "Man's chief end is to glorify *himself* and try to enjoy *himself* as much as he can," we will always discover that these earthly pleasures we grasp so tightly eventually pour through our fingers onto a floor of sand. In the words of the poem "Tam o' Shanter" by Robert Burns:

But pleasures are like poppies spread,
You seize the flow'r, its bloom is shed.

14. Thomas Krüger notes: "In reports on their great deeds, rulers of the ancient Near East and the Hellenistic period boasted not only of their wisdom and wealth but also about the promotion of religious cults and the welfare of their subjects . . . . King Qoheleth, by contrast, reports exclusively on works and deeds that he has done for himself." *Qoheleth*, ed. Klaus Baltzer, trans. O. C. Dean Jr., Hermeneia (Minneapolis: Fortress, 2004), 65. "It is indicative of King Qoheleth's perspective that in his striving for his own happiness, he wastes no thought on the happiness or unhappiness of the people who contribute to his happiness and carry out his 'great works' for him (cf. 4:1–3)" (66).

15. Michael V. Fox, *Ecclesiastes*, JPS Bible Commentary (Philadelphia: Jewish Publication Society, 2004), 13. As Fox also notes, "This emphasis on 'myself' exposes a sort of consumerism, an obsessive striving to fill an undefined but gnawing spiritual need by material goods."

Pleasure has a way of promising more than it can produce. David Hubbard explains that its "advertising agency is better than its manufacturing department." The "one drink, one sexual fling, one contest won, one project accomplished, one wild party—none of these, nor all of them put together, can be enough to bring satisfaction."[16]

THE SIN OF IDOLATRY

The sin of selfishness won't satisfy, and neither will the sin of idolatry. Putting pleasure first fails, ironically, to give pleasure. Rabbi Harold Kushner's book on Ecclesiastes is titled *When All You've Ever Wanted Isn't Enough.* While this might not be the best summary of the whole book, it is an excellent summary of Ecclesiastes 2:1–11. Why isn't everything we want enough? It isn't enough if God isn't first.

For his journal entry on January 2, 1777, John Wesley wrote:

> I began expounding, in order, the book of Ecclesiastes. I never before had so clear a sight either of the meaning or the beauties of it. Neither did I imagine that the several parts of it were in so exquisite a manner connected together; all tending to prove that grand truth, that there is no happiness out[side] of God.[17]

Many of the pleasures mentioned here—such as laughing, planting vineyards, drinking wine, creating and maintaining a garden—are all commendable biblical pleasures. In fact, in the wisdom literature of the Bible—think especially of the book of Proverbs and the beginning and end of Job's story— pleasures and possessions are God's rewards for righteousness (cf. Abraham, Gen. 12:5; 13:2). Even throughout Ecclesiastes, pleasure is commended (e.g., Eccl. 2:24; 3:12; cf. 1 Kings 3:13). So what is the problem with the pleasures listed in Ecclesiastes 2:1–11? The problem is that some of these pleasures are immoral and all of them are idolatrous. Solomon put pleasures before the worship of the Lord his God. He broke the first commandment: "I am the LORD your God, who brought you out of the land of Egypt, out of the

---

16. David Hubbard, *Ecclesiastes, Song of Solomon,* Mastering the Old Testament 15B (Dallas: Word, 1991), 35.

17. *Journals from September 13, 1773 to October 24, 1790,* in *The Works of John Wesley,* 14 vols. (1872; repr., Grand Rapids: Baker, 2007), 4:91.

house of slavery. You shall have no other gods before me" (Ex. 20:2–3). We need to worship God by receiving every pure pleasure as a gift from him. Our pleasures are to be God-centered!

The lesson here, of course, is that God comes first, and that with divine worship first, genuine human satisfaction follows. The poet Christina Rossetti put it like this: "Lord, I have all things if I have but Thee,"[18] and the gospel singer George Beverly Shea like this:

I'd rather have Jesus than silver or gold;
I'd rather be His than have riches untold;
I'd rather have Jesus than houses or lands;
I'd rather be led by His nail-pierced hands
Than to be the king of a vast domain and be held in sin's dread sway.
I'd rather have Jesus than anything this world affords today.[19]

Christ alone "satiates the soul."[20] In the book of Philippians, Paul commands Christians to "rejoice in the Lord" (Phil. 3:1; 4:4, 10). Why? We can rejoice because Jesus "in humility count[ed] others more significant than" himself, so much so that he "made himself nothing, taking the form of a servant, being born in the likeness of men. And being found in human form, he humbled himself by becoming obedient to the point of death, even death on a cross" (2:3, 7–8). King Jesus is the epitome of selflessness, of putting God the Father first. For our sake and our salvation, he denied "the desires of the flesh and the desires of the eyes and pride in possessions" (1 John 2:16). When Jesus was tempted by Satan and later by Peter to take the crown before or instead of the cross (Matt. 4:1–11; 16:21–23), he would not bow the knee to the idol of temporary power and worldly pleasures. Rather, it was "for the joy that was set before him" that he "endured the cross" (Heb. 12:2). You see, our Lord, who taught us to deny ourselves and pick up our cross daily (Mark 8:34), did not do so because he was a cosmic killjoy, but rather because he knows the way to the pleasures of God—"in

18. From Christina Rossetti, "Jesus Alone," in *Christina Rossetti: The Complete Poems* (New York: Penguin Classics, 2001), 588.

19. George Beverly Shea, quoted in Philip Graham Ryken, *King Solomon: The Temptations of Money, Sex, and Power* (Wheaton, IL: Crossway, 2011), 185.

20. From Anne Bradstreet, "The Vanity of All Worldly Things," in *Chapters into Verse: Poetry in English Inspired by the Bible*, ed. Robert Atwan and Laurence Wieder (New York: Oxford University Press, 1993), 1:354.

your presence there is fullness of joy; at your right hand are pleasures forevermore" (Ps. 16:11).

Jesus alone knows how and where to enter into the Master's joy (Matt. 25:23). "For what does it profit a man to gain the whole world and forfeit his soul?" (Mark 8:36). Nothing. It is vanity. The house of hedonism is hollow. But what does it profit a man to lose his life for Jesus' sake and the sake of his kingdom? Everything!

So why do we fool around with drink and sex and ambition when infinite joy is offered us? Why, like children making mud pies in a slum when the offer of an oceanside vacation is given to us, do we fail to consider our Lord's unblushing promises of reward and the staggering nature of his rewards? Why are we so easily pleased? Why?[21] Let us flee from the hollow house of hedonism into the hallowed presence of God.

21. Phrases taken from C. S. Lewis, *The Weight of Glory* (San Francisco: HarperCollins, 2001), 26.

5

ENJOYMENT EAST OF EDEN

Ecclesiastes 2:12–26

*There is nothing better for a person than that he should eat and
drink and find enjoyment in his toil. This also, I saw, is from the
hand of God, for apart from him who can eat or who can have
enjoyment? For to the one who pleases him God has given wisdom
and knowledge and joy, but to the sinner he has given the business
of gathering and collecting, only to give to one who pleases God.
This also is vanity and a striving after wind.* (Eccl. 2:24–26)

In Genesis 2:15–17, we read:

> The LORD God took the man and put him in the garden of Eden to work it
> and keep it. And the LORD God commanded the man, saying, "You may surely
> eat of every tree of the garden, but of the tree of the knowledge of good and
> evil you shall not eat, for in the day that you eat of it you shall surely *die*."

Contrast those verses with Genesis 3:4, where the serpent says to Eve,
"You will not surely die." Then what happens? Eve eats. Adam eats. And as
the serpent slinks away from the scene, death marches into the world. Apart
from the God-pleasing Enoch, who was "taken up so that he should not see
death" (Heb. 11:5; cf. Gen. 5:24), every person in Genesis from Adam to

Joseph dies. Listen to the lines from the sad litany. The first to go is Abel: "Cain rose up against his brother Abel and killed him" (Gen. 4:8c). The first death is a murder—one brother killing another! Then we come to Genesis 5, which records what might be termed *the death genealogy*. It begins, "This is the book of the generations of Adam" (5:1). So far, so good. But look what happens at the end of verse 5, where we read: "Thus all the days that Adam lived were 930 years, *and he died.*" Note next the repetition found at the end of verses 8, 11, 14, 17, 20, 27, and 31: "and he died." But what about righteous Noah? Sorry. "All the days of Noah were 950 years, and he died" (9:29). How about the holy patriarchs? Sorry again: "Abraham breathed his last and died" (25:8); "and Isaac breathed his last, and he died" (35:29); and of Jacob we read that a message was sent to Joseph, which said, "Your father gave this command before he died" (50:16). Not surprisingly, Genesis ends: "So Joseph died . . . . They embalmed him, and he was put in a coffin in Egypt" (50:26).

Who was right—God or Satan? The One who said, "You shall surely die"!

The book of Ecclesiastes assumes the sinful actions and consequences of the fall, and provides the Bible's most thorough exposition of its effects. What does life after Genesis 3 look like? Open Ecclesiastes and see it illustrated in living color. Thus far, we have seen enough cursedness for one sermon series. In Ecclesiastes 1:1–11 Solomon illustrated how our work doesn't work out; in 1:12–18 how our wisdom doesn't add up; and in 2:1–11 how our pleasures don't please. Next, in 2:12–26, he returns to wisdom again. This time, however, he encounters something worse than unanswered questions and increased sorrow. Here he finds that the Grim Reaper plays no favorites among the foolish *and the wise* children of Adam.

Consider Wisdom

Before we back into death ourselves, let us consider wisdom again. After testing pleasure, we read about Solomon's next consideration:

> So I turned to consider wisdom and madness and folly. For what can the man do who comes after the king? Only what has already been done. Then I saw that there is more gain in wisdom than in folly, as there is more gain in light than in darkness. The wise person has his eyes in his head, but the fool walks in darkness. (Eccl. 2:12–14)

Here, as folly parallels darkness, so wisdom parallels light:

there is more gain	in wisdom	than in folly, . . .
there is more gain	in light	than in darkness. (Eccl. 2:13)

When placed up against profitless "madness and folly"—that is, the immoral and idolatrous pleasures of Ecclesiastes 2:4–8—wisdom yields "more gain" (twice in verse 13). Compared to the fool who "walks in darkness," wisdom shows the wise the way to "succeed in life right now."[1] Though with earthly wisdom no one gains an edge on death or finds eternal value in his accomplishments—"the man . . . who comes after the king . . . [will do] what has already been done" (v. 12)—nevertheless, in the meantime, wisdom has its advantages. As Michael Eaton summarizes:

> To possess wisdom will give success (10:10), preserve life and protect (7:12). It gives strength (7:19) and joy (8:1), and is better than mere brute strength (9:16). Man is guided by it (2:3), toils by it (2:21), tests and weighs experiences by it (7:23). Even the practical politics of delivering cities involves wisdom (9:15). Limited it may be, but it is still indispensable.[2]

Thus, we would be stupid not to take hold of it and use it like a flashlight in a power outage. Why tumble down the stairs when we can use the light to find our way? It is better to live like smart Samuel than stupid Samson. It is better to play the game of life with our eyes in their sockets rather than in our pockets.[3]

WHAT MAKES WISDOM LIKE WIND

Wisdom has its downside, however.

After considering the benefits of wisdom in Ecclesiastes 2:12–14, next Pastor Solomon files his complaints against it. Four times he repeats the

---

1. Tremper Longman III, *The Book of Ecclesiastes*, New International Commentary on the Old Testament (Grand Rapids: Eerdmans, 1998), 98.

2. Michael A. Eaton, *Ecclesiastes: An Introduction and Commentary*, Tyndale Old Testament Commentaries 16 (Downers Grove, IL: InterVarsity Press, 1983), 69.

3. "To have one's eyes in one's head is a Hebraism, which we express commonly in German this way: 'Whoever wants to play chess, had better not hide his eyes in his pocket.' By this we mean that he must not only be an expert at the game but must also be a watchful and diligent player." Martin Luther, "Notes on Ecclesiastes," in *Luther's Works*, trans. and ed. Jaroslav Pelikan, 56 vols. (St. Louis: Concordia, 1972), 15:40.

phrase "this also is vanity," and adds the phrase "for all is vanity" (v. 17). Wisdom has its vanities as well as its values, and these vanities can be summarized under two headings.

First, *wisdom offers no protection against death*:

> And yet I perceived that the same event [death] happens to all of them. Then I said in my heart, "What happens to the fool will happen to me also. Why then have I been so very wise?" And I said in my heart that *this also is vanity.* For of the wise as of the fool there is no enduring remembrance, seeing that in the days to come all will have been long forgotten. How the wise dies just like the fool! So I hated life, because what is done under the sun was grievous to me, *for all is vanity* and a striving after wind. (Eccl. 2:14–17)

Duane Garrett summarizes this section well when he writes, "Future generations will no more remember the scholar than they will the beggar on the street."[4] After a few years in the grave, Einstein's dead bones are virtually indistinguishable from Joe Bum's or Jane Doe's.

When my wife and I were first married, we lived in Hyde Park three blocks from the University of Chicago, ranked as one of the best schools in the world. Needless to say, we lived in a highly intellectual environment. Even our neighbor downstairs in our three-flat, who taught salsa dancing, had a Ph.D. in mathematics.

During this time, I worked at Ex Libris Theological Books, a small bookstore that was the local intellectual hub for theological banter. Many notable scholars from Chicago and around the world came through its doors daily. The owner was an eccentric man who loved to put these celebrated scholars in their place with his biting sarcasm. One of his favorite put-downs went like this. First, he would ask Dr. Renowned Scholar, "So how's that book you've been working on?" If the scholar would say, "Oh, it just came out last week," or something similar, the owner would reply (and this was his favorite joke), "So is it out of print yet?" The joke is this: few books, especially scholarly ones, stay in print very long. But the theological point is this: your work is soon to be "out of print," no longer relevant or interesting.

---

4. Duane A. Garrett, *Proverbs, Ecclesiastes, Song of Songs*, New American Commentary 14 (Nashville: Broadman & Holman, 1993), 294. As Roland E. Murphy notes, because of death, "the superiority of wisdom therefore is seen to be quite theoretical." *Ecclesiastes*, Word Biblical Commentary 23A (Nashville: Thomas Nelson, 1992), 22.

People have stopped buying the book. Your wisdom is out of date. Its time of significance has expired.

These scholars would always laugh, but it is really no laughing matter. You can have worldly wisdom—have the best mind, be the most learned, understand how and why things work—but you cannot understand everything, and you cannot expect to be remembered for long. Your book will soon be out of print. Your significance will be as lasting as the beautiful bouquet of flowers that a loved one will place by your grave on the day of your burial. While I like Woody Allen's joke—"I don't want to achieve immortality through my work. I want to achieve it by not dying"[5]—it is no joke to those of us who take life *and death* seriously. Both the wise and foolish are equal heirs of Genesis and its fatal refrain: "and he died."

Second, *wisdom offers no protection against ill-deserved inheritors*:

> I hated all my toil in which I toil under the sun, seeing that I must leave it to the man who will come after me, and who knows whether he will be wise or a fool? Yet he will be master of all for which I toiled and used my wisdom under the sun. *This also is vanity.* So I turned about and gave my heart up to despair over all the toil of my labors under the sun, because sometimes a person who has toiled with wisdom and knowledge and skill must leave everything to be enjoyed by someone who did not toil for it. *This also is vanity* and a great evil. What has a man from all the toil and striving of heart with which he toils beneath the sun? For all his days are full of sorrow, and his work is a vexation. Even in the night his heart does not rest. *This also is vanity.* (Eccl. 2:18–23)

Rashi, the renowned medieval commentator, likely was right that here the aged King Solomon foresaw that his glorious kingdom would, within a short time, fracture in the days of his son Rehoboam (cf. 1 Kings 11:41–12:24). Whether this misfortune was on Solomon's mind or not (and whether we are royalty or not), we must all admit that there is a sense of powerlessness when it comes to the final word on our whole life's work. After we die, we have absolutely no control over how our heirs will spend our life earnings. Will they wisely invest it in reliable stock, or will they

5. Woody Allen, quoted in Philip Graham Ryken, *Ecclesiastes: Why Everything Matters*, ed. R. Kent Hughes, Preaching the Word (Wheaton, IL: Crossway, 2010), 63.

blow it all on expensive pot? Will they give it away to fight the troubles people face, or they will bet it all on Percy's Revenge in the third race at Pimlico? "It is bad enough that one person will receive what another toiled for. How much worse if the recipient is a fool!"[6]

Please allow another Ex Libris illustration. One day the widow of a prominent historian from the University of Chicago came into the bookstore. She relayed the sad news of her husband's death. We consoled her. She then asked whether the store would be interested in buying his library. She consoled us! After she headed for the door, the owner whispered to me his second-favorite line—about our bookstore's offering "free book removal." You see, the best scenario for the business was for some great scholar to die, to have a loved one come in and offer the books to us for about a dollar each, and then for us to offer the service of removing those volumes without cost. I don't know whether my dear wife (upon my parting) is poised to pocket the chump change gained from some bookstore's "free book removal" service, but it remains a steady concern of mine. I trust her in everything but that!

On a more serious note (although I'm serious enough about who will get my library), I worry about who will inherit my pulpit. As a student of church history, I know that many of America's once-orthodox pulpits are now filled by a bunch of unorthodox liberals. What a galling thought it is for me that in the next thirty years, in the very place I stand to preach, a man or a woman might be spouting heresy. Or, who knows, maybe the church will be a convenience store. That's at least a more reassuring thought.

Disgust and Delight

Wisdom. What good is it? Pastor Solomon is right: wisdom offers no protection against either death or ill-deserved inheritors. What, then? His answer might surprise you: disgust, and then delight.

First the disgust. An appropriate question to ask when reading Ecclesiastes is: "How does this make you feel?" That question can be a recipe for exegetical disaster at an everyday Bible study, but Ecclesiastes is not

---

6. Michael V. Fox, *Ecclesiastes*, JPS Bible Commentary (Philadelphia: Jewish Publication Society, 2004), 17.

an everyday Bible text. Listen to the emotions expressed here (ones that we should feel ourselves). If we go back to Ecclesiastes 2:17, Solomon admits, "So I hated life." To that he adds in verse 18, "I hated all my toil," in verse 20, "I . . . gave my heart up to despair," and in verse 23, that his days have been "full of sorrow" and his nights full of insomnia. This brother needs some Prozac! He sounds nothing like the famous California preacher, smiling ear-to-ear in his sun-filled Crystal Cathedral while he recites his second Be-Happy Attitude: "I am really hurting, but I will bounce back." Rather, Solomon sounds like Job on the ashes ("I loathe my life; I will give free utterance to my complaint; I will speak in the bitterness of my soul," Job 10:1), Jeremiah in the stocks ("Cursed be the day on which I was born! The day when my mother bore me, let it not be blessed!" Jer. 20:14), and Jesus on the cross ("My God, my God, why have you forsaken me?" Matt. 27:46).

Herman Melville labeled Ecclesiastes "the truest of all books,"[7] and part of its truth is the true emotions expressed. Solomon's gloomy confessions sound real because they are realistic. Whoever takes a sober look at what becomes of even the wise will have a hard time answering "Fine" to the common question, "How's it going?" As Daniel Fredericks observes, "We have been brainwashed by the heresy of 'fineness' when even as believers we live lives punctuated by 'cursedness.'"[8] We should not cower from feeling disgust when it is our Christian duty.

DELIGHT IN GOD'S GIFTS

But let us also feel the delight; for it, too, is our duty. Like Job, Solomon undergoes testing (Eccl. 1:12–2:26). Yet unlike Job's situation, these tests are not God-imposed but self-imposed. The test question found in our text is: Will human smarts bring lasting meaning and fulfillment to earthly life? The answer is a resounding "no." The shadow of death covers everybody's grave—the atheist ("there is no God"), the agnostic ("who knows if there is a God?"), the hedonist ("pleasure is my god"), the

7. Herman Melville, quoted in Leland Ryken, *Words of Delight: A Literary Introduction to the Bible*, 2nd ed. (Grand Rapids: Baker, 1992), 319.

8. Daniel C. Fredericks, "Ecclesiastes," in Daniel C. Fredericks and Daniel J. Estes, *Ecclesiastes and the Song of Songs*, Apollos Old Testament Commentary 16 (Downers Grove, IL: InterVarsity Press, 2010), 107. I am indebted to Fredericks for his allusion to Robert Schuller and the "I'm fine" reference.

nihilist ("who cares if there is a God?"), and even the clever believer ("I know that my Redeemer lives!" *and* "I know that the square root of 596 is 24.4131112315"). Again similar to Job's story, however, there is some light at the end of the drama. God arrives on the scene with an inspired answer that is sufficient to move us from despairing lamentation to a consoling resolution:

> There is nothing better for a person [*adam*] than that he should eat and drink and find enjoyment in his toil. This also, I saw, is from the hand of God, for apart from him who can eat or who can have enjoyment? For to the one who pleases him God has given wisdom and knowledge and joy, but to the sinner he has given the business of gathering and collecting, only to give to one who pleases God. This also is vanity and a striving after wind. (Eccl. 2:24–26)

Because this section begins with seemingly reluctant optimism ("there is nothing better") and ends with the same refrain heard earlier ("This also is vanity"), some scholars take this conclusion to express a *carpe diem* ("seize the day") attitude: whoever dies with more food in his stomach and the best wine in his mouth wins (1 Cor. 15:32). Such a reading is wrong, however, because it fails to see how disgust and delight might blend in one cup. One is reminded of the cartoon in which Charles Dickens is approached by his publisher, who asks, "Mr. Dickens, either it was the best of times or it was the worst of times. It can't be both."[9] As in life, so here in Ecclesiastes—it is indeed *both!* The curse is the curse. We all live *and die* under its sovereignty. Yet we serve a God who is in the business of bringing life out of death and of cursing the curse itself by his Son who became a curse for us. And while it might go too far to call Pastor Solomon a "Preacher of Joy," as R. N. Whybray famously did over three decades ago,[10] I can agree with Phil Ryken, who wrote that "these verses are an oasis of optimism in a wilderness of despair."[11] They are an oasis because God is there! The shadow of the Almighty can cover the shadow of death, as it does here. God's *presence* and God's *presents* are the reasons to rejoice.

9. Quoted in Ryken, *Ecclesiastes*, 72.
10. R. N. Whybray, "Qoheleth, Preacher of Joy," *Journal for the Study of the Old Testament* 7, 23 (1982): 87–98.
11. Ryken, *Ecclesiastes*, 71.

God's Gift of Justice

Unlike Paul's letters, where God is mentioned in nearly every breath, in Ecclesiastes we hold our breath until we finally hear something said about God. We come to the end of two chapters of a book in the Bible and God has hardly been mentioned. This does not mean that his existence and power haven't been assumed. But Pastor Solomon has been preaching about life without God in view. Now and finally, God is set before our eyes. Look what is said about him, and conversely about us: to "the one who pleases God" (Eccl. 2:26c; cf. 26a), God gives the gifts of justice and joy.

This *justice* part is spelled out in Ecclesiastes 2:26: "For to the one who pleases him God has given wisdom and knowledge and joy, but to the sinner he has given the business of gathering and collecting, only to give to one who pleases God." To those who have overly egalitarian or squeamish sensibilities when it comes to justice, this verdict is a foreign concept. But to those who are steeped in the theology of biblical wisdom literature (e.g., Job 27:16–17; 28:8; Prov. 13:22), as well as a humble understanding and appreciation of God's grace, it resounds as truthful as does Jesus' parable of the ten minas. We say "Amen" when Jesus pronounces his just verdict: "I tell you that to everyone who has, more will be given, but from the one who has not, even what he has will be taken away" (Luke 19:26; cf. v. 27!). And to those of us who lived through a life of suffering for righteousness' sake and were persistently oppressed under the injustice of evildoers, that decree of final justice answers a cry from the depths of the human soul: "Free at last, free at last, thank God Almighty, we are free at last." When the Red Sea covered the Egyptian army, when Sisera fell into the hands of Jael, and when Haman was hanged "on the gallows that he had prepared for Mordecai" (Esth. 7:10), God's people rightly rejoiced in God's justice. So, too, when Jesus comes again to judge the wicked at the final judgment, God's people will rightly and eternally rejoice in the justice of God.[12] We will sing a hallelujah chorus:

> After this I heard what seemed to be the loud voice of a great multitude in heaven, crying out,

---

12. For more on the theme of God's people's rejoicing in God's justice, see Douglas Sean O'Donnell, *God's Lyrics: Rediscovering Worship through Old Testament Songs* (Phillipsburg, NJ: P&R Publishing, 2010), 145–57.

"Hallelujah!
Salvation and glory and power belong to our God,
    for his judgments are true and just;
for he has judged the great prostitute
    who corrupted the earth with her immorality,
and has avenged on her the blood of his servants."

Once more they cried out,

"Hallelujah!
The smoke from her goes up forever and ever." (Rev. 19:1–3)

God's Gift of Joy

Justice is one of the gifts God gives to "the one who pleases him" (Eccl. 2:26a) by trusting and obeying him (12:13).[13] The other gifts are stated at the beginning of verse 26: "For to the one who pleases him God has given wisdom and knowledge and joy." Thus far, Pastor Solomon has been searching for wisdom and using "wisdom" or "knowledge" (which here again is synonymous with "wisdom"). But now, for the first time, *God* is mentioned in relation to wisdom. Finally and explicitly, wisdom is seen as a divine gift.

The same thought is expressed differently in Ecclesiastes 2:24–25, with the addition of food, drink, and toil. Verse 24 begins, "There is nothing better for a person than that he should eat and drink and find enjoyment in his toil." This claim raises an obvious question: "How is it possible to enjoy such pre-fall pleasures (Gen. 2:15–16)?" The answer is given: "This also, I saw, is from the hand of God, for apart from him who can eat or who can have enjoyment?" (Eccl. 2:24b–25). God is the One who gives gifts, and God is also the One who gives the ability to enjoy such gifts.

When Solomon explored enjoyment (the pleasure test of Ecclesiastes 2:1–11) as if it were independent from God, as an autonomous human experiment, he found that grabbing hold of joy from idolatrous and immoral pleasures was like trying to staple the wind. If we neglect God in our pursuit of joy, everything good in life—for example, possessions and pleasures—slips through our grasp. But if we give "thanks to God the Father" through Jesus Christ (Col. 3:17; cf. 1 Tim. 4:4–5) for every good gift, then whatever

13. "Without faith"—or "fear[ing] God" (Eccl. 12:13)—"it is impossible to please" God (Heb. 11:6).

we receive from him—practical wisdom, daily bread, red table wine, our lifetime of labors, and so on[14]—is seen as a gift that brings genuine joy.

This principle is reiterated throughout the New Testament, including in two texts from 1 Timothy: "Now there is great gain in godliness with contentment, for we brought nothing into the world, and we cannot take anything out of the world. But if we have food and clothing, with these we will be content" (1 Tim. 6:6–8); "as for the rich in this present age, charge them not to be haughty, nor to set their hopes on the uncertainty of riches, but on God, who richly provides us with everything to enjoy" (6:17). But perhaps the closest New Testament commentary on our text comes from Jesus himself, in his parable of the rich fool. After our Lord taught, "Take care, and be on your guard against all covetousness, for one's life does not consist in the abundance of his possessions" (Luke 12:15, an apt application of Ecclesiastes 2:1–11), he illustrates his principle with a parable:

> The land of a rich man produced plentifully, and he thought to himself, "What shall I do, for I have nowhere to store my crops?" And he said, "I will do this: I will tear down my barns and build larger ones, and there I will store all my grain and my goods. And I will say to my soul, Soul, you have ample goods laid up for many years; relax, eat, drink, be merry." But God said to him, "Fool! This night your soul is required of you, and the things you have prepared, whose will they be? [i.e., who will inherit them?]" So is the one who lays up treasure for himself and is not rich toward God. (Luke 12:16b–21)

Here, by not properly acknowledging the unpredictable nature and irresistible power of death, the foolish rich man adopts an attitude opposite to the one encouraged in Ecclesiastes. Instead of acknowledging God as the Gift-Giver, enjoying what God has given, and keeping busy about his daily labors, the rich man boasts in his seemingly self-acquired goods ("my crops," "my barns," and "my grain") as he hoards what he has, kicks up his feet on

---

14. It was not uncommon in patristic and rabbinic exegesis of Ecclesiastes to allegorize sensual pleasures—including eating and drinking—into spiritual ones (for rabbinic readings, see Fox, *Ecclesiastes*, 18). For example, Jerome comments: "Furthermore, as the Lord's flesh is the true food, and his blood the true drink, on an anagogical level all the good we have in the present age is to feed on his flesh and drink his blood, not just at the sacrament but also in our reading of the Scriptures; because the true food and drink, which is gained from the word of God, is knowledge of the Scriptures." *Commentary on Ecclesiastes*, trans. Richard J. Goodrich and David J. D. Miller, Ancient Christian Writers 66 (New York: Newman, 2012), 60; cf. 54.

the sofa, leans back, and says, "Chill out, eat up, drink down, have a good time." The fool does not take God seriously or honor his gifts properly. Thus, he not only fails to enjoy for a day what he has gained but also loses it all that very night.

Do not be a rich fool. Be a poor-in-spirit servant. Serve God with all that you think (wisdom) and all that you do (toil). Never stop lifting your hands up in praise for each and every gift that falls from heaven's hands. "So, whether you eat or drink [those simple, common samplings of daily pleasures], or whatever you do [you'd better be doing something!], do all to the glory of God" (1 Cor. 10:31). The pursuit of such a goal is our "inescapable sacred duty."[15]

The Table

After preaching Ecclesiastes 2:1–11 ("The Hollow House of Hedonism"), someone from my congregation came up to me and said, "That is the most visual sermon I have ever heard . . . or seen." If I were to suggest a picture of Ecclesiastes 2:12–26, the image of *a table* comes to mind. In fact, three tables come to mind. The first table is the ordinary kitchen table where a Christian family gathers to eat and drink, enjoying what God has given and acknowledging their gratitude by saying grace before the meal. The second table is the one mentioned in Psalm 23. In verses 4–5, David writes not only about God's presence that sustains him as he walks through the valley of the shadow of death, but also of God's having prepared a table for him in the presence of his enemies. I envision David's many conquered enemies as either being held so far at bay that they are enchained around the table, envying him as he eats, or else being so completely subdued that *they are serving* him the meal. Whether that is the precise imagery of Psalm 23 or not, it is very close to the imagery of Ecclesiastes 2:24–26. Certainly the overall picture of both sections of Scripture is a celebration of God's gifts of justice and joy.

The final table is the table of the Last Supper and, for us now, the Lord's Supper. Jesus walked in the same world in which Solomon walked. Sin was

---

15. I borrowed this phrase, in a slightly different context, from Robert Gordis, who wrote: "Since he insists that the pursuit of happiness with which man has been endowed by the Creator is an inescapable sacred duty, it follows that it must be an inalienable right." *Koheleth—The Man and His World*, 3rd ed. (New York: Schocken, 1968), 129.

crouching at the entrance; death was knocking down everyone's door. But in that fallen world Jesus celebrated many feasts, turning water into wine (John 2:1–11), dining with sinners at Matthew's house (Matt. 9:10–15), and feeding the multitudes (14:14–21; 15:32–38). Then, finally, he reclined at the table with his disciples to celebrate the final Passover meal.

> Now as they were eating, Jesus took bread, and after blessing it broke it and gave it to the disciples, and said, "Take, eat; this is my body." And he took a cup, and when he had given thanks he gave it to them, saying, "Drink of it, all of you, for this is my blood of the covenant, which is poured out for many for the forgiveness of sins. I tell you I will not drink again of this fruit of the vine until [ah, there's going to be resurrection of the body!] that day when I drink it new with you in my Father's kingdom." (Matt. 26:26–29)

Whenever we celebrate the Lord's Supper, we give thanks, break the bread, and drink from the cup. In so doing we "proclaim the Lord's death *until he comes*" (1 Cor. 11:26). We proclaim his death because it is the only death that has the power to kill death. When Abel died, he was finished; when Jesus died, it was finished. The power of death was dead—and death died. Through the cross and resurrection of Jesus, death was "swallowed up in victory" (15:54).

6

THE TERRIFIC TRUTH
ABOUT TIME

Ecclesiastes 3:1—15

*I perceived that whatever God does endures forever; nothing can
be added to it, nor anything taken from it. God has done it, so
that people fear before him. (Eccl. 3:14)*

hen I preached the sermon that became the third chapter in this volume—"A Crack in the Window of Wisdom"—I began by stating how for five hours and nine minutes Daniel Tammet recited 22,514 digits of π (pi) from memory without error. Then I confidently attempted my own three-digit recitation, stating that Tammet had begun with the numbers "3.41 and the rest." The effect of my mistake was astounding. Schoolchildren fainted in astonishment. My wife laughed out loud. And various mathematicians in my congregation (there are many, too many!) gasped in horror. In fact, these unmerciful mathematicians waited with bated breath to be the first to tell me after the service of my grievous error: that pi starts with 3.14. All in all, it was a good illustration of the limits of my own wisdom.

One wonders whether William Ernest Henley felt just as dumb on his deathbed, or any other moment after he wrote his pompous and preposterous poem, "Invictus" (Latin "unconquered").[1] It begins:

---

1. While elsewhere Henley acknowledged his own death (see his poem "Margaritae Sorori," which ends: "The sundown splendid and serene, Death"), and while he penned "Invictus" to voice his resilience

Out of the night that covers me,
Black as the Pit from pole to pole,
I thank whatever gods may be
For my unconquerable soul.

And it ends:

It matters not how strait the gate,
How charged with punishments the scroll,
I am the master of my fate:
I am the captain of my soul.

Dear Mr. Henley, were you really unconquerable? Henley died more than a century ago, at the age of fifty-three. Was he indeed the master of his fate and the captain of his soul?

THE TICK AND TOCK OF TIME

Another famous poem—perhaps the most famous in the Bible—develops nearly the opposite theme of Henley's poem.

First we have the poem itself, which baby boomers are tempted to sing to The Byrds' famous tune "Turn! Turn! Turn!"

For everything there is a season, and a time for every matter under heaven:

a time to be born, and a time to die;
a time to plant, and a time to pluck up what is planted;
a time to kill, and a time to heal;
a time to break down, and a time to build up;
a time to weep, and a time to laugh;
a time to mourn, and a time to dance;
a time to cast away stones, and a time to gather stones together;
a time to embrace, and a time to refrain from embracing;
a time to seek, and a time to lose;

---

after his foot was amputated as the result of a tuberculosis infection, I still find his famous poem both arrogant and ironic. William Ernest Henley, "Double Ballade of the Nothingness of Things," in *Poems* (London: David Nutt, 1919), 162.

a time to keep, and a time to cast away;
a time to tear, and a time to sew;
a time to keep silence, and a time to speak;
a time to love, and a time to hate;
a time for war, and a time for peace. (Eccl. 3:1–8)

There are four key observations to make about this poem. First, it is a poem. This is the simplest observation to make, but also the most founda-tional. While this isn't the first poetic portion in Ecclesiastes (1:13–18 was poetically structured), it is certainly abruptly different from any other sec-tion and "quite unlike anything in the Hebrew Bible."[2]

I won't point out every unique and common poetic device used—we simply don't have *time* (!) for that—but I will point out two. First is the rep-etition of the word *time*, used in the introductory sentence (Eccl. 3:1) and then repeated twenty-eight times in the poem (vv. 2–8), covering fourteen pairs (2 × 7 = 14), with seven serving as the Bible's perfect number. Thus, this is the perfect poem about time. Seriously. The repetition gives rhythm to the poem, making it both memorable and beautiful. As the activities of creation—the sun, wind, and streams in 1:5–7—had circular motion to them, here in 3:1–8 we have a back-and-forth effect to describe human activity. It is like the tick and tock of a clock. Or, to borrow Pastor Solomon's favorite metaphor—*hebel* ("vanity" or "breath")—this poem "*breathes* rhythmically with metrical inhaling and exhaling. A time for this, a time for that (a cadence of polarity and opposition); inhale, exhale; inhale, exhale."[3]

The second poetic device is the poem's parallel structure. Parallelism is the basic construct of Hebrew poetry. Every biblical poem uses it—from Adam's ode to Mary's *Magnificat*. Therefore, Christians who must adhere to the doctrine of the Trinity and ought to be able to recite the Ten Commandments, the Lord's Prayer, and the Apostles' Creed must also comprehend parallelism in poems. How else can you rightly read your Bibles? The Psalms, the Song of Songs, Proverbs, and Lamentations are wholly poetic; the Prophets, Job, and Ecclesiastes are mainly poetic.

2. Eric S. Christianson, *Ecclesiastes through the Centuries*, Blackwell Bible Commentaries (Malden, MA: Blackwell, 2007), 165.
3. Daniel C. Fredericks, "Ecclesiastes," in Daniel C. Fredericks and Daniel J. Estes, *Ecclesiastes and the Song of Songs*, Apollos Old Testament Commentary 16 (Downers Grove, IL: InterVarsity Press, 2010), 111.

God's Word is filled with poetry. God loves poetry. If you love God, you should love poetry, too.

What is wonderful about this simple art form—parallelism—is that it can easily be translated from Hebrew into hundreds of other languages without losing its form. Isn't God's wise providence amazing? Below, Sidney Greidanus identifies the three basic types of parallelisms, all of which are employed in this poem:

> Repetition shows up particularly in the parallel constructions in the poem. The poem consists of fourteen lines, each line constructed in the form of antithetic parallelism. For example,
>
> A time to be born, and a time to die [A—B].
>
> Most verses of two lines are constructed in the form of regular parallelism (either synonymous or synthetic). For example:

| A time to be born, | and a time to die; | [A—B] |
| A time to plant, | and a time to pluck up what is planted | [A'—B'] |

> Verse 8, by contrast, has inverted parallelism:

| A time to love, | and a time to hate; | [A $\diagdown$ B] |
| A time for war, | and a time for peace | [B' $\diagup$ A']⁴ |

As demonstrated above, this is a poem. Further, this is a poem about life in a fallen world. That is not to say that the actions listed here are always or inherently evil. For example, those who claim that killing, war, and hatred are always evil have not carefully read their Bibles. The Bible contains regulations for capital punishment, examples of just wars, laws on sacrificing animals, and exhortations to hate what God hates. But after verse 2 introduces the beginning and end (birth and death), the rest of the poem follows with a summary of everything in between those two times within the context of a fallen world. Words such as *kill, weep, mourn, hate,* and *war,* as well as the reality of death, did not exist before Adam ate from

---

4. Sidney Greidanus, *Preaching Christ from Ecclesiastes: Foundations for Expository Sermons* (Grand Rapids: Eerdmans, 2010), 72.

the tree of the knowledge of good and evil. So we should read this poem, in part, as a sad poem—a reminder of paradise lost. We also take the promises of Revelation 21:3–4—"Behold, the dwelling place of God is with man. . . . He will wipe away every tear from their eyes, and death shall be no more, neither shall there be mourning, nor crying, nor pain anymore"—to cover all the former realities of the curse in play here.

Third, this poem is a busy poem. Note all the activity going on: planting and plucking, mourning and dancing, breaking down and building up, tearing and sowing, and so on. While some of these activities are not to be classified as *toil*—for example, mourning and dancing—most of them fall under the category of *work*. This perhaps explains why the poem is followed by the question, "What gain has the worker from his toil?" (Eccl. 3:9). The fourteen pairs of opposite activities and emotions, which have no discernible order and an intentionally elastic application,[5] attempt to illustrate comprehensively the entirety of an individual's life. These pairs also highlight some of the major decisions to be made between the day of birth and the day of death, the two decisions that no one has sovereignty over.

There is a right time "to plant" (in the spring) and a right time "to pluck up what is planted" (at the harvest); a right time "to break down" (to destroy idols) and a right time "to build up" (to construct the temple); a right time "to mourn" (when a loved one has died) and a right time "to dance" (as David did before the ark of the covenant); a right time "to cast away stones" (to cultivate a field or ruin one in a time of war) and a right time "to gather stones together" (to build a home for one's family or a fortress for one's city); a right time "to embrace" (on your wedding night) and a right time "to refrain from embracing" (a person with leprosy);[6] a right time "to keep" (when Joseph gathered grain for seven years during famine) and a right time "to cast away" (for instance, throwing Jonah overboard!); a right time "to tear" (when Job tore his robe after he lost his children) and a right time "to sew" (like the wife in Proverbs 31 clothing her household in scarlet); a right time

5. I agree with Graham S. Ogden that "in seeking the meaning or significance of the poem as a whole, it is unnecessary that we assign a meaning to every element." *Qoheleth*, 2nd ed., Readings: A New Biblical Commentary (Sheffield, UK: Sheffield Phoenix Press, 2007), 57.

6. As the realities of Genesis 1–3 are assumed, so, too, are the rules of the Pentateuch. Ecclesiastes 3:2, 5, 6, 7, and 8 seem to assume that God's law is in place. For example, according to Leviticus 15:24, a man was to refrain from embracing (i.e., having sexual intercourse) when his wife was ritually unclean (i.e., menstruating).

"to keep silence" (as did Jesus on trial before the Sanhedrin) and a right time "to speak" ("a word fitly spoken is like apples of gold in a setting of silver," Prov. 25:11); a right time "for war" (when the walls of Jericho came tumbling down) and a right time "for peace" (when the walls between God and man and Jews and Gentiles were broken down by Jesus' death). There is an appropriate time for everything done "under heaven," and we need to have the wisdom to set our clocks by *divine time*—which is set by our Father "in heaven" (Eccl. 5:2).

Fourth, the poem ends with the word *peace* (*shalom* in Hebrew), and yet we are left with anything but *shalom*. The lack of peace has to do with the unsettledness of mind. I feel as the Ethiopian eunuch felt after reading Isaiah—that I need someone to explain this text to me. I feel as Jesus' disciples often felt after he spoke in parables: "Explain to us the parable of the weeds of the field" (Matt. 13:36). So here I say and pray (and you can join me in saying and praying), "Lord, explain to us the purpose of this poem."

THE TIMELY TRUTH

Thankfully, the Lord hears our prayer and interprets the poem in Ecclesiastes 3:9–15. These verses should settle any unsettledness (mentally, not necessarily spiritually) related to the poem's meaning. Note the structure: There is a question (v. 9), followed by three perceptions ("I have seen," v. 10, and "I perceived," vv. 12, 14). The poem in verses 1–8 summarizes what we do in time. The question in verse 9 naturally follows, asking, "All for what?" Then verses 10–15 explain what God does with time and, in light of that, what we should do in time with God.

God and Time

We begin with Ecclesiastes 3:9–11, where we read about what God does with time:

What gain has the worker from his toil? I have seen the business that God has given to the children of man to be busy with. He has made everything beautiful in its time. Also, he has put eternity into man's heart, yet so that he cannot find out what God has done from the beginning to the end.

73

Before I lay out the lesson, notice how the camera lens has shifted. In Ecclesiastes 3:1–8, as human life under the sun is depicted seemingly in its entirety, there is no mention of God. The lens is focused on us. Then, in verses 9–15, the camera shifts to God, who is mentioned eight times! Now we see something of what God sees. The purpose of seeing from a heavenly perspective the tick and tock of time on earth is, first of all, so that we might *embrace the beauty of God's comprehensive control of everything*. This is the lesson we learn from verses 9–11.

In his book *Joy at the End of the Tether: The Inscrutable Wisdom of Ecclesiastes*, Douglas Wilson uses the oft-repeated illustration of a tapestry on a loom to illustrate man's view of the ways of God. Wilson writes:

> From the vantage underneath, little is visible but snarls and knots. But above, the beautiful pattern of the work on the loom can be seen. As Solomon has shown, we live our lives under the loom, and everything we see is vanity. So how can we see the pattern above? The only possible answer is through faith in a sovereign God.[7]

The first part of that faith is shown here. Just because God has placed eternity in our hearts—"an etching of the eternal on our soul"[8]—does not mean that we understand how God's ordering of everything works. We are like Augustine, who said that he understood the concept of time up to the point when someone asked him to explain it.[9] God has made us inquisitive about eternity. But just because he has given us a key to open some lock does not mean that he has shown us where on earth the door is.

The right response to this frustration is joy-filled faith. Enjoy what God has given, as we will learn in Ecclesiastes 3:12–13. And enjoy the mystery as well. Humbly concede that God alone is great, and boldly bow before "the Potentate of time."[10] Look above the loom, not below, and see something of God's beautiful design.

---

7. Douglas Wilson, *Joy at the End of the Tether: The Inscrutable Wisdom of Ecclesiastes* (Moscow, ID: Canon Press, 1999), 41.

8. Fredericks, "Ecclesiastes," 124.

9. "What, then, is time? I know well enough what it is, provided that nobody ask me; but if I am asked what it is and try to explain, I am baffled." Augustine, *Confessions*, trans. R. S. Pine-Coffin (New York: Penguin, 1961), 9.14 (264).

10. The phrase comes from Matthew Bridges's hymn "Crown Him with Many Crowns." Twice Fredericks calls verse 11 "the greatest statement of divine providence in the whole Scripture." "Ecclesiastes," 117, 124.

When we struggle to acknowledge that God fits everything, even the fallen world's ugliness, into his sovereignly fitting plan—or to borrow a similar sentiment from Romans 8:28 that "all things work together for [our] good" as well as God's good—the incarnation puts an exclamation point over any and all question marks. We can trust in God's timing because in "the fullness of time" (Gal. 4:4) Jesus came to fulfill God's perfectly timed plan of salvation (John 7:30; 13:1). Jesus, who certainly has time under control (see Rev. 22:13; cf. Heb. 13:8; Rev. 1:8; 21:6), began his earthly ministry by announcing, "The time is fulfilled, and the kingdom of God is at hand" (Mark 1:15). Even the hour of his death was timed by God's watch: "Now before the Feast of the Passover, . . . Jesus knew that his hour had come to depart out of this world to the Father" (John 13:1; cf. Mark 8:31).[11] This is why, years after Jesus' earthly life, Paul wrote that "at *the right time* Christ died for the ungodly" (Rom. 5:6).

Like the apostles before Jesus' ascension, we want to know the fullness of God's plan. But Ecclesiastes gives the same answer that Jesus gave his apostles on that occasion: "It is not for you to know times or seasons that the Father has fixed by his own authority" (Acts 1:7). "The secret things belong to the LORD our God, but the things that are revealed belong to us and to our children forever" (Deut. 29:29). So let us rejoice in the revelation that we have been given. Let us be wise enough to recognize that our times are in God's hands (Ps. 31:15). Let us embrace the beauty of God's comprehensive control of everything.

Holy and Happy

Moving from the topic of God's sovereignty over time, Pastor Solomon next turns our attention to the related topic of human holiness and happiness in time. In Ecclesiastes 3:12–13, he writes:

> I perceived that there is nothing better for them than to be joyful and to do good as long as they live; also that everyone should eat and drink and take pleasure in all his toil—this is God's gift to man.

We may summarize the lesson from these two verses as follows: *Under the sunlight of God's sovereignty, we should be holy and happy.* The word

11. For this compilation of *time*-texts, I'm indebted to Greidanus, *Preaching Christ from Ecclesiastes*, 77–78.

holy is derived from the imperative "do good," which "should be taken in its moral and ethical sense" (i.e., that to "do good" is to do what is pleasing to God and in the best interest of others).[12] The word *happy* comes from the imperative "be joyful," and also from what is said in Ecclesiastes 3:13 about eating and drinking and taking pleasure in one's work. The concept of *God's sovereignty* flows from everything else that is said in verses 10–15. By *God's sovereignty* is meant what the Westminster divines meant when they wrote long ago: "God, from all eternity, did, by the most wise and holy counsel of His own will, freely, and unchangeably ordain whatsoever comes to pass" (WCF 3.1). Or, put more simply, as our Lord Jesus put it: "Are not two sparrows sold for a penny? And not one of them will fall to the ground apart from your Father" (Matt. 10:29).

Some Christians think that if God is exhaustively sovereign, there is little need to strive for holiness. But that idea is opposite to the motive given throughout the Bible. For example, in Romans 12:1, Paul reasons that God's sovereignty in salvation history and personal salvation (read Romans 4–11) is the basis for godly living: "I appeal to you therefore, brothers, by the mercies of God, to present your bodies as a living sacrifice, holy and acceptable to God, which is your spiritual worship."

Other Christians think that if God is exhaustively sovereign, they cannot possibly be happy. But acknowledging God as exhaustively sovereign is the only foundation for happiness. There are war cries and peace treaties, famines and feasts, acts of terrorism and kindness; on the face of this ever-turning terrestrial ball, we sleep and work, sow and harvest, cry and chuckle, live and die. But through it all, "the ever-constant swings of time's pendulum are suspended and held firmly by God."[13] We should acknowledge and appreciate these divine sovereign swings.

We live in a culture of control. Either we have control or we want control of everything around us—from the television in front of our eyes to the weather over our heads. But sometimes the world doesn't submit to our control. The television remote doesn't work. The weather won't cooperate.

Moreover, as much as our culture is obsessed with control, we also indulge in the mystery of what is obviously beyond our control. Storms that do not

12. Philip Graham Ryken, *Ecclesiastes: Why Everything Matters*, ed. R. Kent Hughes, Preaching the Word (Wheaton, IL: Crossway, 2010), 94.
13. William P. Brown, *Ecclesiastes*, Interpretation (Louisville, KY: Westminster John Knox, 2000), 42.

fit into the patterned predictions scare us and fascinate us. A thunderstorm still awes us, especially when we are driving through the middle of one. It is doubly awesome (if not terrifying) to walk through a forest during a storm and to hear trees fall around you (ask Martin Luther!).

Happily, insurance companies still call the destruction caused by hurricanes, tornadoes, and the like *acts of God.* It would be better, however, if *everyone* acknowledged that "God the great Creator of all things doth uphold, direct, dispose, and govern all creatures, actions, and things, from the greatest even to the least, by His most wise and holy providence, according to His infallible foreknowledge, and the free and immutable counsel of His own will, to the praise of the glory of His wisdom, power, justice, goodness, and mercy" (WCF 5.1). Put differently, it would be better if we acknowledged that God is in control. We cannot declare "the end from the beginning and from ancient times things not yet done" (Isa. 46:10). We cannot change the world's times and seasons or enthrone and dethrone its rulers (see Dan. 2:21; 7:12).

We are completely known by God, but we cannot completely know the plans or purposes of God because we are not God. The mirror before our faces is murky (1 Cor. 13:12), and our window into heaven narrow. What, then, should we do? Under the sunlight of God's sovereignty, we should be holy and happy. Rejoice in the Lord. Obey Christ's commands. Do good to others. Eat your roast-beef sandwich. Sip your Scotch. Smile, God loves you. Seriously.

The Purpose of Time

To review, there are three lessons to learn from our text. First, we should embrace the beauty of God's comprehensive control of everything. Wow! Second, under the sunlight of God's sovereignty, we should be holy and happy. Amen and amen. Third, *because of God's enduring, complete, and just providence, we should fear God.* That lesson is derived from Ecclesiastes 3:14–15:

> I perceived that whatever God does endures forever; nothing can be added to it, nor anything taken from it. God has done it, so that people fear before him. That which is, already has been; that which is to be, already has been; and God seeks what has been driven away.

77

God's work in the world is enduring, complete, and just. The idea of God's providence—his constant care of the world being *just*—comes from the final line: "and God seeks what has been driven away" (Eccl. 3:15), or, as the NIV translates it, "and God will call the past to account." This is a difficult phrase to translate and even more difficult to interpret. The sense seems to be that in the way God controls the times, he ends up balancing the scales of justice. For those who have lost out in life as the result of injustice, he redeems the time; and for those who have done injustice, he renders judgment in his time. On the last day, God will certainly call every action into account (11:9; 12:14)!

So here we are taught what God has done, is doing, and will do. We are taught something about his providence. We are also taught, in a brief but significant phrase, precisely what we should do. "I perceived that whatever God does endures forever; nothing can be added to it, nor anything taken from it. God has done it, *so that people fear before him*" (Eccl. 3:14).

As we are a culture that is obsessed with control, so we are also a culture obsessed with time. Think about how many times you look at a watch or a clock throughout the day. And each time we look at the time, how many of us acknowledge what is taught here—that the purpose of time is to fear God?

In the previous chapter, I talked about my precious library. It is now mostly housed in my beautiful church office. On one whole wall is a built-in bookcase. A man in the church built it for me. On the header above all the books, another man engraved the Greek letters *alpha* and *omega* intersecting each other. There is one engraving on the far left, another on the far right. Between those symbols he also engraved in Hebrew script Proverbs 1:7: "The fear of the LORD is the beginning of knowledge; fools despise wisdom and instruction." Not only is the fear of the Lord to be above my head or yours, but it is to be in our hearts, because without it we will not rightly relate with God.

The fear of the Lord is a central concept of the wisdom literature. But what does it mean to "fear the LORD," as Job, the Psalms, and Proverbs phrase it, or to "fear God," as Ecclesiastes has it? Does the word *fear* mean "awe," "reverence," "honor," "obedience," "faith," "hope," or "love"? Or does its meaning encompass all of the above? In chapter 1, I summarized this concept as *trembling trust*. It is not merely *trust*, but a trust that trembles before God. Those who want to neuter the word *fear* in the sense of removing terror before God miss just how *terr-ific* our God is![14] When Isaiah stood before the holy, holy, holy Lord, he said, "Woe is me!" (Isa. 6:5). When Peter witnessed Jesus' power in the miraculous catch of fish, "he fell down at Jesus' knees, saying, 'Depart from me, for I am a sinful man, O Lord'" (Luke 5:8). As viewing the fearful symmetry of a tiger's stripes in the wild would quickly bring you to acknowledge the tiger's awesome power over you, so witnessing the fearful symmetry of time is to bring us to our knees before our Creator—the Author and Sustainer of all things. When Paul wrote that we are to work out our salvation "with fear and trembling" (Phil. 2:12), he wasn't kidding. When the author of Hebrews wrote about the church's duty to offer to God "acceptable worship, with reverence and awe" (Heb. 12:28; cf. 4:1), he wasn't making a mere suggestion. When Jesus said, "And do not fear those who kill the body but cannot kill the soul. Rather fear him who can destroy both soul and body in hell" (Matt. 10:28), he wasn't giving advice that we should heed or not heed. The fear of God is a *fearful* thing.

The command to "fear God" is a central command in Ecclesiastes, and it is used at key points throughout the book (Eccl. 5:7; 7:18; 8:12–13; 12:13). Each context is slightly different, and each sheds further light on the concept of fearing God. In the context of 3:1–15, I will add the idea of a reverent recognition that we are *not* God (or that God is God!) to my definition of *trembling trust*. What God does lasts forever (v. 14). What we do (our "toil") doesn't (vv. 9, 15). What God does with time is to make everything beautiful according to his sovereign plan. But we cannot comprehend that plan fully (vv. 11, 15). This recognition that God is God and that we are not should lead us to trust in him (v. 14) and rejoice in his gifts (v. 13).

KING OF THE WORLD!

The movie *Titanic* has a famous scene in which Jack (Leonardo DiCaprio) mounts the ship's bow, throws out his arms, and shouts, "I'm the king of the world!" He pumps his fist and lays his head back in the wind. A few scenes

14. "Walther Eichrodt rightly observes that the fear of Yahweh simultaneously combines the *mysterium tremendum* ('repulsive mystery') and *mysterium fascinans* ('mysterious attraction') of God." Craig G. Bartholomew and Ryan P. O'Dowd, *Old Testament Wisdom Literature: A Theological Introduction* (Downers Grove, IL: InterVarsity Press, 2011), 25.

later, Jack isn't claiming such omnipotence over creation as the "unsinkable ship" sinks and he eventually descends into his watery grave.

Only God is the King of the world, and every tick and tock of its time is his. And our response to that terrific truth is to bow low and throw up our hands—not in despair or desolation, but in fear and faith. It is also to join Job in closing our mouths before the Almighty: "Behold, I am of small account; . . . I lay my hand on my mouth" (Job 40:4). And it is also to join Paul in raising our voices: "Oh, the depth of the riches and wisdom and knowledge of God! How unsearchable are his judgments and how inscrutable his ways! . . . For from him and through him and to him are all things. To him be glory forever. Amen" (Rom. 11:33, 36).

7

SIGHTS UNDER THE SUN

Ecclesiastes 3:16–22

Moreover, I saw under the sun that in the place of justice, even there was wickedness, and in the place of righteousness, even there was wickedness. I said in my heart, God will judge the righteous and the wicked, for there is a time for every matter and for every work. (Eccl. 3:16–17)

s that Mr. Scrooge?" "A Merry Christmas to you!" "And to you." "Bah! Humbug!" "Look! There's Papa and Tiny Tim!" "And God bless us, every one!" These are a few of the lines that were heard around my house one Christmastime, as my two oldest daughters prepared for their acting debut in a school production of Charles Dickens's *A Christmas Carol*. That classic tale is the story of the change that takes place in Ebenezer Scrooge, whom Dickens describes as "the squeezing, wrenching, grasping, scraping, clutching, covetous, old sinner!"[1] As the ghosts of Christmas past, present, and yet to come show Scrooge what his life has been, is, and will be, his eyes are opened to his sins.

1. Charles Dickens, *A Christmas Carol*, Everyman's Library Children's Classic (New York: Knopf, 1994), 13.

In Ecclesiastes, Pastor Solomon guides us on a tour of his life, showing us what he has seen under the sun so that we might see ourselves, our world, and God as we really should. The motif of *seeing* is not new. In Ecclesiastes 1:14, Solomon said, "I have seen everything that is done under the sun, and behold, all is vanity and a striving after wind." But he has also seen beyond the vanity to the value of wisdom over folly ("Then I saw that there is more gain in wisdom than in folly," 2:13) and the virtue of thanksgiving ("There is nothing better for a person than that he should eat and drink and find enjoyment in his toil. This also, I saw, is from the hand of God," 2:24). Yet in chapters 3 and 4, this theme of sight is more prominent. In 3:10, 12, and 14 we read the phrases "I have seen" and "I perceived." In 3:16, 22; 4:1, 4, 7, and 15 we find the phrase "I saw." So that we might change something about our own sinful perceptions and actions, we will focus on two sights that Solomon saw under the sun.

A Righteous Judge at the Right Time

Our tour begins in Ecclesiastes 3:16–17:

> Moreover, I saw under the sun that in the place of justice, even there was wickedness, and in the place of righteousness, even there was wickedness. I said in my heart, God will judge the righteous and the wicked, for there is a time for every matter and for every work.

The phrase "moreover, I saw" (which could be translated "I saw something *else*")[2] syntactically links us to the preceding verses. Old themes resurface: death, vanity, and enjoyment in our toil. New themes arise: wickedness and God's justice (continuing on from Ecclesiastes 3:15). Solomon saw human wickedness in verse 16 and divine justice in verse 17. Here the wickedness is that of injustice and unrighteousness. The shock here is not that injustice and unrighteousness exist, but where they exist. Injustice is rife everywhere in our world. The shock, however, is that

2. Iain Provan, *Ecclesiastes/Song of Songs*, NIV Application Commentary (Grand Rapids: Zondervan, 2001), 92.

82

it is even "in the place of justice" (i.e., a court of law). When we learn that a judge took a bribe, a lawyer misrepresented the facts, a witness lied under oath, or a murderer got off scot-free, we cringe.

Throughout the world, courts of law typically contain representation—often a sculpture—of Lady Justitia. Blindfolded, she holds balanced scales in her right hand and a large sword in her left. The blindfold represents impartiality (she judges everyone "without passion and prejudice"), the scales fairness, and the sword her swift and final justice. But here in Ecclesiastes, the blindfold is off, the scales off-balanced, and the sword stolen. Outside the courthouse the witches of Shakespeare's Macbeth are chanting, "Fair is foul and foul is fair."

The other location of unexpected immorality is "the place of righteousness" (i.e., the temple). Notice the synonymous parallelism of verse 16:

I saw under the sun that
   in the place of justice,   even there was wickedness, and
   in the place of righteousness,   even there was wickedness.

Both the court of law and the house of God are filled with evil people. Shocking!

Today the media makes a big deal about a prominent pastor who falls into some sexual sin or the CEO of a not-for-profit organization who embezzles funds. They do so because the story sells. As immoral and amoral as our culture is, we still expect certain people to be above such evils, or at least have the willpower to avoid immoralities. But sadly, even the reverends are irreverent. Some were in Pastor Solomon's day, and some are in ours as well.

If we will find wickedness even in the highest court and the holiest place, where do we go for justice and holiness? There is only one place to go, and that is above the sun—to the heavens (Eccl. 5:2). We go to God—who alone is "good" (Mark 10:18) and who alone will judge "the world with righteousness; . . . the peoples with uprightness" (Ps. 9:8; cf. 75:2). This is where Ecclesiastes 3:17 takes us: "I said in my heart, *God* will judge the righteous and the wicked, for there is a time for every matter and for every work." This is also a shocking statement. We might well have expected Solomon to say, "This too is vanity. It's like trying to bottle a hurricane." Instead, he gives us one of the most amazing confessions of faith in the Bible. He meets the bad news of verse 16 with the good news of verse 17.

Throughout the Old Testament, we read how a righteous God sees, hates, and judges injustice and unrighteousness.[3] Here Solomon stands on the character and promises of God. In effect, he stands alongside God incarnate. We know of Jesus' trial before unrighteous religious leaders and an unjust Roman court of law. We also know that, in the words of 1 Peter 2:22–23: "He committed no sin, neither was deceit found in his mouth. When he was reviled, he did not revile in return; when he suffered, he did not threaten, but continued *entrusting himself to him who judges justly*." Immediately before these verses, Peter gives the exhortation, "For to this you have been called, because Christ also suffered for you, leaving you an example, so that you might *follow in his steps*" (v. 21). We follow in Jesus' steps by entrusting ourselves to God, knowing that the Father (along with his Son) will right every wrong.[4] With equity, fairness, and justice, he will balance the scales, wield the sword, and render his verdict with his always-unbiased eyes wide open.

Sometimes this verdict occurs within our lifetimes. We witness the bad boss fired, the corrupt politician sentenced, the dictator fallen. But whether God's justice comes during our lifetime, and through natural means (e.g., a court of law), or else after our lifetime (i.e., on the judgment day),[5] we need faith to believe what Ecclesiastes 3:17 teaches: God will judge everyone ("the righteous and the wicked") at the right time ("for there is a time for every matter and for every work"). Believe that promise. Wait patiently for it to happen. In the meantime, cry out, "O Sovereign Lord, holy and true, how long before you will judge and avenge . . . ?" (Rev. 6:10; cf. Ps. 4:2).

---

3. For example, note the words from the prophets (Isa. 5:22–23; Amos 5:12; Mic. 7:3) as well as from Solomon himself (2 Chron. 6:23; 19:6–7; Prov. 17:15; 22:22–23; 24:23–25, 28–29).

4. E.g., Matt. 25:41–46; John 5:22; Acts 17:30–31; 1 Cor. 4:4–5; 1 Peter 4:5.

5. Thomas Krüger notes two studies—Michel (*Untersuchungen*) and Schwienhorst-Schönberger (*Nicht im Menschen*)—that argue that Ecclesiastes 3:16 is a "statement about the future judgment of God in the world, before which (or to which) wickedness will be sent." *Qoheleth*, ed. Klaus Baltzer, trans. O. C. Dean Jr., Hermeneia (Minneapolis: Fortress, 2004), 91.

There is "a time for every matter under heaven" (Eccl. 3:1), including the day that God has fixed to right every wrong. On that day, we will see how all the wicked knots and snarls under the loom were necessary for the beautiful end design. We will see how God made "beautiful in its time" (v. 11) every moral monstrosity, even evils in the courts and the churches. We live under the loom now. We look up and see only the mess. We are "under the sun." But someday we will see "above the sun" the beauty of the tapestry, a sight that will cause us to lift our hands in praise of God and to bow our heads in awe of him.[6]

OUR MORTALITY—A MOTIVE FOR JOY?

We may summarize Ecclesiastes 3:16–17 like this: The sight of wickedness in unlikely places should help us to turn in faith and hope to God, who will rightly judge at the right time. What comes next in verses 18–22 may be summarized as follows: The sight of our own mortality should motivate us to work with joy.

Note that both reactions to the realities of wickedness and death are unexpected and ironic. While we would expect to arrive at hopelessness after viewing wickedness in places that we do not expect to find it, instead we are told to hope in God. And while we would expect to arrive at despair after seeing that we die and return to dust just like every animal in the fallen world, instead we are told to rejoice in our God-given work. The Bible is an odd book at times. How are we to make some sense of this second application? Is our mortality really a motive for joy?

The Reality

Before we get to the joy at the end of the tether, we must first feel the strength of the tether itself. We may subdivide Ecclesiastes 3:18–22 by using

---

6. Daniel Fredericks takes Ecclesiastes 3:1–22 as a unit and argues that in the later verses we are given six reasons to fear God. While I'm not convinced by his division, his fifth and sixth reasons are right: we should fear God "because of his justice (3:17) and his imposition of the curse of death (3:19)." Daniel C. Fredericks, "Ecclesiastes," in Daniel C. Fredericks and Daniel J. Estes, *Ecclesiastes and the Song of Songs*, Apollos Old Testament Commentary 16 (Downers Grove, IL: InterVarsity Press, 2010), 120.

three *R*s—the *reality*, the *reason*, and the *reaction*. The *reality* and the *reason* are discussed and illustrated in verses 18–21. In verse 18 we read, "I said in my heart with regard to the children of man that God is testing them that they may see that they themselves are but beasts."

In what sense are we like beasts? Solomon continues:

> For what happens to the children of man and what happens to the beasts is the same; as one dies, so dies the other. They all have the same breath, and man has no advantage over the beasts, for all is vanity. All go to one place. All are from the dust, and to dust all return. Who knows whether the spirit of man goes upward and the spirit of the beast goes down into the earth? (Eccl. 3:19–21)

Pastor Solomon is not denying that human beings are made in the image of God and the pinnacle of creation (Gen. 1:27–30). As Psalm 8:5–8 testifies, God has made us a little lower than the angels, crowned with glory and honor, and given dominion over all creation. Neither is he denying some form of life after death; he has just talked about God's future judgment (Eccl. 3:17) and will conclude the book with the ominous warning that "God will bring every deed into judgment, with every secret thing, whether good or evil" (12:14). Such a verdict assumes that people are alive, not annihilated, after death. Thus, when Solomon wonders, "Who knows whether the spirit of man goes upward and the spirit of the beast goes down into the earth?" (3:21), he is making an observation from experience. He is asserting that no one has "direct first-hand empirical evidence of what happens to the human spirit after death."[7] At the funeral parlor or the gravesite, no one can verify that the soul went out, down, up, or anywhere else.

What we all know, however, is what he states in Ecclesiastes 3:19–20: as, in a sense, both bodies share "the same breath," so both bodies will share the same ashes. We all know the brute fact that our bodies die and turn to dust in the same way as the brute beasts. After death, the most beautiful woman and the ugliest hyena return to the same "place"—both

---

7. Jeffrey Meyers, *A Table in the Mist: Meditations on Ecclesiastes*, Through New Eyes Bible Commentary (Monroe, LA: Athanasius Press, 2006), 94.

"disintegrate equally into dust."[8] In verse 20, Solomon is merely paraphrasing the final phrases of Genesis 3:19—"By the sweat of your face you shall eat bread, till you return to the ground, for out of it you were taken; *for you are dust, and to dust you shall return.*" Adam and Eve's scheme—to be like God—failed miserably.

Human beings can do many things that animals cannot do. We can read, write, draw, cook, fall in love, and lament that our bodies will turn to dust. And we can drink spinach smoothies, pop vitamins, and invent all sorts of incredible gizmos such as treadmills and life-support machines, but nothing we can do or make changes the reality that our mortality makes us more like the animals than like God, that "man in his pomp will not remain; he is like the beasts that perish" (Ps. 49:12).

The Reason

In 2 Peter 3:9, Peter answers the question "Why is God's justice delayed?" by stating that God is graciously giving time for sinners to repent. Here in Ecclesiastes, however, the focus is on the step before repentance, which is a recognition of our fallen frame. This is the *reason* given in Ecclesiastes 3:18: "I said in my heart with regard to the children of man that God is testing them that they may see that they themselves are but beasts." (In Hebrew the final phrase, "that they themselves are but beasts," strongly emphasizes the point with the use of assonance: *shehem-behemah hemmah lahem.*) We die like beasts because we wanted to be like God (Gen. 3:17–19). The curse of Genesis 3 makes it absolutely clear that we are in the "finite mammal" category, not the "transcendent God" category. Martin Luther said to Erasmus, "Your God is too small!" To this we might add, "And we are too big."

The Response

The *response* to the reality and reason for God's reminder of our fallen frame can be varied. People can be bitter, as Ernest Hemingway was when he wrote, "Life is just a dirty trick from nothingness to nothingness."[9]

---

8. Jerome, *Commentary on Ecclesiastes*, trans. Richard J. Goodrich and David J. D. Miller, Ancient Christian Writers 66 (New York: Newman, 2012), 63.

9. Ernest Hemingway, quoted in Alister McGrath, *Doubting: Growing through the Uncertainties of Faith* (Downers Grove, IL: InterVarsity Press, 2006), 60.

Or they feel dejected, as John Updike was when he wrote, "I have time at last to consider my life, this its stubby stale end."[10] People can feel deep sorrow, as Nicholas Wolterstorff did when he wrote about the loss of his son, "There's a hole in the world now."[11] At the right time, each of these can be the right response. After all, there is a time to weep and mourn (Eccl. 3:4). But in Ecclesiastes 3:22, our reaction is to be rejoicing: "So I saw that there is nothing better than that a man should rejoice in his work, for that is his lot. Who can bring him to see what will be after him?"

The Masoretes of the Middle Ages assigned a Jewish holiday to each of the Five Megilloth: Song of Songs (Passover), Ruth (Pentecost), Lamentations (Fast of the Ninth of Ab), Esther (Purim), and Ecclesiastes (Feast of Tabernacles). Yes, the scholars paired that joyous harvest celebration—similar to Thanksgiving—with Ecclesiastes! We might have had Solomon conclude by saying, "So I saw that there is nothing better than that a man should *break down and cry* or *break it down and party on*." Instead, he calls us to cheer up and look up and bear down. His ironic application is to get back to work and be glad in it!

Some authors have the attitude that "writing is agony," as expressed by Gene Fowler: "Writing is easy: All you do is sit staring at a blank sheet of paper until the drops of blood form on your forehead."[12] In her book *Take Joy*, Jane Yolen seeks to move us past that attitude, "to learn to write not with blood and fear, but with joy."[13] In a similar and more expansive vein, Pastor Solomon is calling for a change in attitude. Admittedly, he has been a downer for most of Ecclesiastes 1–3. But here, as he did in 2:24–26 and 3:12, and as he will do in 5:18–20; 8:15; 9:7–9; and 11:7–10, he reminds us of "the gospel of enjoyment."[14] As Daniel

---

10. John Updike, "Downtime," in *Americana* (New York: Knopf, 2001), 46.

11. Nicholas Wolterstorff, *Lament for a Son*, quoted in Bryan Chapell, *The Hardest Sermons You'll Ever Have to Preach* (Grand Rapids: Baker, 2011), 221.

12. Gene Fowler, quoted in Jane Yolen, *Take Joy: A Writer's Guide to Loving the Craft* (Cincinnati: Writer's Digest, 2006), 2.

13. Yolen, *Take Joy*, 2.

14. Roland E. Murphy rightly states that Qoheleth "hardly merits" R. N. Whybray's title "Preacher of Joy." Yet Murphy admits, "There are several passages in the book that can be advanced in favor of the gospel of enjoyment." *The Tree of Life: An Exploration of Biblical Wisdom Literature*, Anchor Bible Reference Library (New York, Doubleday, 1990), 53, 55.

Fredericks notes, "Though we may be as transient as the beasts, our advantage and reward in life is to enjoy our work and its fruits."[15] Both animals and humans can work, but only humans can enjoy their work and the results of their labors. The beaver can build his dam, but he can't sit down after a hard day's work, thank God for his job, his family, and his food, and then enjoy all that he has accomplished and all that he has been given.

In her poem "Mindful,"[16] Mary Oliver describes her own daily delights in creation. She speaks of losing herself "inside this soft world," and of teaching herself to rejoice in what she witnesses. Similarly, and more in line with Solomon's shift of thought, Billy Collins's "Memento Mori"[17] moves from human transience to human delight. The poet moves from the imagery of himself as "a soap bubble floating over the children's party" to the reality of death pulling him up "by the reins" and settling him "down by a roadside, grateful for the sweet weeds and the mouthfuls of colorful wildflowers."

In what you see, what you hear, and what you do—take joy! Reminders of our mortality should motivate us to rejoice. We should rejoice in what we see. We should rejoice in what we do. We should rejoice in our God-given, God-rewarded work.

TILL ONE GREATER MAN

But wait a minute. Why? Why should the sight of our own mortality motivate us to work with joy? Ecclesiastes 3:22 gives a reason. After we read, "So I saw that there is nothing better than that a man should rejoice in his work, for that is his lot," we read the question, "Who can bring him to see what will be after him?" (v. 22). Despite what the best-selling books claim, the assumed answer is "No one." There is no ghost of life-beyond-the-grave who reveals to us now the events of

15. Fredericks, "Ecclesiastes," 122.
16. Mary Oliver, "Mindful," in *Why I Wake Early: New Poems* (Boston: Beacon, 2005), 58.
17. Billy Collins, *Horoscopes for the Dead* (New York: Random House, 2011), 13–14. Cf. his poem "Roses" on the death of "the roses in the gardens" (96–97).

the afterlife. Put simply, since the "future remains veiled," enjoy your "time-bound lot in life."[18]

As Christians, however, we can add an additional and all-important reason for rejoicing: "our Savior Christ Jesus, who abolished death and brought life and immortality to light through the gospel" (2 Tim. 1:10). It is difficult to discern precisely what Pastor Solomon believed and taught about the afterlife. But the revelation of God in Christ is plain on these matters.

The New Testament clears up any potential misunderstanding, teaching us that the human spirit or soul survives death. In Philippians 1:21–23, Paul assumes an afterlife:

> For to me to live is Christ, and to die is gain. If I am to live in the flesh, that means fruitful labor for me. Yet which I shall choose I cannot tell. I am hard pressed between the two. My desire is to depart and be with Christ, for that is far better.

And if any fog hangs over what is assumed in that text, it is cleared up by Jesus when he said to Martha at Lazarus's tomb, "I am the resurrection and the life. Whoever believes in me, though he die, yet shall he live" (John 11:25), and later gave his disciples a promise so rightly read at funerals:

> Let not your hearts be troubled. Believe in God; believe also in me. In my Father's house are many rooms. If it were not so, would I have told you that I go to prepare a place for you? And if I go and prepare a place for you, I will come again and will take you to myself, that where I am you may be also. (John 14:1–3)

We can rejoice in our work because Jesus has been raised from the dead. He has conquered the curse. John Milton expressed it this way:

> Of Man's First Disobedience, and the Fruit
> Of that Forbidden Tree, whose mortal taste

---

18. Richard Schultz, "Ecclesiastes," in *Baker Commentary on the Bible*, ed. Gary M. Burge and Andrew E. Hill, 2nd ed. (Grand Rapids: Baker, 2011), 588.

Brought Death into the World, and all our woe,
With loss of Eden, till one greater Man
Restore us, and regain the blissful Seat . . . .[19]

RESTORED SIGHT

The Tuesday before I first preached Ecclesiastes 3:16–22 was the day before All Saints' Day. Some call it *All Hallows' Eve*; others label it *Halloween*. Some Christians avoid celebrating this religious holiday for religious reasons. Many non-Christians, who have no idea that it has any religious connections at all, celebrate Halloween more religiously than Christmas, or so it seems from their extravagant decorations.

I like it when people get festive, and I admire decorative creativity. But why do people feel the need to cover their houses and lawns with death decorations for Halloween? I suppose I can understand having a black light here and a plastic pumpkin there. But please explain why one of my neighbors has a stuffed body posted to a tree with a bloodstained shirt, a knife through the chest, and a leg chopped off. Someone also explain to me why another neighbor lines his yard with dismembered limbs, skeletal remains, and a gravesite with two hands rising above the ground to depict someone buried alive. Why the obsession with violence, evil, and the occult? Why the preoccupation with death?

The irony is that if someone knocked on the doors of these homes and told the owners that if they like death so much they should attend church because the pastor talks about death in nearly every sermon, they would not only turn down the invitation but think it more than a little bizarre. Why does a culture obsessed with death refuse to hear the truth or talk soberly about death? Why is it that a culture that loves to decorate with death, and watch people die on television and in the movies, do everything in its power to remove the sight and sound of *real* death? Why would an invitation to a sermon series on Ecclesiastes be declined but an invitation to a seminar on seven sure ways to be happy be accepted? And why does Ecclesiastes say that

19. John Milton, *Paradise Lost*, bk. 1, lines 1–5.

thinking seriously about wickedness and death is the only path to hope and happiness?

Solomon has helped us to *see* the answer. The sight of wickedness in unlikely places might help us, as "frail children of dust,"[20] to turn in faith and hope to God, who will rightly judge at the right time. And the sight of our own mortality motivates us to work with joy.

20. Robert Grant, "O Worship the King" (1833).

8

IT IS NOT GOOD FOR THE CHILDREN OF MAN TO BE ALONE

Ecclesiastes 4:1–16

Two are better than one, because they have a good reward for their toil. For if they fall, one will lift up his fellow. But woe to him who is alone when he falls and has not another to lift him up!
(Eccl. 4:9–10)

y wife surprised the children by making them hot chocolate. Afterward, our five-year-old, Charlotte, came into the room where Emily and I were sitting, and she said, "Mommy, I have an idea." "What's that?" Emily replied. Charlotte paused, grinned, and timidly announced, "That we say thank you . . . to you." I smiled and said, "Aw, that's sweet." Charlotte said, "I mean together . . . all the kids." Ten minutes passed. Some organization was going on in the other room. Charlotte finally called out, "Okay, everybody . . . all the kids . . . come into the room." The other three came in. Evelyn counted, "1, 2, 3," and all joined in together, "Thank you, Mommy." Charlotte closed the sweet scene by declaring, "Hugs," and she went around hugging each member of the family.

When I was in Ireland for seventeen days away from my family, I missed moments like that. At times I enjoyed the alone time (the quiet, that is!);

at other times the quietness was haunting—"O solitude, beautiful word: crabgrass grows between your syllables!"[1] In Genesis 2:18 the Lord God said, "It is not good that the man should be alone." So the Lord created out of the man woman, and the two became one, and all was well in the world. But then came the first sin, followed by the immediate manifestations of separation—the man from the woman (it's her fault), the woman from creation (it's the snake's fault), and God from the man and woman (sorry, it's your fault, so out you go). Even the first brothers—Cain and Abel—were separated from each other by Cain's murder of Abel. And as much as God's judgment upon Adam affects us all (we "sinned in him, and fell with him," WSC 16), so God's curse upon Cain illustrates the isolation that we all feel at times: "You shall be a fugitive and a wanderer on the earth" (Gen. 4:12).

In the previous chapter, we saw two sights under the sun; here in Ecclesiastes 4 we add four more sights to the tour, all of which center on "the need of companionship."[2] In verses 1–3, Solomon saw those oppressed without anyone to comfort them; in verses 4–6, he saw envy of others as the ambition for industry; in verses 7–12, he saw the isolation of avarice; and in verses 13–16, he saw that it is lonely even at the top.

Oppression

Extending his observations of evil earthbound activities from Ecclesiastes 3:16, in 4:1–3 Solomon saw those oppressed without anyone to comfort them. Verse 1 states the raw deal that some have been dealt, and verses 2–3 give Solomon's sad commentary on it. First, we read verse 1: "Again I saw all the oppressions that are done under the sun. And behold, the tears of the oppressed, and they had no one to comfort them! On the side of their oppressors there was power, and there was no one to comfort them." The theme is easy to spot. The repetition of the word *oppress* in its various forms—*oppressions*, *oppressed*, and *oppressors*—along with the phrase "no one to comfort them," tells us the sorry story of the powerful oppressing the powerless.

1. Pablo Neruda, "Ode to Solitude," in *Odes to Opposites* (New York: Bulfinch, 2008), 99.
2. Michael A. Eaton, *Ecclesiastes: An Introduction and Commentary*, Tyndale Old Testament Commentaries 16 (Downers Grove, IL: InterVarsity Press, 1983), 90.

Iain Provan defines *oppression* as "accumulation—seeking after profit—without regard to the nature, needs, and rights of other people."[3] Then he illustrates this sin from Scripture:

> In the Bible, oppression involves cheating one's neighbor of something (Lev. 6:2–5 associates it with expropriation, stealing, retaining lost property that has been found, and swearing falsely), defrauding him, and robbing him. It involves making an unjust gain, including the profit made from interest on loans (e.g., Ezek. 22:1–29, esp. vv. 12, 29). It is the abuse of power, financial and otherwise, perpetrated on those who are not so powerful and are indeed vulnerable—the poor, the widows, orphans, and strangers (e.g., Ezek. 22:7, 29; Amos 4:1, Mic. 2:1–2). Thus it is often associated with violence and bloodshed in the Old Testament and with the denial of rights and justice (e.g., Jer. 22:17, Ezek. 22:6–7, 12, 29; cf. also Prov. 1:10–19).[4]

Then and now, oppression is an awful evil. "Under the sun" many people live "under the thumb" of abusive husbands, gang leaders, mobsters, and dictators. Think on the genocides of Bosnia and Rwanda, the ideological purges of Darfur, the attacks and suppressions of Islamic terrorists, the sexual abuse and slavery of children, and the unborn child with no voice (not even her mother's voice) to cry out to spare her life.

Isolation increases the pain of oppression. Those oppressed have "no one to comfort them." As much as Job's three friends eventually were unhelpful and hurtful (Job 16:2), they were, for a time, true friends—sitting alongside Job in silence, comforting him by their mere presence (2:11–13). But here in Ecclesiastes, where are the friends to offer any such comfort? And where is "the God of all comfort" (2 Cor. 1:3)? God is not mentioned in these sixteen verses of Ecclesiastes 4. Here, we are looking at life "under the sun," deep under the sun.

How should we respond to this reality? Shed streams of tears (John 11:35)? Rend our robes (Job 1:20)? Overturn tables (Mark 11:15)? Pastor Solomon gives a reserved, but certainly not stoical, cynical, or suicidal, reply to life's ugliness:

3. Iain Provan, *Ecclesiastes/Song of Songs*, NIV Application Commentary (Grand Rapids: Zondervan, 2001), 103.
4. Ibid., 104.

And I thought the dead who are already dead more fortunate than the living who are still alive. But better than both is he who has not yet been and has not seen the evil deeds that are done under the sun. (Eccl. 4:2–3)

Put simply, under the darkness of oppression, Solomon says that nonexistence—whether already dead or not yet alive—is preferable to existence. He gives a seemingly unorthodox equation: that "zero is better than one."[5] And yet Solomon, following Job ("Let the day perish on which I was born," Job 3:3), Jeremiah ("Why did I come out from the womb to see toil and sorrow, and spend my days in shame?" Jer. 20:18), and even Jesus on Judas ("It would have been better for that man if he had not been born," Matt. 26:24), simply admits what we all admit at times: that those who are sorely oppressed, cruelly persecuted, and inhumanly tortured would be better off dead.

With that said, it is hard to know where Solomon is spiritually. Has he so soon forgotten his great confession of faith in Ecclesiastes 3:17? Does he need to return to "the house of God" (5:1; see also Ps. 73:17)—to sense the presence of God and the promises of God—in order to remind himself that the highest One above the oppressors (Eccl. 5:8) will right every wrong at the right time?[6]

Whatever Solomon's spiritual disposition when writing chapter 4, our disposition when reading chapter 4 should be that of Jesus Christ and his earliest disciples.

Near the end of the previous chapter, I threw in a line from the hymn "O Worship the King." I called us "frail children of dust." The full verse goes:

Frail children of dust, and feeble as frail,
in Thee do we trust, nor find Thee to fail:
Thy mercies how tender, how firm to the end,
our Maker, Defender, Redeemer, and Friend.[7]

Jesus is not only a friend to sinners, but also a friend to the oppressed. With holy indignation, he ousted the oppressors in the Court of the Gen-

---

5. Jeffrey Meyers, *A Table in the Mist: Meditations on Ecclesiastes*, Through New Eyes Bible Commentary (Monroe, LA: Athanasius Press, 2006), 99.

6. Cf. Ernst Wilhelm Hengstenburg's reading of Ecclesiastes 5:8–9. *Commentary on Ecclesiastes, with Treatises on the Song of Solomon, Job, Isaiah, Sacrifices, etc.*, trans. D. W. Simon (Edinburgh: T. & T. Clark, 1869), 140.

7. Robert Grant, "O Worship the King" (1833).

tiles (Luke 19:45–46). And with compassion, he lamented the lost but also healed the afflicted:

> And Jesus went throughout all the cities and villages, teaching in their syna-
> gogues and proclaiming the gospel of the kingdom and healing every disease
> and every affliction. When he saw the crowds, he had compassion for them,
> because they were harassed and helpless, like sheep without a shepherd.
> (Matt. 9:35–36)

As Christians, we must know that "religion that is pure and undefiled before God, the Father, is this: to visit orphans and widows *in their afflic-tion*" (James 1:27). Moreover, we must be doers of the Word by feeding the hungry, satisfying the thirsty, welcoming the stranger, clothing the naked, and visiting the imprisoned (see Matt. 25:34–40). The church needs more William Wilberforces, but it also needs quiet Good Samaritans who are busy mending one wounded traveler, visiting one shut-in, adopting one orphan, funding one refugee.

ENVY

In Ecclesiastes 4:1–3, we examined the topic of oppression. In verses 4–6, we turn next to the topic of envy. Verse 4 reads, "Then I saw that all toil and all skill in work come from a man's envy of his neighbor. This also is vanity and a striving after wind." Why do we work? Here Pastor Solomon claims that the primary motive (although he uses the hyperbole of "*all* toil and *all* skill") is "competitive envy."[8] Envy is the ambition for industry! Rather than joy in our God-given labor (3:22) being the "caffeine" that gets us up in the morning, covetous competitiveness oils our engines. Contrary to the law of Leviticus 19:18, which is echoed by our Lord Jesus, "You shall love your neighbor as yourself" (Matt. 22:39), we embrace such mottos as "you gotta look out for number one." Such cutthroat rivalry, which rots the bones (Prov. 14:30), nev-ertheless rules the roost. To climb to the top, you step on other people's heads.

The antithesis to this inferiority-complex, anti-neighbor ambition is illustrated next in Ecclesiastes 4:5–6. One natural response to the reality

---

8. Richard Schultz, "Ecclesiastes," in *Baker Commentary on the Bible*, ed. Gary M. Burge and Andrew E. Hill, 2nd ed. (Grand Rapids: Baker, 2011), 589–90.

that envious ambition drives our toil would be to stop working altogether. Wise Solomon answers that attitude with the proverb "The fool folds his hands and eats his own flesh" (v. 5). It is hardly a lovely picture. Someone who folds his hands cannot or does not work. The "grotesque imagery of self-cannibalism"[9]—"of a foolish man sitting with his hands clasped together and gnawing on his knuckles"[10]—illustrates that the one who refuses to work will only destroy himself. "His sloth is slow suicide" (*The Message*). Elsewhere, Solomon puts it this way:

> How long will you lie there, O sluggard?
>   When will you arise from your sleep?
> A little sleep, a little slumber,
>   a little *folding of the hands* to rest,
> and poverty will come upon you like a robber,
>   and want like an armed man. (Prov. 6:9–11)

The fool-headed notion that not working will solve the envy issue fails. A better solution is offered, also in proverbial form, in Ecclesiastes 4:6: "Better is a handful of quietness than two hands full of toil and a striving after wind." Here, *hand*-images are paired against each other: a handful of quietness and two handfuls of greed. The pictures are plain enough. The phrase "two hands" depicts someone cupping his hands in order to possess as much as possible. People whose hands are cupped can carry more of the weight of this world. It looks good to carry the big house, the big car, and the big bank account, but it's heavy. It weighs you down. And it requires overtime all the time—toil, toil, toil.

Everyone has a choice: be the workaholic who has everything but rest and genuine success (in the end, it is all "a striving after wind"), or else be a worker who is content (i.e., the guy with "a handful of quietness"). Envision the imagery! Instead of two greedy hands cupped to gain everything one can, it is simply one hand extended. The hand is *full*, but not of stuff; it is filled with "quietness." His work (note: his hand is not folded but unfolded or extended out) is full of joyous contentment. With one hand he works

9. Choon-Leong Seow, *Ecclesiastes*, Anchor Bible 18C (New York: Doubleday, 1997), 179.
10. Michael V. Fox, *Ecclesiastes*, JPS Bible Commentary (Philadelphia: Jewish Publication Society, 2004), 28.

for the glory of God (which brings its own reward), and with the other . . . well, one wonders what he is doing. Perhaps he is helping the oppressed of verses 1–3, as Zacchaeus did when he was saved—half to the poor, half to those he oppressed, and all to Jesus (Luke 19:8). Or maybe he is just relaxing. Either way, he is the poster boy for Paul's super-slogan, "there is great gain in godliness with contentment" (1 Tim. 6:6; cf. 2 Thess. 3:10–12). Comfort and contentment are the antidotes for oppression and envy.

ISOLATION

In Ecclesiastes 4:1–3, Solomon saw the oppressed without anyone to comfort them, while in verses 4–6 he saw envy of others as the ambition for industry. Next, he saw the isolation of avarice:

Again, I saw vanity under the sun: one person who has no other, either son or brother, yet there is no end to all his toil, and his eyes are never satisfied with riches, so that he never asks, "For whom am I toiling and depriving myself of pleasure?" This also is vanity and an unhappy business. (Eccl. 4:7–8)

Here is a snapshot of "the compulsive money-maker"[11] who never stops to think, "What is the worth of my work?" The word *one*, which is repeated five times in Ecclesiastes 4 (vv. 8, 9, 10, 11, and 12), is important here. Truly, "One is the loneliest number."[12] The "*one* person" who never stops working ("there is no end to all his toil," v. 8) never discovers that money has failed to fill the void in his heart's desires ("his eyes are never satisfied with riches," v. 8) and that no one will happily gain from all his unhappy labors (he has neither a "son [n]or brother"[13] to inherit it all, v. 8). This loner has lost. He has money, but no family or friends. His avarice has left him alone, much like the rich young ruler who came to Jesus all by himself, who refused to

---

11. Derek Kidner, *The Message of Ecclesiastes: A Time to Mourn, and a Time to Dance*, The Bible Speaks Today (Downers Grove, IL: InterVarsity Press, 1976), 46.

12. This is a line from Harry Nilsson's song "One," made famous by Three Dog Night's cover in 1969. The line is used in Jeffrey Meyers's commentary.

13. A son and a brother would be "the two closest male relations across two generations and also the two relatives who might benefit from his toil through inheritance." Tremper Longman III, *The Book of Ecclesiastes*, New International Commentary on the Old Testament (Grand Rapids: Eerdmans, 1998), 140. "Money is (his) only kin." Duane A. Garrett, *Proverbs, Ecclesiastes, Song of Songs*, New American Commentary 14 (Nashville: Broadman & Holman, 1993), 307.

give his wealth to others and join Jesus' band of ragamuffins, and who thus walked away alone and unhappy (Mark 10:17–22).

When Solomon saw such a man and examined his motives and movements, he gave his intentional isolation and his awful inclusio: "I saw vanity . . . . This also is vanity" (Eccl. 4:7–8). It is an inclusio that we Christians are to hear and heed: Don't be a selfish, greedy workaholic, or you will find your work worthless and yourself all alone, even at your own funeral. Order your flowers now, because no one else will!

Thankfully, Solomon moves us pastorally from the miseries of solitude to the profits of companionship. In reading Ecclesiastes 4:9–12, notice the word *two*, in contrast with the words *one* and *alone*:

> *Two* are better than *one*, because they have a good reward for their toil. For if they fall, *one* will lift up his fellow. But woe to him who is *alone* when he falls and has not another to lift him up! Again, if *two* lie together, they keep warm, but how can *one* keep warm *alone*? And though a man might prevail against *one* who is *alone*, *two* will withstand him—a threefold cord is not quickly broken.

Jeffrey Meyers smartly says that "one helpful way to understand this passage is to see it as inspired arithmetic." He explains:

> In verses one through three of chapter 4, zero is better than one. Then, in verses four through six, we read that one [handful] is better than two. Climactically, in verses seven through twelve we find that two are better than one.[14]

Four benefits to companionship are given. First, two can work better than one and so have a larger profit ("a good reward for their toil," Eccl. 4:9); second, they can help each other in time of need ("if they fall, one will lift up his fellow," v. 10); third, they give emotional support (and physical warmth)

---

14. Meyers, *A Table in the Mist*, 97–98. In a similar vein, Graham S. Ogden labels his section on Ecclesiastes 4:1–12 "Mathematically Speaking," and writes: "Structurally we note three observations in vv. 1–2, 4–5, 7–8, rounded off with conclusions in vv. 3, 6, 9. Each conclusion has two features: (1) The 'Better' proverb; (2) a mathematical theme using the numerals 1 or 2 . . . . This opening trilogy of sub-sections is followed by three conditional clauses in 4.10–12a, bearing a mathematical theme. The entire unit is then brought to an end with a numerical quotation, v. 12b." *Qoheleth*, 2nd ed., Readings: A New Biblical Commentary (Sheffield, UK: Sheffield Phoenix Press, 2007), 69.

to each other ("if two lie together, they keep warm," v. 11); and fourth, they give each other protection ("two will withstand him," v. 12).[15]

While it is appropriate to extend the application of these benefits to many areas of life, including marriage (this text is read at weddings), the contrast is between the man of Ecclesiastes 4:7–8, who has no men around him (neither a son nor a brother), and the man of verses 9–12, who has at least one other person next to him at all times. The image is that of business partners on a sales trip, or two other men on some journey together.

This journey is set in the ancient Near East, of course. In that time and place, it was hazardous to travel, especially overnight. Without flashlights, one could easily fall into a pit. Jesus tells a parable about this threat: "Can a blind man lead a blind man? Will they not both fall into a pit?" (Luke 6:39). He also spoke of the threat of robbers who waited on travel routes for solo travelers. The parable of the Good Samaritan begins: "A man was going down from Jerusalem to Jericho, and he fell among robbers, who stripped him and beat him and departed, leaving him half dead" (10:30). The men needed each other for protection, as well as for warmth. Back then and there, if two men stopped for the night to sleep, they would likely lay their garments over their bodies and lie close to each other to keep warm. We should not be squeamish about this just because our homosexualized culture has trained us this way. In parts of Africa, men hold hands. In Italy, men greet each other with a kiss on the cheek. At a Serbian Orthodox wedding, men kiss one another on the lips. (Trust me, I know. I'm still a bit squeamish over that surprise!)

With that original context in mind (and, I hope, the thought of where my lips have been *out* of your mind), when we move from one to two to three (!) in the pinnacled final phrase (a lovely numerical parallelism in Hebrew)—"a threefold cord is not quickly broken" (Eccl. 4:12)—we must refrain from spiritualizing. The threefold cord is not the Trinity.[16] The threefold cord is not "knowledge of Scripture and Mishnah and right conduct."[17] The threefold cord is not a husband, his wife, and God.[18] And the threefold cord (likely)

---

15. Garrett, *Proverbs, Ecclesiastes, Song of Songs*, 308.

16. For example, Jerome, *Commentary on Ecclesiastes*, trans. Richard J. Goodrich and David J. D. Miller, Ancient Christian Writers 66 (New York: Newman, 2012), 69.

17. See *Qiddushin* 1.10, in Eric S. Christianson, *Ecclesiastes through the Centuries*, Blackwell Bible Commentaries (Malden, MA: Blackwell, 2007), 183.

18. This is another traditional Jewish interpretation (Koh. R), noted in Fox, *Ecclesiastes*, 30.

is not a husband, wife, and their first child, although that interpretation at least stays with the life-under-the-sun emphasis. Rather, the "threefold cord" is simply a statement that we all know to be true: in the most "dangerous and difficult situations" and "for everything from work to warfare," there is comfort, success, and safety in numbers.[19] Michael Fox hits the nail on the head (or the goad into the side of a sheep): "If the companionship of two people is beneficial, how much the more so the fellowship of three!"[20] And in this way, while the original context is clear, the universal application is elastic. Stretch it into your marriage. Stretch it around your workplace. Pull it into your church.

Pastor Solomon's "commendation of community" is a welcome "antidote to the individualism that infects" every local church.[21] Just as the body of Christ "does not consist of one member but of many" (1 Cor. 12:14), we need each other for service ("The eye cannot say to the hand, 'I have no need of you,' nor again the head to the feet, 'I have no need of you,'" v. 21). We also need each other for mission (and Jesus "called the twelve and began to send them out two by two," Mark 6:7), perseverance in holiness ("And let us consider how to stir up one another to love and good works, not neglecting to meet together, as is the habit of some, but encouraging one another, and all the more as you see the Day drawing near," Heb. 10:24–25), and even church discipline ("Truly, I say to you, whatever you bind on earth shall be bound in heaven, and whatever you loose on earth shall be loosed in heaven. Again I say to you, if two of you agree on earth about anything they ask, it will be done for them by my Father in heaven. For where two or three are gathered in my name, there am I among them," Matt. 18:18–20).

When Paul wrote 2 Timothy under house arrest in Rome, he was tired, cold, and discouraged. What he wanted and needed was a few friends to pick up his spirits—to be with him and pray with him. This was his garden of Gethsemane. When Paul writes in 2 Corinthians 7:6 about being "downcast" ("depressed" is how the NASB translates the word) because his body needed rest, and because he was fighting affliction without and fear within, he says,

---

19. Philip Graham Ryken, *Ecclesiastes: Why Everything Matters*, ed. R. Kent Hughes, Preaching the Word (Wheaton, IL: Crossway, 2010), 118.

20. Fox, *Ecclesiastes*, 30.

21. The first phrase comes from Provan, *Ecclesiastes/Song of Songs*, 105–6, and the second from Sidney Greidanus, *Preaching Christ from Ecclesiastes: Foundations for Expository Sermons* (Grand Rapids: Eerdmans, 2010), 107.

"God, who comforts the downcast, comforted us *by* the coming of Titus." At the conclusion of 2 Timothy, Paul lists his friends—old friends such as Prisca and Aquila and new friends such as Linus and Carpus—because he wants them all to stand by him in the hour of his death. Paul also enlists Timothy (not merely lists him), his good friend and "soul-son," as Kent Hughes calls him,[22] because he wants Timothy to stand literally by him at the hour of his death.

Second Timothy is loaded with imperatives—such as "share in suffering" (1:8) and "preach the word" (4:2). In 4:9–22, the imperatives are comparatively few, and *every one of them* has to do with Timothy's coming to visit Paul:

- "*Do your best* to come to me soon" (v. 9). Come on, timid Timothy, venture up to the front line!
- "Luke alone is with me. *Get Mark* and bring him with you, for he is very useful to me for ministry" (v. 11).
- "Tychicus I have sent to Ephesus [your temporary replacement is on his way, so then] when you come, *bring the cloak*," books, and so forth (vv. 12–13).
- "*Do your best* to come [get here soon] before winter" (v. 21).

Are you discouraged? Depressed? Do you need a friend to comfort you and pull you through? Well, embrace the ecclesia! "A cord of three strands is not quickly broken" (Eccl. 4:12 NIV). Even more, a cord of two hundred or two thousand strands is impossible to break. As Paul leaned on his friends in his hour of need, so we must do the same. Fellowship is more than sharing a cup of coffee after the service; it is sharing life together—sharing sorrows, fears, and pains—so that together we might fight the good fight, finish the race, keep the faith, and long for the glory of Christ's appearing.

Even at the Top!

After we have seen with Solomon the sights of the oppressed (Eccl. 4:1–3), the envious (vv. 4–6), and the isolated (vv. 7–12), finally we come to the king (vv. 13–16). In the Beatles' "Eleanor Rigby," the chorus goes:

22. R. Kent Hughes and Bryan Chapell, *1–2 Timothy and Titus*, Preaching the Word (Wheaton, IL: Crossway, 2000), 258.

> All the lonely people
> Where do they all come from?
> All the lonely people
> Where do they all belong?

As the song progresses, the Beatles sing of the old maid Eleanor Rigby and the forgotten Father McKenzie. Like the song "Eleanor Rigby," the final verses of this section of Ecclesiastes picture an alone and forgotten person. Yet it is not the commoner who is in view, but a seemingly unforgettable king! With our fourth and final "better than" proverb (cf. Eccl. 4:3, 6, 9), we read:

> Better was a poor and wise youth than an old and foolish king who no longer knew how to take advice. For he [the youth; here's his unforgettable story] went from prison to the throne, though in his own kingdom he had been born poor. I saw all the living who move about under the sun, along with that youth who was to stand in the king's place. There was no end of all the people, all of whom he [the young king who rose to the throne] led. Yet those who come later will not rejoice in him. Surely this also is vanity and a striving after wind. (Eccl. 4:13–16)

The story is straightforward. There were two kings. The first king was an old monarch, yet unexpectedly foolish. He clogged his ears to the advice of others. He ruled alone, and thus he ruled foolishly. The second king, who succeeded the first king, lived the American Dream—he went from rags to riches. He went from the poorhouse (and the prison house) to the White House. Perhaps he reminds you of Joseph in Genesis, who rose from humble origins up through the Egyptian prison system to rule alongside Pharaoh.

Yet like Joseph, this second king was soon forgotten. In Exodus we read, "Now there arose a new king over Egypt, who did not know Joseph" (Ex. 1:8). Like that true story, this truthful tale teaches the same lesson: the popularity of the high and mighty is short-lived. Even the praise of praiseworthy politicians evaporates. "The whims of the masses and the reign of the wise are as momentary as the direction of the wind" is how Daniel Fredericks puts it.[23] It is not that his approval rating went down after he lost the election; it is

---

23. Daniel C. Fredericks, "Ecclesiastes," in Daniel C. Fredericks and Daniel J. Estes, *Ecclesiastes and the Song of Songs*, Apollos Old Testament Commentary 16 (Downers Grove, IL: InterVarsity Press, 2010), 138.

that his name has been buried in Sheol. The reporter's question "What do you think of King So-and-So?" is met with the reply, "King Who?"

> How low men were, and how they rise!
>> How high they were, and how they tumble!
> O vanity of vanities!
>> O laughable, pathetic jumble![24]

This is where Solomon leaves us at the end of Ecclesiastes 4: staring at this what's-his-face king as we listen to that now-familiar refrain, "Surely this also is vanity and a striving after wind" (Eccl. 4:16). We look at a man who "has reached a pinnacle of human glory, only to be stranded there."[25] It's lonely at the top.

TWO GREAT COMMANDS; ONE GREAT CHRIST

In this passage, Solomon seems to be a poor pastor, for he leaves us without hope or joy. He gave us those enjoyment exhortations in the previous passage, but not in this one. Here his climax is anticlimactic. But we may leave on a cheerful note—not a deep, sad note that sings about our "ultimately empty achievements,"[26] but a high and happy note that sings of our Savior King and his unforgettable acts of salvation. Comfort, contentment, and community are the antidotes for oppression, envy, and isolation, and Christ is the answer to it all.

When our Lord was asked, "Teacher, which is the great commandment in the Law?" (Matt. 22:36), he replied, "You shall love the Lord your God with all your heart and with all your soul and with all your mind. This is the great and first commandment. And a second is like it: You shall love your neighbor as yourself" (vv. 37–39). Both commands are relational: we are to relate to God in love and we are to relate to people in love.

But how? Going back to the beginning of this chapter, which went back to the beginning of human life on earth, let me ask: How do fallen human beings who are separated from God and each other get back a right relationship

---

24. From William Thackeray's 1885 edition of *Vanitas Vanitatum*, quoted in Christianson, *Ecclesiastes through the Centuries*, 127.

25. Kidner, *The Message of Ecclesiastes*, 52.

26. Ibid.

with God and other human beings? The answer: by the incarnation and the death of the God-man. One of the ironies of the atonement is not just that Jesus suffered and died to renew certain relationships, but that he suffered and died *alone* to do so. Abandoned by God and people, Jesus made it possible for people to be in a right relationship with God and neighbor. From Gethsemane to Golgotha, a slow, sad separation occurred. Jesus was forsaken by Israel. He was forsaken by the Twelve. Finally, in some inexplicable way, he was forsaken by the Father—"My God, my God, why have you forsaken me?" (Matt. 27:46). Some read this God-forsakenness as Jesus' descent into hell. Hell is the ultimate place of isolation. Not three, nor two, but one—you are alone with yourself, your sin, and your shame forever. But out of hell, Jesus arose victorious! Out of his solitude of suffering, the stairway to heaven was opened and the pathway to brotherly love was paved around the whole wide world.

This is the high and happy note that I'll leave you with. It is a tune you can hum when you comfort the oppressed, hold out a handful to others, and selflessly protect and profit a friend. It is a song to sing because you know (however high you climb in this life and however many people will forget what you did to get there) that God will rejoice in you just as he rejoices in his beloved Son.

9

SANDALS OFF, MOUTH SHUT

Ecclesiastes 5:1—7

*Guard your steps when you go to the house of God. . . . God is
the one you must fear.* (Eccl. 5:1, 7)

any years ago, I was a part of a wealthy suburban church
that had sermon titles such as "What Would Jesus Say to
Bart Simpson?" and that, for its youth day, had its teenag-
ers stream down the aisles, dressed like inner-city gangsters, as they rapped
out the opening "hymn," with the appropriate ganglike hand gestures. More
recently, I attended a church that showed hilarious homemade video clips to
season the sermonette. I have also heard about one church that hands out
free popcorn as you enter the "sanctuary," and another one where everyone
bounces around a beach ball during the "worship" band's performance.
Although these examples are perhaps extreme, they show a growing trend.
Today, as our churches overflow with folksy entertainment and raw "authen-
ticity," we live in one of the most sacrilegious and blasphemous church
cultures in the history of Christianity. No joke.

Yet each generation has troubles of its own. In New Testament times,
James criticized those in the church who were showing favoritism toward the
rich (James 2:2–4). Paul decried those in the Corinthian church who were

getting drunk on the communion wine (1 Cor. 11:21). Jesus got out a whip for those making a profit on the pilgrims to Jerusalem, treating the temple like a den of thieves (John 2:13–17). In Old Testament times, the prophets called out the hypocrites who walked through the sacrificial motions (e.g., Isa. 29:13; Mal. 1:14). And in Ecclesiastes 5:1–7, Pastor Solomon prophetically shares some choice words of his own for the recreationally religious person who is oblivious that his "worship" is highly offensive to God. Put simply, he warns the "fool" (vv. 1, 3, 4) to fear God (v. 7). Put differently and more broadly, he instructs all of God's people at all times on how to worship wisely.

Establishing a Safe Distance

As we approach God in worship, Pastor Solomon wants to establish a safe distance between us and the transcendent God. He does this with two imperatives given at the top (Eccl. 5:1) and tail (v. 7) of our text. At the top we are charged to watch out when we go to worship ("Guard your steps when you go to the house of God," v. 1), and at the tail we are given the central charge of wisdom literature: to fear God. This inclusio of admonitions counsels "caution, reverence, restraint, moderation, and sincerity" before the Lord,[1] as well as recognition that God is God.

The first Sunday evening of every month, my church gathers for our Community Chat. After a potluck meal, we "chat" about the life of the church. At one chat, the pastors answered questions that covered everything from "Is Santa for real?" to "What's the definition of moralistic therapeutic deism?" Another question, related to preaching, was posed to me: "Will you ever preach a topical sermon?" I said, "A what—a topical sermon? Never!" I tore my garments. Once I composed myself, I did reply, more moderately, "Well, yes, I have been thinking about preaching a sermon on the topic of *the implications of the doctrine of double predestination on effective child-rearing.*" Slightly more seriously, I said that from time to time, especially as a significant issue arises in our culture (e.g., homosexuality) or a Christian doctrine needs defending (e.g., justification), I would not be opposed to tackling a topic; but I would do so based on the exegesis of a Bible text or texts. One of the reasons to refrain from picking a topic to preach on,

1. Choon-Leong Seow, *Ecclesiastes*, Anchor Bible 18C (New York: Doubleday, 1997), 197.

however, is that most topics would center on our felt needs. To put a clearer point on that reason: topical sermons can sometimes focus on ourselves and our issues *at the expense* of focusing on God.[2] That is a problem not only if you claim to be a God-centered church, but also if you seek to meet people's most foundational need.

In his book *The Supremacy of God in Preaching*, John Piper begins:

> People are starving for the greatness of God. But most of them would not give this diagnosis of their troubled lives. The majesty of God is an unknown cure. There are far more popular prescriptions on the market, but the benefit of any other remedy is brief and shallow. Preaching that does not have the aroma of God's greatness may entertain for a season, but it will not touch the hidden cry of the soul: "Show me thy glory!"[3]

With our need for glory in mind, consider what we learn about *God* in Ecclesiastes 5:1–7. This is appropriate to do for the reason stated above (that God's greatness is the remedy for our troubles), as well as the emphasis of the text itself. In Ecclesiastes 4, God is never mentioned. In the first seven verses of chapter 5, however, God is mentioned seven times (including the pronoun *he* in verse 4)! This is the highest concentration of *God*-talk in the book,[4] and for that reason it is unusual and important.

In Ecclesiastes 1–4 we have learned a number of things about God, including that whatever God does endures forever (3:14), that God has given us work to be busy with (3:10), that God grants enjoyment in our work (2:24–25; 3:13) and the reward of wisdom, knowledge, and joy (2:26), that God has made everything beautiful in its time (3:11), and that in his time he will judge the righteous and the wicked (3:15, 17).

Here in Ecclesiastes 5:1–7, we learn three truths about God. First, God has a house. In verse 1, "the house of God" references Solomon's temple, built in the tenth century B.C. and destroyed in 587 B.C. While it stood, the temple was a visible testimony to God's absolute holiness. There Isaiah saw "the Lord sitting upon a throne, high and lifted up"

---

2. Iain Provan summarizes a recent study on sermons by stating that "over 80 percent of these [sermons] made God and his world spin around the surrogate center of the self." *Ecclesiastes/Song of Songs*, NIV Application Commentary (Grand Rapids: Zondervan, 2001), 122.

3. John Piper, *The Supremacy of God in Preaching* (Grand Rapids: Baker, 1990), 9.

4. For a very close second, see Ecclesiastes 3:10–18; cf. 5:18–6:2; 8:12–17.

(Isa. 6:1) as the seraphim called to one another, "Holy, holy, holy is the LORD of hosts" (v. 3). The temple symbolized God's holiness—that is, he was inaccessible except by sacrifice through a priestly mediator, and even such a priestly mediator could be incinerated by God's consuming fire (Lev. 10:1–3; cf. 15:31; 1 Sam. 6:19–20). Of course, God was not limited to this human-made house. In Solomon's dedication of the temple in 1 Kings 8:27, he says as much: "But will God indeed dwell on the earth? Behold, heaven and the highest heaven cannot contain you; how much less this house that I have built!" Solomon echoes that prayer in Ecclesiastes 5:2, proclaiming that "God is in heaven." Is God in the temple *and* in heaven? Yes, he is: "the whole earth is full of his glory!" (Isa. 6:3; cf. Deut. 4:39). Wherever God is, there is a distance and difference between the Creator and his creation. He is not our peer. "I am God and not a man, the Holy One" (Hos. 11:9).

Second, God knows and judges the way we worship. He sees into the heart—the attitudes behind the actions—and judges whether our worship is "acceptable worship" (Heb. 12:28) or not. If not, he renders his judgment against the "appearance of godliness" (2 Tim. 3:5). He gets "angry" at the blabbering fool and "destroys" (i.e., does not accept) his sacrificed animal and retracted vow (Eccl. 5:6).

Third, unlike the gods of the Gentiles, which are deaf and dumb, Israel's God hears and speaks. In the temple God's people were told "to draw near to listen" (Eccl. 5:1), and in the temple God heard and accepted sincere sacrificial vows.

So, then, in light of God's transcendence, omnipresence, omniscience, and holiness (God has a house), justice (God knows and judges our worship), and forgiveness and accessibility (God hears and speaks), "God is the one you must fear" (Eccl. 5:7).

But again, what does it mean to fear the Lord? I could flesh out such "fear" by giving a long definition (but I won't),[5] or a short definition (which I might whisper—*trembling trust*), or an illustration (which I will give now).

---

5. Here is my definition from Proverbs that fits wisdom literature in general (*The Beginning and End of Wisdom: Preaching Christ from the First and Last Chapters of Proverbs, Ecclesiastes, and Job* [Wheaton, IL: Crossway, 2011], 37):

According to the book of Proverbs, "the fear of the LORD" is a continual (23:17), humble, and faithful submission to Yahweh, which compels one to hate evil (8:13) and turn away from it (16:6) and brings with it rewards better than all earthly treasures (15:16)—the rewards of a love for and

In *The Lion, the Witch, and the Wardrobe*, when Mr. and Mrs. Beaver tell the four children that Aslan (the Christ-figure) is a lion, Susan replies:

"Ooh! . . . Is he—quite safe? I shall feel rather nervous about meeting a lion."

"That you will, dearie, and make no mistake," said Mrs. Beaver; "if there's anyone who can appear before Aslan without their knees knocking, they're either braver than most or else just silly."

"Then he isn't safe?" said Lucy.

"Safe?" said Mr. Beaver. . . . "Who said anything about safe? 'Course he isn't safe. But he's good. He's the King, I tell you."[6]

Our perpetual posture before the Lord should be that of humility, awe, reverence, and faith. We are to come with boldness and confidence before our good, approachable King (mixed, of course, with a bit of shaking in our boots).

Drawing Near Wisely

In Ecclesiastes 5:1–7, more than anywhere in the first eighty-two verses we have studied thus far, we are introduced to God. We learn that God is holy in his temple, that he knows and judges the way we worship him, and that he hears and speaks, and thus he is to be feared. The psalmist summarizes these truths well when he writes:

> The Mighty One, God the Lord,
>   speaks and summons the earth
>   from the rising of the sun to its setting.
> Out of Zion, the perfection of beauty,
>   God shines forth.
>
> Our God comes; he does not keep silence;
>   before him is a devouring fire,
>   around him a mighty tempest.
> He calls to the heavens above
>   and to the earth, that he may judge his people. (Ps. 50:1–4)

a knowledge of God (1:29; 2:5; 9:10; 15:33), and long life (10:27; 14:27a; 19:23a), confidence (14:26), satisfaction, and protection (19:23).

6. C. S. Lewis, *The Lion, the Witch, and the Wardrobe* (New York: HarperCollins, 1994), 79–80.

This God "in heaven" (Eccl. 5:2), who rules time (3:1–15) and judges all peoples (3:16–22), nevertheless can be approached. The isolation we felt as we walked through chapter 4 can be remedied by other humans *as well as* the One who is wholly other. "We stand in need of an altogether greater" companion, and that companion is *Elohim*.[7] Solomon emphasizes this approachability by changing from his "reflective 'journaling' style" to sermonizing.[8] That is, he moves from first-person observations (e.g., "I saw," "I considered") to second-person imperatives ("you"—e.g., "[you] pay what you vow," and "you must fear"). This is the first time in the book that the reader is addressed and admonished. This is Solomon's application of 1:1–4:16, an application similar to the one he gives at the end of the book (12:13–14).

Having looked at *God*, let us turn our attention to *you*. Between the two imperatives that frame our text, we find a number of negative admonitions: "Be *not* rash with your mouth" (Eccl. 5:2), "do *not* delay paying it" (v. 4), and "let *not* your mouth lead you into sin" (v. 6). There are a total of four negative admonitions. All the admonitions are warnings about words in worship, about nouns and verbs related to verbal communication: "Be not rash with your mouth, nor let your heart be hasty to utter a word" (v. 2), "a fool's voice . . . many words" (v. 3), "vow a vow" (v. 5), "let not your mouth . . . do not say . . . your voice" (v. 6), and "words grow many" (v. 7).

Listen First

When I was in high school, my class went on a weekend spiritual retreat (this was a Catholic high school). We must have been told twenty times that the boys couldn't be on the girls' floor and vice versa. Well, 50 percent of the boys-who-will-be-boys decided to test this policy. We (yes, I include myself in that pronoun) ventured down after the official bedtime. We quickly learned that the school was quite serious about the policy: we were caught almost immediately and bused home early the next morning.

One by one we were called into the dean's office. The dean was also the head football coach. Of course. Now, what do you think I did when I sat before him? I'll tell you what I did: I sat still and shut my mouth. I didn't

---

7. Michael A. Eaton, *Ecclesiastes: An Introduction and Commentary*, Tyndale Old Testament Commentaries 16 (Downers Grove, IL: InterVarsity Press, 1983), 97.

8. Kathleen A. Farmer, *Who Knows What Is Good? A Commentary on the Books of Proverbs and Ecclesiastes*, International Theological Commentary (Grand Rapids: Eerdmans, 1991), 167.

speak unless I was asked to speak. When I was asked to speak, I humbly and truthfully (for the record) gave my story and admitted my guilt. He then loudly lectured me, scared me with the threat of suspension, issued a week's detention, stood up, walked over to me, punched me hard in the shoulder (this is when deans were deans!), and said in his strong Chicago accent, "O'Donnell, get out of here!"

We all know from various experiences that there are times to be quiet. Drawing near to God is such a time. Drawing near to God requires that we first listen before we speak. But before I tackle that theme, allow me to say a few words about the historical context and structure. If there is any proof that Ecclesiastes is an ancient Israelite document, it is this section. Besides being written in Hebrew (always a good clue), it uses Hebrew poetic structures and assumes Israel's cultic conduct. The mention of "the house of God" (i.e., the temple), the offer of a sacrifice, and vows clues us in on the fact that the "God" of Ecclesiastes is the "Lord" of the Torah, the Prophets, and the Psalms. This section, in its entirety, is about temple worship.

The structure is a basic Hebrew poetic structure. After the opening command ("Guard your steps," Eccl. 5:1) and reason (because "to draw near to listen is better," and so on, v. 1), there is a command followed by a reason followed by a proverbial illustration. That pattern is repeated three times in verses 2–7. The final line—"but God is the one you must fear" (v. 7)—is intentionally outside this pattern because, like many of Jesus' parables, the last line is the punch line (what Bible scholars term the *law of end stress*). Alexander Maclaren once used this image of good preaching: The preacher touched the text "with a silver hammer, and it immediately broke up into natural and memorable divisions."[9] That is precisely what Pastor Solomon has done with his "sermon" structure. The structure of these verses is easy to see and remember.

Beyond the silver-hammered structure, we return now to the theme of Ecclesiastes 5:1–3. Listen to what these verses say about listening:

> Guard your steps when you go to the house of God. To draw near to listen is better than to offer the sacrifice of fools, for they do not know that they are doing evil. Be not rash with your mouth, nor let your heart be hasty to utter

9. Alexander Maclaren, quoted in Sidney Greidanus, *Preaching Christ from Ecclesiastes: Foundations for Expository Sermons* (Grand Rapids: Eerdmans, 2010), 124–25.

a word before God, for God is in heaven and you are on earth. Therefore let your words be few. For a dream comes with much business, and a fool's voice with many words. (Eccl. 5:1–3)

Temple sacrifices were offered in silence. In effect, the silence shouted out the steadfast love of a holy, holy, holy God for undeserving sinners. Then the silence was broken by a reading from the law of Moses and an explanation for the people. The response to hearing from God would be to speak to God—through prayers, songs, and sometimes personal vows. The service closed with a benediction.

The emphasis in Ecclesiastes 5:1–3 is on listening to the Word of God. This listening ear is contrasted to the mouths of fools. Here the foolish worshipers are not necessarily those who bring blind, lame, or sick animals to be sacrificed ("they do not know that they are doing evil," v. 1); rather, the foolish are those who sin with their mouths. Instead of being like Moses before the burning bush—with their sandals off, mouths shut, and ears open (respectfully revering the Lord, Ex. 3:5)—they chatter on before their Creator. They are mumbling mantras before the Almighty! With hollow hearts and blank minds they offer up "empty phrases" (Matt. 6:7), thinking that the more they talk, the more God will listen.

One is reminded of Jesus' parable of the Pharisee and the tax collector, which begins:

> Two men went up into *the temple* to pray, one a Pharisee and the other a tax collector. The Pharisee, standing by himself, prayed thus: "God, I thank you that I am not like other men, extortioners, unjust, adulterers, or even like this tax collector. I fast twice a week; I give tithes of all that I get." (Luke 18:10–12)

The Pharisee gives God all the gossip as he goes on about his own personal holiness. In all likelihood, his prayer lasted the length of a double-overtime football game. "But the tax collector," Jesus continues, "standing far off, would not even lift up his eyes to heaven, but beat his breast, saying, 'God, be merciful to me, a sinner!'" (Luke 18:13). With a posture that acknowledges God's superiority, the tax collector offers a short, simple, God-honoring prayer—much like the one that Jesus taught us to pray, which begins, "Our Father in heaven, hallowed be your name" (Matt. 6:9), and ends focusing on our deepest spiritual needs: "forgive us our debts, . . . lead us not into temptation, . . . deliver us from evil" (vv. 12–13).

In the temple, Israel was to listen first. As Christians, we know and appreciate that through Jesus' death, our Lord judged the temple (Matt. 21:13; 23:38) and replaced it (12:6; 24:2; 26:61; 27:40, 51). We do not journey to Jerusalem to some building to worship God. Under the new covenant in Jesus' blood, we have a perfect and permanent sacrifice and intercessor for our sins (Heb. 7:23–28), as well as the gift of the Holy Spirit, who dwells within everyone who worships God in spirit and in truth (John 4:23–24; Eph. 2:13–22). Jesus is the temple we go through to rightly worship God, and in him we become the temple of the living God (1 Cor. 3:16; Eph. 2:19–22; 1 Peter 2:5). Nevertheless, like Israel of old, we are to hear ("Hear, O Israel," Deut. 6:4) before we speak to God. In all walks of life, but especially in public worship, we are to "be quick to hear, slow to speak" (James 1:19). The words of God, rather than the words of the worshiper, are to take priority.

Our words should be few because many words do not mediate between God and man. In prayer, the number of words counts for nothing. D. L. Moody memorably said it this way: "Some men's prayers need to be cut short on both ends and set on fire in the middle."[10] Augustine put it like this: "Remove from prayer much speaking, not much praying."[11] And Martin Luther, with his usual blend of bluntness and humor, said that prayers should be "brief, frequent, and intense"[12] because "God has no need of such everlasting twaddle."[13] He also said:

Remember your situation: God is such a great majesty in heaven, and you are a worm upon earth. You cannot speak about the works of God on the basis of your own judgment. Let God rather do the speaking; do not dispute about the counsels of God and do not try to control things by your own counsels. It is God who can arrange things and perfect them, for He Himself is in heaven. We express all of this in German by saying: "Don't use many words, but: keep your mouth shut!"[14]

10. D. L. Moody, quoted in Luis Palau, *So You Want to Grow* (Eugene, OR: Harvest House, 1986), 13.

11. Augustine, quoted in Frederick Dale Bruner, *The Christbook: Matthew 1–12*, 2nd rev. ed. (Grand Rapids: Eerdmans, 2004), 290.

12. Martin Luther, quoted in ibid., 289.

13. Luther, quoted in ibid., 291.

14. Martin Luther, "Notes on Ecclesiastes," in *Luther's Works*, trans. and ed. Jaroslav Pelikan, 56 vols. (St. Louis: Concordia, 1972), 15:78.

The Irish say it this way: "It is better to remain silent and be thought a fool than to open your mouth and remove all doubt" (one of Murphy's Laws). Or, less crassly, the Hebrews put it like this: "When words are many, transgression is not lacking, but whoever restrains his lips is prudent" (Prov. 10:19). Wise worship starts with locked lips.

Speak Second

Those lips should not stay locked, however. Worshiping wisely also involves right words at the right time. We are to listen to God first and *speak* to God *second*. The second half of our text covers the boundaries for this second lesson:

> When you vow a vow to God, do not delay paying it, for he has no pleasure in fools. Pay what you vow. It is better that you should not vow than that you should vow and not pay. Let not your mouth lead you into sin, and do not say before the messenger that it was a mistake. Why should God be angry at your voice and destroy the work of your hands? For when dreams increase and words grow many, there is vanity; but God is the one you must fear. (Eccl. 5:4–7)

If it is not obvious from the repetition of the word *vow* (five times), this section centers on temple vows. Such a vow involved a conditional promise; a worshiper coming to the temple asked God for something in return for something—usually money or an animal sacrifice (Lev. 27:1–25), although it could be just about anything or *anyone*. For example, barren Hannah vowed to give God her son if she was able to conceive and give birth (1 Sam. 1–2).[15] So the problem being addressed in Ecclesiastes is not the vow itself (it was a condoned but not commanded biblical practice), but the temptation to "delay" (Eccl. 5:4) or "not pay" (v. 5) the vow once the request has been granted. To say to the temple "messenger" (the spiritual bill collector sent to retrieve the coins for the temple treasury) that "it was a mistake" or "it was unintentional" is intentionally sinful (Num. 15:30–31; Deut. 23:21). It is better not to vow than to vow and refrain from keeping your end of the deal. "Simply let your 'Yes' be 'Yes' and your 'No,' 'No'; anything beyond this

15. Other examples of vows are Jacob's vowing that if God protected and provided for him, he would give God "a full tenth" (Gen. 28:20–22), and David's vowing that he wouldn't go to bed until the temple was built (see the poetic exaggeration in Psalm 132:2–5).

116

comes from the evil one" (Matt. 5:37 NIV), as a wise man once said. Why? Because God doesn't take kindly to the Ananias and Sapphira vowing club (Acts 5:1–11). Or, as Solomon exhorted, God "has no pleasure in fools" (Eccl. 5:4) and "Why should God be angry at your voice and destroy the work of your hands?" (v. 6). All toying with God will be exposed ("You blind fools," e.g., Matt. 23:16–22) and judged ("a rod for his back," Prov. 14:3). All lame excuses will be leveled by the Lord.

We all make vows to God and to one another. I vowed to remain faithful to my wife "till death do us part." As an ordained minister, I vowed "to be zealous and faithful in maintaining the truths of the Gospel and the purity, peace and unity of the Church, whatever persecution or opposition may arise." At your baptism, you might have vowed to "live in faithful and joyful obedience" to Christ. In church membership vows, you might have vowed to "faithfully participate in the service and activities of this church, seeking to bring about the unity of this body of believers and the glory of our great God." If you are a witness in a court of law, you will vow (with your hand on a Bible, no less!) to "tell the whole truth and nothing but the truth," so help you God. Making vows is not the issue. Making impulsive promises that you have no intention of keeping or without any real idea what you are saying is foolish (cf. Prov. 20:25). It is a dream-induced fantasy.

Twice Solomon compares "many words" (Eccl. 5:3; "words grow many," v. 7) to dreams. The sense of verse 3 is that just as an extremely busy day produces sound sleep (and the dreams that come with such sleep), so a fool produces verbosity. And the sense of verse 7 is that pious phrases uttered by "the mouth . . . [that] pours out evil things" (Prov. 15:28)—reciting God's covenant statutes (Ps. 50:16)—will prove to be as futile as the fantasies created in slumberland. Poof! They are gone the moment you awake.

The night before Jesus' arrest, Peter vowed to Jesus, "Even if I must die with you, I will not deny you!" (Matt. 26:35). That vow was made shortly before he vowed three times, "I do not know the man" (26:74; cf. vv. 70, 72). While we will never find ourselves in Peter's precise predicament, we should nonetheless watch out for making our own dreamlike oaths. We should avoid making promises such as these:

- Lord, if you give me a wife, I promise that we won't kiss before we are married.

117

- Lord, if you give us children, we will promise to read them the Bible every day, take them to church every Sunday, and save monthly for their college education.
- Lord, if you get me that much-needed raise, I will give half of it to the poor, and I promise I'll come home early every night and spend my evenings playing with the kids and not watching any television.
- Lord, if I happen to overeat on Thanksgiving, I promise to exercise next week and eat less than a thousand calories a day until Christmas.

If we are to vow, let us "make [our] vows to the LORD [our] God and perform them" (Ps. 76:11). Let us not say to the Lord, "I will do this," and then fail to do it (e.g., the parable of the two sons, Matt. 21:28–30). There is no value in mindless muttering and great danger in rash vows (e.g., the story of Jephthah's daughter, Judg. 11:29–40). Perhaps the only vow we should make, certainly the safest but never the easiest, is the vow to fear God. Pledge to do that today! "Lord, I will listen to you when you speak, and Lord, when I speak to you I will not come before you with aimless chatter or deluded daydreaming, but with humble and honest admiration and heartfelt and reasonable requests."[16] Be warned, however, that even this can be a rash vow if not taken seriously.

Listen first; speak second.

No Fear of God

Beyond our speak-first, listen-second (if ever) world, the more foundational issue is the absence of the fear of God in the culture as well as the church. Paul's quotation of Psalm 36:1, "There is no fear of God before their eyes" (Rom. 3:18), could be the contemporary church's motto. If it is not found in our actual vision statements, it is found in many worship services every Sunday. We have made glorious Jesus into our own inglorious image and serve him up to accommodate everyone's personal tastes.

Ecclesiastes 5:1–7 is the antidote for such cultural and religious rubbish. It especially protests against this new Protestantism. It gives us a sorely needed vision of God and picture of wise worship. It moves us beyond God

---

16. The phrase "aimless chatter or deluded daydreaming" comes from Carl Schultz, "Ecclesiastes," in *Evangelical Commentary on the Bible*, ed. Walter A. Elwell (Grand Rapids: Baker, 1989), 441.

as "the Big Guy upstairs" and Jesus as our "homeboy." Instead, it takes us to the feet of "the One who is high and lifted up, who inhabits eternity, whose name is Holy" (Isa. 57:15), and of his Son, Jesus Christ, "the firstborn of the dead, . . . the ruler of kings on earth" (Rev. 1:5), the One whose eyes are a flame of fire, whose voice is like the roar of many waters, and whose face is like the sun shining in full strength (vv. 14–16), and the One who nevertheless "loves us and has freed us from our sins by his blood" (v. 5). In view of such a God, it compels us to take our sandals off, keep our mouths shut, and . . . listen first.

10

GRIEVOUS EVILS, GREAT JOYS

Ecclesiastes 5:8–6:9

*Behold, what I have seen to be good and fitting is to eat and
drink and find enjoyment in all the toil with which one toils
under the sun the few days of his life that God has given
him, for this is his lot. Everyone also to whom God has given
wealth and possessions and power to enjoy them, and to
accept his lot and rejoice in his toil—this is the gift of God.*
(Eccl. 5:18–19)

My favorite tale from Chaucer's *Canterbury Tales* is the Pardoner's Tale. After the physician has finished has tragic tale, the host then turns to the pardoner and asks him to tell a more upbeat story. Others disagree and ask for a moral tale, which the immoral pardoner agrees to tell only after he has had his fill of food and drink. So with a full stomach and in a drunken stupor, the gluttonous and greedy cleric reveals the trick of his trade: how he cheats people of their money by preaching on money as the root of all evil.

His tale is this. Three lawless young men go in search of Death. They think that if they can find Death, they will be able to kill him. As they are searching, they meet an old man who tells them that Death can be found at the foot of an oak tree. Off they go to the tree. There, instead of finding Death, they find eight bushels of gold. With death now out of mind and greed in hand, they decide to sleep there that night, guard the treasure, and sneak away with it in the morning.

Meanwhile, the youngest man goes into town to buy some food and drink. He also buys some rat poison, and poisons the wine. He wants the gold all to himself. But the other two also want the gold for themselves, so they plot to kill him when he returns. Sure enough, that is what they do. The man returns, and they stab him to death. Then, to celebrate, they lift their cups and drink the poisoned wine. They, too, die. The old man was right: all three greedy men found Death under the tree.

Like the Pardoner's Tale, Ecclesiastes 5:8–6:9 introduces us to the dark and dangerous side of riches. It tells the tragic tale that those who hunger and thirst for money will not be satisfied. And it calls us to *abandon* the sad, bad investment of the love of money as well as to *embrace* the wise investment of trusting God by enjoying his good gifts.

THE STRUCTURE OF THE TEXT

Pastor Solomon, with the artistic mind that he surely possessed (think of the design of the temple and the imagery of the Song of Songs), presents his message as a chiasm, a common literary device in the ancient Near East that uses parallel concepts or words to make a point. The three common types of parallelism that we have seen before are found here. There is synonymous parallelism:

He who loves money will not be satisfied   with money,
nor he who loves wealth   with his income. (Eccl. 5:10; cf. 5:11)

There is antithetic parallelism:

Sweet is the sleep of a laborer, whether he eats little or much,
but the full stomach of the rich will not let him sleep. (Eccl. 5:12)

121

And there is synthetic parallelism:

> All the toil of man is for his mouth,
> yet his appetite is not satisfied. (Eccl. 6:7)

But there is also the parallelism of all parallelisms—the glorious chiasm! The term *chiasm* derives its name from the Greek letter *chi*, because the basic form resembles the left half of that letter (X). A chiasm is a structural device in which the point of the text is highlighted both by its separateness (it alone has no parallel) and by its central placement (it is found in the middle). This can be depicted as follows:

A People Who Cannot Be Satisfied (5:8–12)
  B People Who Cannot Enjoy (5:13–17)
    C What Is Good (5:18–19)
      D Enjoy the Moment (5:20)
    C' What Is Bad (6:1–2)
  B' People Who Cannot Enjoy (6:3–6)
A' People Who Cannot Be Satisfied (6:7–9)[1]

Notice how the author takes several similar themes and, starting from both ends, works his way to the center. If we begin from the outside, the themes in the first and last sections are similar. Then, as we continue to move from the outside inward, we see how the theme of an earlier section parallels a later theme. This narrowing in on the main theme takes us to the center: the poetic and practical point of the passage.

An even simpler way to see and preach this text is to view the "chiasm as a step pyramid."[2]

---

1. Choon-Leong Seow, *Ecclesiastes*, Anchor Bible 18C (New York: Doubleday, 1997), 217. Cf. Daniel C. Fredericks, "Chiasm and Parallel Structure in Qoheleth 5:9 [Eng. 5:10]–6:9," *Journal of Biblical Literature* 108, 1 (1989): 17–35; and Daniel C. Fredericks, "Ecclesiastes," in Daniel C. Fredericks and Daniel J. Estes, *Ecclesiastes and the Song of Songs*, Apollos Old Testament Commentary 16 (Downers Grove, IL: InterVarsity Press, 2010), 147–49.

2. For much of the structure and outline for my sermon, I am indebted to Sidney Greidanus, *Preaching Christ from Ecclesiastes: Foundations for Expository Sermons* (Grand Rapids: Eerdmans, 2010), 137–56. Once I saw how Greidanus laid out the text, I scrapped my outline and gladly borrowed his.

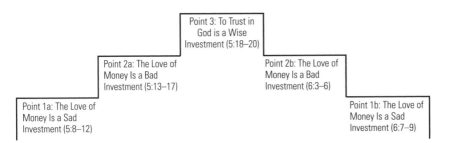

Whichever visual helps best, both display the central point of Ecclesiastes 5:8–6:9. A deliberate structure gives us a definite message: to *embrace* the wise investment of trusting God by enjoying his good gifts.

A SAD INVESTMENT

The first point in this passage is that the love of money is a sad investment; it cannot bring ultimate satisfaction. Money can't buy joy any more than it can buy love. Or, as Pastor Solomon summarizes: "He who loves money will not be satisfied with money" (Eccl. 5:10). This theme is found in 5:8–12 and 6:7–9. Starting with the end of our text, we read:

All the toil of man is for his mouth, yet his appetite is not satisfied. For what advantage has the wise man over the fool? And what does the poor man have who knows how to conduct himself before the living? Better is the sight of the eyes than the wandering of the appetite: this also is vanity and a striving after wind. (Eccl. 6:7–9)

We all have an appetite for food and work to get it. When we do get it, we consume it. Yet we soon discover that a particular meal didn't permanently satisfy our basic craving, because a few hours later the same cycle recurs. So also is the appetite for wealth. Whether we are rich or poor, smart or dumb, we can feed our money-loving appetite all we want, but we will always want more. As Horace said on this theme: "Greed is not decreased either by surplus or by shortage"[3] Thus, it is better to see rightly and be content with our daily bread than to be blind to the law of diminishing

3. Horace, quoted in Jerome, *Commentary on Ecclesiastes*, trans. Richard J. Goodrich and David J. D. Miller, Ancient Christian Writers 66 (New York: Newman, 2012), 76.

returns and keep biting into *hebel* helping after *hebel* helping, hoping to find eternal sustenance.

The theme of *no satisfaction* and the comparison between the rich and the poor touched on in Ecclesiastes 6:7–9 also surface at the start of the text. In 5:8–12 we read:

> If you see in a province the oppression of the poor and the violation of justice and righteousness, do not be amazed at the matter, for the high official is watched by a higher, and there are yet higher ones over them. But this is gain for a land in every way: a king committed to cultivated fields.
>
> He who loves money will not be satisfied with money, nor he who loves wealth with his income; this also is vanity. When goods increase, they increase who eat them, and what advantage has their owner but to see them with his eyes? Sweet is the sleep of a laborer, whether he eats little or much, but the full stomach of the rich will not let him sleep.

Here the poor have it both good and bad. What is good is their sleep. Unlike the insomnia caused by overindulgent indigestion ("the full stomach of the rich will not let him sleep"), the sleep of the working-class man is "sweet . . . whether he eats little or much" (Eccl. 5:12). Perhaps part of the reason he sleeps well is that he is not worrying about the business—its employees, profits/losses, lawsuits, or a sudden financial swing or crash. The lack of fatty foods milling around in his digestive system helps, too. Bread and water digest better than the beer and meat consumed by the rich.

Yet sometimes the poor would trade in sweet sleep for better wages and working conditions. Those verses are notoriously difficult to translate and explain, but my sense is that unjust oppression of the poor (Eccl. 5:8) is caused by bureaucratic business hierarchy that is corrupt from the top ("a king") down (v. 9). The whole system is run by guys who love money (v. 10). The higher-ups line their pockets on the labor of the poor. Trickle-down economics has not trickled down here. The rich hoard their wealth while the poor make it for them. "You shall love your neighbor as yourself" (Lev. 19:18; Matt. 19:19) has been erased from the lawbooks.

Pastor Solomon tells us not to be "amazed" at this (the fallen world is what it is, and there is very little we can do about it), but he does call it a "violation of justice and righteousness" (Eccl. 5:8). In that sense, we should do whatever we can do and at the very least grieve over how unloving the lovers of money are to others.

There is a flaw in their system, however—a God-designed flaw. When the rich get money, they do not get satisfaction from it—not the satisfaction they thought it would bring. There is a God-made and God-shaped void that even a billion dollars can't fill.

Moreover, the accumulation of money comes with some additional and unexpected costs. Loving money and having money to love can be *costly*! How so? Look at Ecclesiastes 5:11. The first half reads, "When goods increase, they increase who eat them." Put differently, wealth attracts a circle of dependents—or, put more graphically, "human leeches."[4]

The second half continues: "and what advantage has their owner but to see them with his eyes?" The answer to this rhetorical question is "none." All that he can do is to watch the leeches slowly suck him dry.

He will need a maid to clean his big house. He will need a personal chef to cook his rich meals. He will need a gardener to trim the trees. He will need an accountant to keep the books. He will need a broker to invest his savings. One by one and week by week, in their different and seemingly subtle ways, they will all leech a little more and more and more from his back pocket. Then there is the family (which seems to continually extend outward the more he makes), and the old friends, and the new acquaintances (who never have enough and want a little more), and finally the tax man (who is usually the first at the front door to collect).

Wealth has its advantages, and the wisdom literature of the Bible is not averse to highlighting them. It also has its disadvantages, some of which are highlighted here. But the love of money is especially disadvantageous. It cannot satisfy the craving of the covetous: the stronger the money addiction, the wider the hole in the human heart.

A BAD INVESTMENT

The first point is that the love of money is a sad investment; it cannot bring ultimate satisfaction. The second point is that the love of money is a bad investment; it can actually bring you harm. This theme is found in

---

4. Duane A. Garrett, *Proverbs, Ecclesiastes, Song of Songs*, New American Commentary 14 (Nashville: Broadman & Holman, 1993), 314.

Ecclesiastes 5:13–17 and 6:1–6 and is summarized in 5:13: "There is a grievous evil that I have seen under the sun: riches were kept by their owner to his hurt."

Hoarding can hurt the hoarder in at least three ways. First, riches can be suddenly and ruinously lost. Verse 14 throws the first match into this bonfire of vanities: "those riches were lost in a bad venture. And he is father of a son [i.e., he has a family to support and heir to think of], but he has nothing in his hand." As wise as it is to diversify earnings, salary and savings can still go up in smoke. Just ask Job. He did not foresee his personal stock-market crash (Job 1:13–19). He lost it all in one day! Or ask business leaders during a recession. They might or might not take their losses in faith, as Job did: "The LORD gave, and the LORD has taken away; blessed be the name of the LORD" (1:21). When the economy falters, some businesspeople take their own lives. In *Counterfeit Gods: The Empty Promises of Money, Sex, and Power, and the Only Hope That Matters*, Tim Keller writes of a tragic string of suicides that followed the global economic crisis that started in 2008:

> The acting chief financial officer of Freddie Mac, the Federal Home Loan Mortgage Corporation, hanged himself in his basement. The chief executive of Sheldon Good, a leading U.S. real estate auction firm, shot himself in the head behind the wheel of his red Jaguar. A French money manager who invested the wealth of many of Europe's royal and leading families, and who had lost $1.4 billion of his clients' money in Bernard Madoff's Ponzi scheme, slit his wrists and died in his Madison Avenue office. A Danish senior executive with HSBC Bank hanged himself in the wardrobe of his £500-a-night suite in Knightsbridge, London.[5]

To such powerful men, money was everything. *It* had power over them. And so when they lost everything, there was nothing worth living for. Thus, the sudden loss of riches is not an exclusively ancient phenomenon. Financial ruin can happen to anyone anywhere at any time.

In any case, riches are certain to disappear at death. This is the second way in which hoarding hurts. At the turn of the century, the Virginia Museum of Fine Arts exhibited fourteen contemporary artists' works on the theme

---

5. Timothy J. Keller, *Counterfeit Gods: The Empty Promises of Money, Sex, and Power, and the Only Hope That Matters* (New York: Dutton, 2009), ix–x.

of vanity. A book was written to display and explain the works—*Vanitas: Meditations on Life and Death in Contemporary Art*. For this exhibit Yukinori Yanagi contributed his work *Dollar Pyramid*. Using colored sand, he carefully replicated an enlarged dollar bill in fifteen fragmented parts enclosed in plastic boxes forming a pyramid, each connected by an invisible tunnel. Eventually the artist released a colony of ants into these sand paintings (contemporary art at its best!). A few weeks later, as the ants worked their way through each box—digging tunnels and carrying grains from one box to another—the image of money eroded.[6]

We find a similar image in Ecclesiastes 5:15–16: "As he came from his mother's womb he shall go again, naked as he came, and shall take nothing for his toil that he may carry away in his hand. This also is a grievous evil: just as he came, so shall he go, and what gain is there to him who toils for the wind?" Just as we were born without any clothes, so we will leave this world—with nothing. In the grave, all our investments add up to zero. "You can't take it with you" is not merely a creative bumper sticker; it is also a true scriptural slogan.

If that is the case (and we all know that it is), then what is the profit in money? Is wealth worth it? If we "cannot take anything out of the world" (1 Tim. 6:7), why toil for dust? If even the rich man "will carry nothing away" with him "when he dies" (Ps. 49:17), why make money our god? For as Martin Luther rightly asked, "What sort of god is it that is not even capable of defending himself against moths and rust?"[7]

Third, without God's gift to enjoy abundance, everything that money can give is joyless. As Luther again put it, "The wicked begin their hell in this life."[8] This touches back on the "I can't get no satisfaction" theme that Solomon explored earlier in Ecclesiastes 2:1–11. It puts an exclamation point on it, however, because of God's clear role in the matter. It is not merely that money can't buy joy; it is also that God makes sure of it.

In skimming through Ecclesiastes 5:17 and 6:1–6, notice that God is mentioned twice. In 6:2 we read that God is the One who has given the particular rich man talked about here "wealth, possessions, and honor,"

---

6. John B. Ravenal, *Vanitas: Meditations on Life and Death in Contemporary Art* (Richmond, VA: Virginia Museum of Fine Arts, 2000), 27–28, 64–65 (plate 14).

7. Martin Luther, "The Sermon on the Mount and the Magnificat," in *Luther's Works*, trans. and ed. Jaroslav Pelikan, 56 vols. (St. Louis: Concordia, 1956), 21:173.

8. Martin Luther, "Notes on Ecclesiastes," in *Luther's Works*, 15:97.

and yet he withholds the ability to enjoy it all—"God does not give him power to enjoy them." Also, the word *darkness* is repeated three times. The second and third references illustrate the darkness of the grave, specifically referring to a stillborn child: "For it comes in vanity and goes in darkness, and in darkness its name is covered" (6:4). The physical darkness (death) of the stillborn child is better (can you imagine!?) than the spiritual and mental darkness that plagues the living rich: "Moreover, all his days he eats in darkness in much vexation and sickness and anger" (5:17).

In biblical times, eating was a social occasion intended to bring great joy. The picture here is the opposite: an unhappy man sitting in the dark eating meal after meal alone. The other picture is even grimmer and more shocking! For an Israelite, the ultimate earthly blessing would be to have wealth, a long life, and many children. Yet we read:

> If a man fathers a hundred children and lives many years, so that the days of his years are many, but his soul is not satisfied with life's good things, and he also has no burial, I say that a stillborn child is better off than he. . . . Moreover, it [the stillborn] has not seen the sun or known anything, yet it finds rest rather than he [the rich man]. Even though he should live a thousand years twice over, yet enjoy no good—do not all go to the one place [the dust of the earth]? (Eccl. 6:3, 5–6)

The stillborn child who never lived a day is better off than the rich man who lived two thousand years and fathered a hundred children. Why? Because the child has found "rest," while nothing can compensate for the rich man's lack of joy. The child rests in peace, while the rich man is choked by what Jesus called "the cares of the world and the deceitfulness of riches" (Matt. 13:22). The point? "A long life without enjoyment . . . is far worse than no life at all,"[9] and a hundred heirs with a thousand cares is a miscarriage of life.

A Wise Investment

The first point is that the love of money is a sad investment; it cannot bring you ultimate satisfaction. The second point is that the love of money is a bad investment; it can actually bring harm. The final point—the point

9. William P. Brown, *Ecclesiastes*, Interpretation (Louisville, KY: Westminster John Knox, 2000), 65.

of all the points (the center of the chiasm!)—is to make the wise investment of trusting God by enjoying his good gifts. Unlike the grievous evils that Solomon has seen in Ecclesiastes 5:8–17 and 6:1–9, in 5:18–20 he writes of great joys:

> Behold [let us look at this another way], what *I have seen to be good* and fitting is to eat and drink and find enjoyment in all the toil with which one toils under the sun the few days of his life that God has given him, for this is his lot. Everyone also to whom God has given wealth and possessions and power to enjoy them, and to accept his lot and rejoice in his toil—this is the gift of God. For he will not much remember the days of his life because God keeps him occupied with joy in his heart.

God is mentioned four times, and for the fourth time in Ecclesiastes eating, drinking, and finding enjoyment are recommended (Eccl. 2:24–25; 3:12–13, 22). What is taught is this: We are to accept our "lot" in life (5:19). We are dust-destined creatures. So, then, work hard. Find enjoyment in that work (vv. 18, 20). Eat up and drink down the simple, everyday pleasures that money can buy (v. 18). And acknowledge the absolute sovereignty of God in all things: as not a drop of rain falls to the ground unless God so wills it, so not an ounce of joy flows through our hearts unless the Lord gives it. God is the Giver of all good things. He alone is the Giver of joy! Just as riches are heaven-sent (2 Chron. 1:11–12; Job 1:21), so, too, is the power to enjoy them.

Too often we are like Israel in the wilderness. Though God promised to provide us with daily manna from heaven, we want to hoard what we are given. We hoard because deep down we do not believe that the Giver will continue to give. But listen: the "insatiable materialistic soul" can be satiated only by total dependence on our always-sovereign and ever-happy Lord.[10] Every day we are to come to God with open hands, admitting our anxieties and confessing our idolatries, and asking him to make us more and more dependent on his plan and provision for us—its molding and unfolding in our lives. We are to work and work hard. But we are to work hardest at sitting at the feet of our Lord, the "one thing . . . necessary" (Luke 10:42).

We sit at the feet of our Maker and Master because he alone gives the days of our lives (Eccl. 5:18), as well as "wealth and possessions *and* power

---

10. Fredericks, "Ecclesiastes," 156.

to enjoy them" (v. 19). To quote the venerable British philosopher Mick Jagger, "You can't always get what you want. But if you try sometimes you just might find you get what you need."[11] What we need is for God to give us the ability to enjoy possessions. If you do not have that joy, pray for it. If you cannot sing, "Rejoice in the Lord always" (Phil. 4:4), ask God for the strength to grab hold of blessed contentment (see 4:10–13).

My Treasure Thou Art

For many people—the finally-rich lottery winner and the little-bit-poorer lottery loser—coveting money is idolatry (Col. 3:5). Against this idol God's Word comes with its hammer: "Hear, O Israel: The LORD our God, the LORD is one. You shall *love* the LORD your God with all your heart and with all your soul and with all your might" (Deut. 6:4–5; cf. Matt. 22:37; Mark 12:30; Luke 10:27). This is the greatest commandment. God first! Jesus restates this command with reference to himself: "Whoever loves father or mother . . . son or daughter [and I will add here *money* or *the things money can buy*] more than me is not worthy of me" (Matt. 10:37; cf. 1 Cor. 16:22). You can't have money first and Jesus second: "No one can serve two masters" (Matt. 6:24).

Christianity seeks to destroy money as the god of our hearts, and erects in its place the understanding that money is a blessing from God and thus a bridge to God—who is to be our highest treasure. As we sing in the classic hymn "Be Thou My Vision":

> Riches I heed not, nor man's empty praise,
> Thou mine Inheritance, now and always:
> Thou and Thou only, first in my heart,
> High King of Heaven, my Treasure Thou art.[12]

Throughout his earthly ministry, Jesus warned about the deceitfulness of riches (Matt. 6:24; 13:22; Luke 12:15) and the futility of greed (Matt. 19:22–24; Luke 12:16–20). Moreover, he admonished us to be "rich toward God" (Luke 12:21), to seek first his kingdom (v. 31), and to trust and thank God for provision (Matt. 6:19–33). Following Jesus (1 Tim. 6:3), Paul speaks

---

11. Rolling Stones, "(I Can't Get No) Satisfaction," *Out of Our Heads* (RCA Studios, 1965).
12. Mary E. Byrne, trans., "Be Thou My Vision" (1905).

of the damnable dangers of the love of money (v. 10) and the uncertainty of riches, charging wealthy Christians instead to "set their hopes . . . on God, who richly provides us with everything to enjoy" (v. 17). Likewise, the author of Hebrews wrote what can serve as a wonderful summary of our text: "Keep your life free from love of money, and be content with what you have, [why?] for he [Jesus!] has said, 'I will never leave you nor forsake you'" (Heb. 13:5).

When it comes to money, we all face the same choice: between acknowledging Jesus as King and submitting to his lordship or else remaining under our own perceived rule over our lives. If we keep the puny crown on our big heads, we will find the investment to be both sad and bad. Greed will not gratify. Even the "green" that greed sometimes gets will not gratify. But if we allow King Jesus (who is King whether we acknowledge it or not) to graciously remove our crowns and toss them into the sea, we will find that seeking first the kingdom of God is the wisest investment of all. Trusting God by enjoying his good gifts brings us all that we truly need. For as the wisest sage ever to live once instructed, "Do not labor for the food that perishes, but for the food that endures to eternal life, which the Son of Man will give to you" (John 6:27).

11

INSTRUCTIONS FROM THE GRAVE

Ecclesiastes 6:10—7:14

*Consider the work of God: who can make straight what he has
made crooked? In the day of prosperity be joyful, and in the day
of adversity consider: God has made the one as well as the other,
so that man may not find out anything that will be after him.*
(Eccl. 7:13–14)

Questions are significant in the ministry of Jesus. Often he answers questions with questions of his own. "Who do you say that I am?" (Matt. 16:15) and "What does it profit a man to gain the whole world and forfeit his soul?" (Mark 8:36) are two of his cut-to-the-core queries. Ask the first question of an honest seeker and see what he says. Ask the second question of a hoarding rich man and watch him squirm.

Our text for this chapter (Eccl. 6:10–7:14) begins with questions. After admitting that there is insufficient information to unravel earth's anomalies, contesting against the curse, and untwisting "God's 'twisting' of the times"[1]—"Whatever has come to be has already been named, and it is known

---

1. Richard Schultz, "Ecclesiastes," in *Baker Commentary on the Bible*, ed. Gary M. Burge and Andrew E. Hill, 2nd ed. (Grand Rapids: Baker, 2011), 593.

what man is, and that he is not able to dispute with one stronger than he" (6:10)—the questions come in verses 11–12: "The more words, the more vanity, and what is the advantage to man? For who knows what is good for man while he lives the few days of his vain life, which he passes like a shadow? For who can tell man what will be after him under the sun?"

While there are three questions here, thematically there are only two. That is, the first question asks the same question in two different ways: "the more vanity" parallels "the few days of his vain life, which he passes like a shadow," and "what is the advantage to man?" parallels "who knows what is good for man while he lives . . . ?" This first question can be summarized as "Who knows what is good for us?" and the second "Who can tell what will happen to us?" To both questions we can add the phrase "during our brief earthly life" (i.e., "vain life" and "under the sun"). The first question is answered in Ecclesiastes 7:1–12 and the second in 7:13–14.

WHAT'S THE GOOD?

Instead of babbling on to ourselves and others ("the more words, the more vanity" or hot air, Eccl. 6:11) about what might benefit us in "the few days" of our transient lives (6:12), we come to 7:1–12 to listen to God's eternal perspective. If our lives pass like a shadow (Ps. 144:4)—like the shadow of a hawk swiftly flying overhead, ready to swoop down on its prey—what actions would be to our advantage? Pastor Solomon provides some pithy proverbs. Using the Hebrew word *tov* (translated "good" or "better") nine times (eleven times in the whole text), he tells us what is good for us, or what is better than something else. There are seven "better than" comparisons, which we can divide into two scenes.

Going to a Funeral

The first scene takes place at a funeral. In Ecclesiastes 7:1–4, we read twice that attending a "house of mourning" is better than going to a "house of mirth":

A good name is better than precious ointment,
and the day of death than the day of birth.
It is better to go to the house of mourning
than to go to the house of feasting,

for this is the end of all mankind,
    and the living will lay it to heart.
Sorrow is better than laughter,
    for by sadness of face the heart is made glad.
The heart of the wise is in the house of mourning,
    but the heart of fools is in the house of mirth.

Pastor Solomon's counterintuitive teaching is reminiscent of Jesus' Beatitudes. Jesus didn't label the courageous, the agreeable, the funny, the intelligent, the attractive, and the fit "blessed." Rather, he attached that title to those who mourn, are persecuted, and are poor in spirit. Similarly, Solomon speaks of sorrow as better than laughter, the day of death as better than the day of birth, and going to a funeral as better than going to a festival.

These three events are better because they help us to focus on our character and reputation. Ecclesiastes 7:1 claims, "A good name is better than precious ointment,"[2] or, as Proverbs puts it, "than great riches, . . . than silver or gold" (Prov. 22:1). The title of Alister Chapman's biography of John Stott, *Godly Ambition*,[3] fittingly summarizes the point. We should be ambitious to make a good name for ourselves by glorifying God's name on earth.

How does a funeral help with this task? At a birthday bash, frat party, wedding reception, or whatever other kind of party one might attend, people do not normally evaluate how well and wisely they are living their lives. Even the most celebratory New Year's Eve parties are superficial. We would do better to stay home that night, shake our heads in dismay, and read Ecclesiastes until falling asleep. Do not underestimate the divinely appointed opportunity that every funeral allows. Outside each funeral home God holds up his picket signs: "Life is brief." "Death is inevitable." "Walk wisely!" And within each funeral home, every casket cautions us ("redeem the time!") and questions us ("how are you spending your time?"). What will be said of you when people gather at the house of mourning to mourn over you? Will you be remembered as someone wise or foolish?

2. Note the wordplay of "name" (*shem*) and "ointment" (*shemen*).
3. Alister Chapman, *Godly Ambition: John Stott and the Evangelical Movement* (New York: Oxford University Press, 2012).

In her brilliant song "Laughing With," Regina Spektor juxtaposes how God can be the butt of a "God-theme joke" at "a cocktail party," but how no one laughs at God "in a hospital . . . in a war . . . when they're starving or freezing or so very poor," how no one laughs at God "when the doctor calls after some routine test . . . when their airplane starts to uncontrollably shake."[4] We may add to Spektor's thought-provoking lyrics that no one laughs at God when asked to sign the death certificate at the hospital or when standing graveside, watching a loved one lowered into the ground.

As much as our culture is a culture of death (we play violent video games, watch documentaries on serial killers, and murder our unborn), nevertheless we deny death when it gets uncomfortably close. This aversion is shown in our language (we say compassionately, "She has passed away" or "gone to a better place," or, crudely, "He has kicked the bucket"), as well as our entertainment. British scholar Carl Trueman bemoans the American obsession with happy endings. In his book *Fools Rush In Where Monkeys Fear to Tread*, he writes:

> I remember my jaw hitting the floor some years ago when I watched a Disney version of *Notre Dame de Paris* where the Hunchback does not die but lives happily ever after . . . . The point of the story of Quasimodo is that the guy with the hump dies at the end and it's all terribly sad. My wife is meant to cry, and I am meant to feel angry at the raw deal Quasimodo has been dealt in the poker game of life.[5]

In a similar but even more serious vein, in his novel *The Second Coming*, Walker Percy writes:

> The present-day unbeliever is crazy because he finds himself born into a world of endless wonders, having no notion how he got here, a world in which he eats, sleeps . . . works, grows old, gets sick, and dies . . . takes his comfort and ease, plays along with the game, watches TV, drinks his drink, [and] laughs . . . as if his prostate were not growing cancerous, his arteries

---

4. Available at http:///www.reginaspektor.com/music/songs/laughing.
5. Carl R. Trueman, *Fools Rush In Where Monkeys Fear to Tread: Taking Aim at Everyone* (Phillipsburg, NJ: P&R Publishing, 2012), 169–70.

turning to chalk, his brain cells dying by the millions, as if the worms were not going to have him in no time at all.[6]

Death is an enemy (1 Cor. 15:26), but also an evangelist. Death "is the great mentor for diligence, sobriety, love, generosity, reverence and humility. Death forces the most profound questions to be asked, but mercilessly mocks those who sleep through its lessons."[7] Death is like a detox clinic. It sobers us up! It is not the emotionally abusive father ("You'll never amount to anything"), but rather the effective drill sergeant ("Attention! Move out. Time is short. Get to a funeral. Sit there. Think.").

Jimmy Carr played football in the NFL. Typical of professional athletes, he thought he was invincible. It wasn't until he was nearing sixty and went to the funeral of a close friend that he saw his invincibility as an illusion. God used the corpse of his close friend as a mirror. For the first time, the great Jimmy Carr reexamined his own less-than-great life. Shortly after the funeral, he gave his life to Christ.

When we go to a funeral, we should think about our reputation. Who are we? What have we done with our lives? How will we stand before God? Moreover, as Christians, we should think beyond our earthly reputation to our heavenly resurrection. While Pastor Solomon believed in an afterlife (Eccl. 12:7, 14), he certainly did not express an exalted view of it. As Christians, however, if we do not hold out hope for the resurrection of our bodies, we are to be most pitied. After the glorious resurrection of Jesus, we are not left groping in the dark. We know for certain that our Redeemer lives and that we will abide with him forever. As Jesus said, "whoever believes in me, though he die, yet shall he live" (John 11:25). In light of Christ's trampling down of death by his death, we see death differently. It is not the exit to extinction but the entrance to eternity. True, our bodies are wasting away. But it is also true that our inner nature is being renewed day by day as we pass through slight momentary afflictions into an eternal glory that is beyond our comprehension (2 Cor. 4:16–18). Thus, we affirm with Paul that "to die is gain"

6. Walker Percy, quoted in Philip Graham Ryken, *Ecclesiastes: Why Everything Matters*, ed. R. Kent Hughes, Preaching the Word (Wheaton, IL: Crossway, 2010), 153–54.

7. Daniel C. Fredericks, "Ecclesiastes," in Daniel C. Fredericks and Daniel J. Estes, *Ecclesiastes and the Song of Songs*, Apollos Old Testament Commentary 16 (Downers Grove, IL: InterVarsity Press, 2010), 177.

(Phil. 1:21). We also affirm with Solomon (in a way that he could not have comprehended!) that "the day of death" *is* better than "than the day of birth" (Eccl. 7:1).

Traveling the Road Less Taken

We have divided the seven "better than" comparisons into two scenes. The first scene takes place at a funeral. The second scene is that of coming to a fork in the road. We can choose between two pathways: the walkway of wisdom and the footpath of folly. Ecclesiastes 7:5–12 uses the language of the fool and the wise person. Verse 4 transitions nicely from one thought to the next: "The heart of the *wise* is in the house of mourning, but the heart of *fools* is in the house of mirth." Then in verses 5–12 we read:

> It is better for a man to hear the rebuke of the *wise*
> than to hear the song of *fools*.
> For as the crackling of thorns under a pot,
> so is the laughter of the *fools*;
> this also is vanity.
> Surely oppression drives the *wise* into madness,
> and a bribe corrupts the heart.
> Better is the end of a thing than its beginning,
> and the patient in spirit is better than the proud in spirit.
> Be not quick in your spirit to become angry,
> for anger lodges in the bosom of *fools*.
> Say not, "Why were the former days better than these?"
> For it is not from *wisdom* that you ask this.
> *Wisdom* is good with an inheritance,
> an advantage to those who see the sun.
> For the protection of *wisdom* is like the protection of money,
> and the advantage of knowledge is that *wisdom* preserves the life of him
> who has it.

The key words unlock this section. *Wise/wisdom* is repeated seven times, *fools* four times, and *heart* five times. In Hebrew, the word *heart* (*lev*) has more to do with thinking and doing than feeling. The heart is the place where reflections and decisions are made. Here the thoughtful decision is between the walkway of wisdom and the footpath of folly.

If Ecclesiastes 7:1–4 is not far removed from the beginning of the Sermon on the Mount (the Beatitudes), then verses 5–12 are not far removed from the end, where Jesus talks about the one who receives his words as being "like a wise man who built his house on the rock" (Matt. 7:24) and the one who rejects them as being "like a foolish man who built his house on the sand" (v. 26). In Ecclesiastes, the wise choose wisdom because the way of wisdom, while narrow and more difficult, is "better." The word *tov* is used four times, with three of its uses rightly interpreted as "better."

The three "better than" comparisons can be summarized under two exhortations: listen to the wise and wait wisely. First, listen to the wise, for as Solomon says in Ecclesiastes 7:5, it is better "to hear the rebuke of the wise than to hear the song of fools." Most people like to listen to foolish songs, of the kind that one might hear in "the house of feasting" (v. 2) or "mirth" (v. 4). Today one thinks of the songs sung at the homecoming dance, during the Super Bowl halftime show, or when Uncle Fred comes home drunk out of his head. We live in the land of silly songs. Nearly everyone has sung silly songs that dull our consciences to the reality of death and to living rightly in its shadow. Perhaps, in your vain life under the sun, you have sung Chubby Checker's "The Twist," Tina Turner's "What's Love Got to Do with It?," Cyndi Lauper's "Girls Just Want to Have Fun," or Justin Bieber's "Baby":

Baby, baby, baby, ohh
Like
Baby, baby, baby, noo
Like
Baby, baby, baby, ohh

I'll stop there before I lose more gray matter. These memorable lyrics, sustained by a good beat and a kid with cool hair, do not get us to dig down deep into the soul, do they?

Similar in sound to "the song of fools" is "the laughter of the fools." Both can be compared to breath ("this also is vanity") as well as "the crackling of thorns under a pot." Not only is the image apt (the idea that silliness erupts into flame, quickly dies down, is carried up, up, up and away like smoke, and thus doesn't last long enough to warm even a thin layer of soup, let alone cook a hearty stew), but the use of assonance *and* onomatopoeia is also apt!

Assonance is the repetition of similar vowel sounds; in onomatopoeia, the very sound of a word or phrase suggests its meaning. In Hebrew, "For as the crackling of thorns under a pot" sounds like, or is intended to sound like, sticks popping in a fire. "The sibilants [š, s, ś] reflect the hissing sound of the fire, while the palatals [k, q] reflect the crackling of the wood."[8] James Moffatt's rendering catches some of the sound in English, "Like nettles crackling under kettles." Literary devices aside, the point of the metaphor is plain: we are to use the *lev* (that is, the heart) to lay aside the levity. The songs and laughter of fools (cf. Eccl. 2:2) are of no use in helping us to gain "a heart of wisdom" (Ps. 90:12), but they are of a great danger to the soul (see Luke 6:25).

Instead of listening to fools, then, and their trivial jokes and Top 40 songs, we are to listen to the wise and their unpopular but constructive criticism: "It is better for a man to hear the rebuke of the wise" (Eccl. 7:5). In Proverbs, Solomon makes this point strongly ("Whoever loves discipline loves knowledge, but he who hates reproof is stupid," Prov. 12:1) and visually ("A rebuke goes deeper into a man of understanding than a hundred blows into a fool," 17:10). I would be half the man I am without a few good rebukes—rebukes that I didn't push aside, argue against, or start a fistfight over. I learned how to write from a professor who marked up every mistake I made and graded extremely low (but on a curve, so sometimes a 67 percent on an essay received an A). I learned how to preach from pastors (and my wife!) who took a scalpel to my earliest sermons. In your line of work, marriage, or anything else in life, isn't the same true for you? It was for Simon Peter. Think of Peter's life (and growth!) without the rebukes he received from wise men. Jesus rebuked him in Galilee. Paul rebuked him in Galatia. And with each rebuke, Peter grew. Listen to the wise. It's for your own good.

The first exhortation in Ecclesiastes 7:5–12 is to listen to the wise; the second is to wait wisely. The theme of waiting arises in verses 7–10:

Surely oppression drives the wise into madness,
    and a bribe corrupts the heart.

8. Choon-Leong Seow, *Ecclesiastes*, Anchor Bible 18C (New York: Doubleday, 1997), 237. For the use of paronomasia, see Ecclesiastes 7:1 (*tov shem mishemen tov*); for assonance, note verse 5 (*sir, sama, is*), verse 6 (*sir, k'sil, sirim*), and verses 8–9 (*ruah, nuah*). Also (and of course), parallelisms are employed: synonymous (7:1, 6, 7, 8, 11), antithetic (7:2, 4, 5), and synthetic (7:12). What a feast of literary devices!

Better is the end of a thing than its beginning,
and the patient in spirit is better than the proud in spirit.
Be not quick in your spirit to become angry,
for anger lodges in the bosom of fools.
Say not, "Why were the former days better than these?"
For it is not from wisdom that you ask this.

The phrase "patient in spirit" is the central concept around which everything in these verses orbits. We all face temptations toward impatience. It might be the quick fix, as addressed in Ecclesiastes 7:7: "Surely oppression drives the wise into madness, and a bribe corrupts the heart." If "oppression" has to do with the loss of money (which I think it does), then even the wise man will be tempted to embrace something that he would otherwise think crazy or evil ("madness"), and take a bribe or extort someone in order to pay off his debts. Beyond the temptation of the quick fix is the temptation to lose our temper, as stated in verse 9: "Be not quick in your spirit to become angry, for anger lodges in the bosom of fools."

Closely related to losing our temper is complaining about the present as we idolize and airbrush the past. "Say not, 'Why were the former days better than these?' For it is not from wisdom that you ask this" (Eccl. 7:10). To paraphrase, "Ah, the good old days! When I was a boy, gas was a nickel a gallon and young men wore their trousers above their bottoms, not below." Nostalgia of this sort nauseates Pastor Solomon, for he knows, as we all should know, that each age has its own unique opportunities and challenges, and we cannot face the challenges of our age by pining after another.[9] Such praise of the past proves our impatience with the present. So let's come down from our pride-in-the-past pedestal (v. 8) and give today's generation a shot! You never know, "the end of a thing" might be better "than its beginning" (v. 8).

When things do not go our way, the wise wisely wait. We are to put on patience, which is a fruit of the Spirit (Gal. 5:22), and to put off impatience, which is the root of the devil. By heaven's strength, we are to shun the easy but immoral solution, temper our tempers (be "slow to anger," Prov. 14:29), and manage the hand that we have been dealt rather than longing for some

9. Michael A. Eaton, *Ecclesiastes: An Introduction and Commentary*, Tyndale Old Testament Commentaries 16 (Downers Grove, IL: InterVarsity Press, 1983), 112.

ideal era. Why? Because while the walkway of wisdom might not be the easy path to travel, it is nevertheless the better one:

> Wisdom is good with an inheritance,
>> an advantage to those who see the sun.
> For the protection of wisdom is like the protection of money,
>> and the advantage of knowledge is that wisdom preserves the life of him
>>> who has it. (Eccl. 7:11–12)

Money has its advantages. If you have money, when adversity strikes—the loss of a job, a sputtering economy, a natural disaster—you have some shelter and security. Similarly, wisdom protects. The wise know how to navigate through life's deep and difficult waters. The wise know the wisdom of tempering the tongue, listening, waiting, and attending funerals. Yet human wisdom without a right relationship with God gets us only so far. Thus, there is another step, a final step forward, that we must take. The last step is the beginning of wisdom: to fear the Lord. This is how Solomon concludes our journey in Ecclesiastes 7:13–14.

CONSIDER GOD

The first question ("Who knows what is good for us?") is answered in Ecclesiastes 7:1–12; the second question ("Who can tell what will happen to us?") is answered in 7:13–14. The second question is rhetorical. The tone is negative, as in: "Who on earth can possibly predict what will become of us in the future? Will tomorrow bring feast or famine, work or unemployment, prosperity or adversity, happiness or sorrow?" What is the answer to these questions? Only God knows. It follows that to God we must go. We go to him not for answers but for shelter under his sovereignty. Here is how Pastor Solomon phrases it:

> Consider the work of God:
>> who can make straight what he has made crooked?
>
> In the day of prosperity be joyful, and in the day of adversity consider: God has made the one as well as the other, so that man may not find out anything that will be after him. (Eccl. 7:13–14)

Phil Ryken says that we should see these verses "not as an expression of fatalism but of Calvinism!"[10] That is, they exhort us to see our situation—whether seemingly straight or certainly crooked—as ordered and smooth in the sovereign mind of God. The Scottish Presbyterian Thomas Boston titled a book after Ecclesiastes 7:13, *The Crook in the Lot*. By this title he did not mean that there was a thief in the backyard; he meant, rather, that things happen in all our lives that we wish we could change, but can't. Boston writes:

> While we are here, there will be cross events, as well as agreeable ones . . . .
> Sometimes things are softly and agreeably gliding on; but, by and by, there
> is some incident which alters that course, grates us, and pains us . . . . Every-
> body's lot in this world has some crook in it.[11]

We all struggle with the twisted expressions of divine administration. Why, when the world is in the hand of a good and sovereign God, is it such a crooked place? And why does the dial of his wheel of fortune more often stop on "Bankrupt" than on "Win a Trip to Hawaii"?

Yet part of the point of the crookedness is to straighten us out, as Pastor Solomon attempts to do in the final two verses. I call these verses Solomon's "Job-moment" because they reflect both the beginning and the end of Job's drama. At the end, in Job 37:14, Elihu exhorts Job to "stop and *consider* the wondrous works of God." Then in chapters 38–41, God cross-examines his creature (Job) with his creation. God summons even the ostrich to testify against human arrogance, ignorance, and ingratitude. Finally, in chapter 42, the righteous man repents. "I have uttered," Job admits, "what I did not understand, things too wonderful for me . . . . I had heard of you by the hearing of the ear, but now my eye sees you" (vv. 3–5). What Job finally sees clearly is that he could not see clearly (cf. 1 Cor. 13:12). He acknowledges that the Lord is lovingly involved in the operations of an exceedingly complex universe; that God's mysterious providence is too wonderful to comprehend; that human perceptions of justice are not the scales on which the righteousness of God is weighed; and that God has an inescapable purpose in whatever he does, even if that purpose is never revealed to the creature it affects.

10. Ryken, *Ecclesiastes*, 163.
11. Thomas Boston, quoted in ibid.

Earlier, at the beginning of Job's story (Job 1–2), the hero experienced a very "crooked" world. Job lost his wealth. He lost his children. He lost his friends' respect. He lost his wife's love. Yet Job acknowledged, as Solomon does here, that God has made the day of prosperity as well as the day of adversity ("The LORD gave, and the LORD has taken away," Job. 1:21). He came to understand that both light and darkness (Isa. 45:7), good and bad (Job 2:10; cf. Lam. 3:38), come from the Lord's sovereign hand. Both are works of God. Both are to be "considered."

That admonishment is given twice in the final two verses of our text. Consider. Consider. If we do not know what the future holds, we can only submit to and trust in the One who holds the future. Martin Luther said it well: "Let us, therefore, be content with the things that are present and commit ourselves into the hand of God, who alone knows and controls both the past and the future."[12] God can twist the times so that a proud boy sold into slavery (a bad thing) is the very man God uses to save thousands of people from starvation (a good thing). God can twist the times so that an evil nation destroys a holy building (a bad thing) so that another nation, which was called to be holy, might repent (a good thing). In both the good days and the bad days, we are to bless the name of the Lord (Job 1:21).

On the good days, be happy—"in the day of prosperity be joyful" (Eccl. 7:14). On the bad days, look to God and look at what God does—"consider the work of God" (v. 13; cf. 3:11; 8:17; 11:5). Trust in the Lord's sovereign purposes, knowing that he once used the worst day in human history— the day of Christ's crucifixion—to bring hope and happiness to the world forever. The Man of Sorrows is the God of joy (Isa. 53:3; John 15:11), and the saints who follow that Savior should rejoice in him always. I will say it again, "Rejoice!" Do you really believe that God works all things together for your good (Rom. 8:28)? Then live like it. Trust God and tremble before him. Trembling trust is the wise way forward in a fallen world. Trembling trust in the risen Christ is the only wise way to overcome the grave.

WAITING FOR SUPERMAN

In a modern world, where the work of God is considered benign, other idols—even in the form of make-believe superheroes—rise to the surface.

12. Martin Luther, "Notes on Ecclesiastes," in *Luther's Works*, trans. and ed. Jaroslav Pelikan, 56 vols. (St. Louis: Concordia, 1972), 15:104.

Waiting for "Superman"—the award-winning documentary about public education in the United States—begins with these words from educator Geoffrey Canada:

> One of the saddest days of my life was when my mother told me that Superman did not exist. I was a comic book reader . . . . And I just loved Superman because even in the depths of the ghetto you just thought, "He's coming, and I don't know when, because he always shows up, and he saves all the good people . . . . I was reading—I don't know, maybe I was in the fourth grade—I said, "Ma, do you think Superman is real?" "Superman is not real." I was like, "He's not. What do you mean, he's not?" "No, he's not real." And she thought I was crying because . . . it's like Santa Claus is not real. I was crying because there was no one coming with enough power to save us.[13]

Not so. Not so at all. There *is* someone strong enough to save (cf. Eccl. 6:10),[14] someone who makes "everything beautiful in its time" (3:11).[15] He is someone that we cannot and should not argue with, but someone that we can and should rest in. Our greatest good is God! God knows what is good for us, and he holds our futures in his sovereign, loving hands. So stop pounding on the door of doubt. Stop trying to squeeze through the doggie flap of purposeless pleasures. Stop shaking the locked gate of grief. Pastor Solomon has shut every door but one: faith! Knock. Open. Walk through. Acknowledge God's greatness. Take death seriously. And for God's sake, enjoy life while you're at it!

---

13. *Waiting for "Superman"* (Paramount Vantage, 2011).
14. Seow convincingly argues that God is the "one stronger" in Ecclesiastes 6:10. *Ecclesiastes*, 233, 250–51.
15. On Ecclesiastes 7:1–14 intentionally echoing 3:1–15, see Sidney Greidanus, *Preaching Christ from Ecclesiastes: Foundations for Expository Sermons* (Grand Rapids: Eerdmans, 2010), 159.

12

FINDING THE FEAR OF GOD IN A CROOKED WORLD

Ecclesiastes 7:15–29

See, this alone I found, that God made man upright, but they
have sought out many schemes. (Eccl. 7:29)

n "The Story of the Bad Little Boy Who Didn't Come to Grief,"
Mark Twain describes the mischief of a boy named Jim. Unlike
what the Sunday-school books say about what happens to such
boys, however, nothing bad happens to Jim. For example, "Once he climbed
up in Farmer Acorn's apple-tree to steal apples, and the limb didn't break,
and he didn't fall and break his arm, and get torn by the farmer's great dog,
and then languish on a sick bed for weeks, and repent and become good!"
Then there was "the time he went boating on Sunday, and didn't get drowned,
and that time that he got caught out in the storm when he was fishing on
Sunday, and didn't get struck by lightning." After recalling one peculiar
providence after another, the story concludes with Jim all grown up. Twain
relays how Jim "got wealthy by all manner of cheating and rascality; and
now he is the infernalist wickedest scoundrel in his native village, and is
universally respected, and belongs to the Legislature."[1]

1. See Mark Twain, *The Best Short Stories of Mark Twain*, Modern Library Classics (New York:
Random House, 2004), 10–13.

Twain makes us laugh at the earth's inequities, such as a bad boy's being rewarded with good things, or at least escaping Providence's punishments. But we all know that injustice is no laughing matter. We struggle with the lazy neighbor who makes more money than we do, the star athlete who kills his wife and gets away with it, the Middle Eastern tyrant who daily grows in power.

Moreover, we also struggle (perhaps more so) with the opposite. There is certainly nothing funny about bad things happening to good people. In his sermon on Ecclesiastes 7:14–22, Brandon Levering shares the story of "a godly young couple, who celebrated their first pregnancy, only to discover that their daughter had Trisomy 18," or Edwards syndrome—a deadly genetic disorder. Their daughter, Elizabeth, lived only five days. A year later, a son was born. They named him Joseph, because Joseph means "the LORD adds." Yet shortly after the boy turned one, Joseph died in his sleep.[2] What do we do with that? And what do we do with our own sad stories? How do we handle our paradoxical world? That is what Pastor Solomon seeks to find out.

A First Finding

Solomon begins his investigation into injustice in Ecclesiastes 7:15–18. He observes:

> In my vain [or "brief and passing quickly"] life I have seen everything.
> There is a righteous man who perishes in his righteousness, and
> there is a wicked man who prolongs his life in his evildoing. (Eccl. 7:15)

Solomon's observation is that some righteous people die too young ("perish"), while some wicked people live too long. In reflecting on that observation, and especially the phrase "a righteous man who perishes *in* his righteousness" (v. 15), the first person who comes to mind is Jesus. Our Lord died in his early thirties. Or think of the young martyrs, such as Abel and Naboth in the Old Testament, Stephen and James in the New Testament, and Perpetua and Felicity in the early church.

---

2. Brandon Levering, "The Puzzle of Pleasing God," a sermon on Ecclesiastes 7:14–22, preached at Westgate Church (Weston, MA), August 26, 2012.

How are we to respond to such travesties of justice? Should we demand that God give us all the answers? Throw in the towel? Party like it's 1999? In Ecclesiastes 7:16–17, Pastor Solomon offers two surprising pastoral applications (note the A-B-C-A'-B'-C' parallelism, as well as the synonymous parallelism):[3]

> Be not overly *righteous,*
>> and do not make yourself too *wise.*
>>> Why should you destroy yourself?
> Be not overly *wicked,*
>> neither be a *fool.*
>>> Why should you die before your time?

Ecclesiastes 7:16 is one of those "What did he just say?" verses. We do a double take. Do *not* be overly righteous!? Should we just be a tiny bit righteous? This sounds doable. But before we draw any conclusions, let's let that strange verse sit in our craniums for a moment. We'll return to it after we see its opposite application in verse 17.

The Bible clearly teaches that everyone is a sinner. Solomon himself will say this in Ecclesiastes 7:19–29. Stay tuned: the pastor will call you all "sinners" shortly. We all recognize, however, that there are some terribly sinful people in this world. They are not law-abiding citizens who sometimes break the rules; rather, they are persistent rule-breakers. It is what they do for a living. Think of the mobster, the drug lord, the gang member, or the pimp. The danger of being that kind of "fool" is obvious. Such professions are hardly known for their retirement homes and good pensions. Ninety percent of the murders in a city such as Chicago occur because the "overly wicked" are killing each other. Do not run with that crowd. If you do, you are likely to "die before your time."[4]

Contrasted with the really bad guys are the goody-two-shoes—or, more precisely, those who embrace what Bryan Chapell humorously calls *sola bootstrapa*: that is, those who take hold of their bootstraps and pick themselves up

---

3. Sidney Greidanus, *Preaching Christ from Ecclesiastes: Foundations for Expository Sermons* (Grand Rapids: Eerdmans, 2010), 180–82.

4. The right "time" to die is by natural causes in old age.

147

so that God might accept and reward them.[5] Solomon calls them the "overly righteous" or the "too wise" (Eccl. 7:16). Obviously, there is a difference between a *righteous* person and an *overly righteous* person. The adjective *overly* is important. So, too, is the question that follows in the second half of the verse: "Why should you destroy yourself?" The sense is this: If anyone—whether righteous or unrighteous—can die young (which, of course, is true), then do not think that somehow obtaining ultra-righteousness will be an absolute insurance against such calamity. It is not that Solomon is against *righteousness*—consistent godly thought, speech, and actions. Rather, he is against attempting to tie God's hands (or open God's hands of blessing) by our behavior.

Normally, righteousness and wisdom are blessed (with long life, no less, e.g., Ex. 20:12; Prov. 3:1–2), while wickedness and folly are punished (with life cut short, e.g., Ps. 55:23; Prov. 10:30). But this is not always the case. We can't count on our perfect righteousness to prolong our lives. So do not kill ("destroy") yourself in trying to do so. You can count only on God, and it is up to him whether life is long or short, hard or easy. This is what we are to *grasp*. As Ecclesiastes 7:18 admonishes: "It is good that you should take hold of this, and from that withhold not your hand." In other words, we should grab hold of God, "for the one who fears God shall come out from both of them," which is perhaps more clearly translated "will succeed either way" (NLT) or "will win through at all events" (NAB). Put it this way: a saint or a sinner can become a winner only by trusting in God alone. We are to grab hold of God—or, better, we are to allow God to grab hold of us. The one who tremblingly trusts God avoids the temptation of irreligious antinomianism (i.e., lawlessness) on one side and religious arrogance on the other. The one who tremblingly trusts God worships him because he is worthy of our worship regardless of the sweet or bitter providences that he brings into our lives.

A Second Finding

The text began, "In my vain life I have seen everything" (Eccl. 7:15), followed by Solomon's first observation. The theme of exploration and observa-

5. Bryan Chapell, *Christ-Centered Preaching: Redeeming the Expository Sermon* (Grand Rapids: Baker, 2005), 289.

tion continues throughout the passage. We can summarize Solomon's first finding in verses 15–18 as follows: It is a crooked world. In verses 19–24, he adds this observation: It is a crooked world *filled with sinners—even the wise!* Here's how he pens it: "Wisdom gives strength to the wise man more than ten rulers who are in a city. Surely there is not a righteous man on earth who does good and never sins" (vv. 19–20).

Wisdom is worth it. In the previous passage, Solomon compared wisdom to money, because like money it brings security (Eccl. 7:12). Here he shows wisdom's strength. He compares the strength it gives to the strength of "more than ten rulers who are in a city" (v. 19)—"a full number of rulers."[6] People call an extraordinarily beautiful woman a "perfect ten." She is super-beautiful. Similarly, these ten rulers are super-strong. But wisdom is super-duper ("more than") strong! Only a fool would fail to desire wisdom, with the security and strength it provides.

Before the wise think themselves "too wise" (Eccl. 7:16), however, Solomon quickly pushes them off their pedestal: "Surely there is not a righteous [recall from verse 16 that *righteous* is synonymous with *wise*] man on earth who does good and never sins" (v. 20). Even the godly are sometimes ungodly; occasionally, the consistently good do bad things. In Psalm 143:2, David acknowledges that "no one living is righteous before you," and in Romans 3:10 Paul writes, "None is righteous, no, not one."[7] Solomon is not alone is this conviction and confession (cf. 1 Kings 8:46; Prov. 20:9).

In case we struggle with the claim that "all have sinned" (Rom. 3:23)—even the wise—Solomon provides an example from one of our tiniest body parts: the tongue.[8] He writes: "Do not take to heart all the things that people say, lest you hear your servant cursing you. Your heart knows that many times you yourself have cursed others" (Eccl. 7:21–22).

Respect the realism here. Ecclesiastes 7:21 essentially says, "I hope you know that sometimes people close to you (i.e., your servant, or in our context perhaps people in your household or at your workplace) slander you, gossip

---

6. Greidanus, *Preaching Christ from Ecclesiastes*, 192.

7. Greidanus points out that Paul's phrase *ouk estin dikaios* is identical to the Septuagint's translation of Ecclesiastes 7:20. Ibid., 186.

8. "So also the tongue is a small member, yet it boasts of great things. How great a forest is set ablaze by such a small fire! And the tongue is a fire, a world of unrighteousness. The tongue is set among our members, staining the whole body, setting on fire the entire course of life, and set on fire by hell" (James 3:5–6).

about you, and even curse you. So you will never be at peace if you are out to tame everyone's tongue. Let it go." Verse 22 adds, "Let it go because I hope you recognize that your friends must be talking behind your back, since you have done the same to them. Right?" Together, these verses teach us an even more sobering truth: our tongue is only the tip of the iniquity iceberg. The proof that "all humans are inescapably flawed" is right between our teeth.[9] This is why Jesus claimed that our words are a reliable judge of our whole being: "I tell you, on the day of judgment people will give account for every careless word they speak, for by your words you will be justified, and by your words you will be condemned" (Matt. 12:36–37).

Beyond our tongues as a testimony of our depravity, the cross of Christ is the ultimate sign of our sin. The cross shows us not only how much God loves us, but also how terribly sinful we are. Paul wrote, "It is a trustworthy statement, deserving full acceptance, that Christ Jesus came into the world to save sinners" (1 Tim. 1:15 NASB). The subject of this sentence is "Christ Jesus," the verb is "came" (he "*came* into the world"), and the direct object of the infinitive phrase is "sinners." That's you and me!

> For while we were still weak, at the right time Christ died for the ungodly. For one will scarcely die for a righteous person—though perhaps for a good person one would dare even to die—but God shows his love for us in that while we were still sinners, Christ died for us. (Rom. 5:6–8)

Note how often sin is mentioned in our text! We find "wicked" (Eccl. 7:15, 17) and "wickedness" (v. 25), "sins" and "sinner" (vv. 20, 26), "evildoing" (v. 15), and "not a righteous man on earth who does good and never sins" (v. 20), as well as evil actions such as gossip and cursing (vv. 21–22), fornication or adultery (v. 26), and humankind's "schemes" (vv. 27–29)—that is, plots and sins against God and neighbor. Ecclesiastes affirms the Bible's view of sin (e.g., Mark 7:20–23; Rom. 3:9–10). We celebrate Jesus as the exception—"[Jesus] who in every respect has been tempted as we are, yet without sin" (Heb. 4:15)—and we rejoice in that "for our sake [God] made him to be sin who knew no sin, so that in him we might become the righteousness of God" (2 Cor. 5:21). The cross exposes us to ourselves.

9. Michael V. Fox, *Ecclesiastes*, JPS Bible Commentary (Philadelphia: Jewish Publication Society, 2004), 49.

In 1908, *The Times* newspaper asked a few authors to contribute on the topic "What's wrong with the world?" G. K. Chesterton submitted the briefest response. He wrote: "Dear Sirs, I am. Sincerely yours, G. K. Chesterton."[10] Whenever I share my testimony, I always include the two truths that led me to submit to "the way, and the truth, and the life" (John 14:6). The first of those truths is that the only relationship that lasts forever is between God and man. The second truth is that I have a sin nature. For my whole life, I had been told that I sometimes sinned—morally missed the mark. But I was never told that I *was* a sinner, that in my very nature I was inescapably sinful, and thus I inescapably sinned. Until we discover in ourselves that Dr. Jekyll *is* Mr. Hyde—that is, that we all have dark impulses and evil actions—we will never get very far on the walkway of wisdom. The crucifixion of God incarnate will make absolutely no sense.

From a recognition of our moral limitations in Ecclesiastes 7:19–22, Solomon moves on to a recognition of our mental limitations in verses 23–24: "All this I have tested by wisdom. I said, 'I will be wise,' but it was far from me. That which has been is far off, and deep, very deep; who can find it out?"

Ultimate, or godlike, wisdom is elusive and incomprehensible. Trying to grasp it is like trying to leap from Boston to Brisbane or like trying to jump into the middle of the Black Sea and touch the bottom. It is too distant and too deep.

These horizontal and vertical challenges, however, are intentional. God alone is God, and God alone is perfectly righteous and perfectly wise. We were never supposed to eat from the tree of the knowledge of good and evil. His thoughts are too high and too deep for us to comprehend (cf. Isa. 55:9; cf. Rom. 11:33). To admit that we don't have the answers shows wisdom on our part. Calvin called it "learned ignorance."[11] Even the wise are not all wise, and sometimes sin.

A THIRD FINDING

In Ecclesiastes 7:15–18, Solomon found that it is a crooked world. Then in verses 19–24, he added that it is a crooked world filled with sinners—even

10. G. K. Chesterton, quoted in D. A. Carson, *The God Who Is There: Finding Your Place in God's Story* (Grand Rapids: Baker, 2010), 35–36.
11. John Calvin, *Institutes of the Christian Religion*, ed. John T. McNeill, trans. Ford Lewis Battles, 2 vols., Library of Christian Classics 20–21 (Philadelphia: Westminster, 1960), 3.21.2.

the wise! Finally, in verses 25–29, he concludes that it is a crooked world filled with sinners—even the wise, *but also the fools.*

We begin in Ecclesiastes 7:25: "I turned my heart to know and to search out and to seek wisdom and [its opposite] the scheme of things, [that is,] to know the wickedness of folly and the foolishness that is madness." Throughout this text, Solomon has been seeking and finding.[12] Here, that motif only intensifies. Words and phrases for the idea of *seeking*—"turned my heart to know," "to search out," "to seek" (v. 25), "my soul has sought repeatedly" (v. 28)—are everywhere. And the word *find/found* is repeated seven times.

Solomon's findings focus on the fools. The first is Lady Folly; the second is de-evolved Adam (bear with my language for a moment). Lady Folly is described in Ecclesiastes 7:26: "And I find something more bitter than death: the woman whose heart is snares and nets, and whose hands are fetters. He who pleases God escapes her, but the sinner is taken by her." Daniel Fredericks provocatively calls her "Slut Folly."[13] I label her *Lady Folly* because the seductive adulteress described here is more than a woman who tempts and traps men. Following Solomon's proverbs in the book of Proverbs, the ensnaring woman in Ecclesiastes is the personification and embodiment of folly, whether sexual or otherwise.

In Proverbs, we are introduced to two voices. Lady Wisdom "cries aloud in the streets," calling everyone to embrace her (Prov. 1:20–33), and for those who do embrace her there is blessing:

> Blessed is the one who finds wisdom,
>   and the one who gets understanding,
> for the gain from *her* is better than gain from silver
>   and *her* profit better than gold.
> *She* is more precious than jewels,
>   and nothing you desire can compare with *her*.
> Long life is in *her* right hand;
>   in *her* left hand are riches and honor.
> *Her* ways are ways of pleasantness,
>   and all *her* paths are peace.

---

12. For the personal (*I*) search motif, see Ecclesiastes 7:15, 23, 25, 26, 27, 28, 29.

13. Daniel C. Fredericks, "Ecclesiastes," in Daniel C. Fredericks and Daniel J. Estes, *Ecclesiastes and the Song of Songs*, Apollos Old Testament Commentary 16 (Downers Grove, IL: InterVarsity Press, 2010), 185.

She is a tree of life to those who lay hold of *her*;
those who hold *her* fast are called blessed. (Prov. 3:13–18; cf. 4:5–13; 7:4)

The other voice comes from Lady Folly. She is "loud and wayward" (Prov. 7:11), and yet her words are "smooth" (v. 5) and "seductive" (v. 21). Those who embrace her are trapped—her "heart is snares and nets" and her "hands are fetters" (Eccl. 7:26). They are also led down into "the depths of Sheol" (Prov. 9:18; cf. 7:27) and, worse, to a more bitter punishment than death itself (Eccl. 7:26). Just as the wise son keeps away from the house of the adulterous (Prov. 5:1–14), so the wise person resists the traps of Lady Folly. As Solomon puts it, "He who pleases God escapes her, but the sinner is taken by her" (Eccl. 7:26).

Once when I tucked my daughter Lily into bed, her Bible was open to Genesis 38. I said, "Oh, the most scandalous chapter in the Bible!" In case you don't know, Genesis 38 tells about Tamar's clever "seduction" of Judah. Foolish Judah gave in. Set against Judah is his brother Joseph, who in Genesis 39 is repeatedly enticed by Potiphar's wife. Unlike his older brother, Joseph flees.

He flees! My brothers and sisters, let us flee from Lady Folly! Do you struggle with pornography? Flee from the unobserved computer. Do you struggle with a drug addiction? Flee from your dealer. Do you struggle with gambling? Flee from the casino. Do you struggle with coveting? Flee from the shopping mall. Do you struggle with sloth? Flee from the sofa. Do you struggle with gossip? Flee from . . . people! (Whoever—your hairdresser or barber, maybe?) Don't let wickedness grab hold of your life. Shake it off, head for the door, and run like mad! Please God instead, not only because it is right, but also because he is more pleasurable than anyone or anything that this crooked world offers.

The first fool is Lady Folly. We can and must escape her. The second fool is de-evolved, or devolved, Adam. We cannot escape from him because he is you and me. Here I use a common visual from the theory of evolution—that homo sapiens gradually evolved from a slouched-over ape to an upright man—and twist it a bit. In Ecclesiastes 7:29, Solomon summarizes his search by saying, "See, this alone I found, that God made man *upright*, but they have sought out many schemes." The theology here comes from Genesis 1–3. The "very good" (Gen. 1:31) man did something very bad. He wanted to be "like God" (3:5), only this didn't work out too well. The image here also comes from Genesis. It is a picture of a once-upright man (whom Genesis 2:20 called "Adam") and his offspring (note the plural, "they") scampering about the earth, scheming against God and each other. They built a tower to reach the heavens (11:4), and they wreaked violence across the earth (6:11). In the end, the sons of Adam are nothing like God. This moral devolution is captured well in the New Living Translation: "I discovered that God created people to be *upright*, but they have each turned to follow their own *downward* path."

This devolved Adam is interestingly and ironically illustrated in women. Listen to what Solomon writes, and then we can try to make sense of it:

> Behold, this is what I found, says the Preacher, while adding one thing to another to find the scheme of things—which my soul has sought repeatedly, but I have not found. One man among a thousand I found, but a woman among all these I have not found. (Eccl. 7:27–28)

What is Solomon saying here? Is he a sexist and misogynist? I will try not to be politically correct, just correct. The answer is "no." Sure, Solomon doesn't think too highly of women, but "he doesn't think too highly of men either."[14] In Ecclesiastes 7:20 and 29, he included (highlighted with the masculine pronoun) man's sinfulness. To him, "iniquity is an equal opportunity employer," and of course, "even the one good man that he found in a thousand was still a sinner."[15]

What, then, does he mean by "One man among a thousand I found, but a woman among all these I have not found" (Eccl. 7:28)? There are three good possibilities. Pick whichever one you like! First, he could be taking a conventional saying ("one man among a thousand I found," i.e., like our "he's one in a million") and adding an exaggerated twist to it ("but a woman among all these I have not found"). In other words, he uses hyperbole to gain a hearing (about what he will say about everyone in verse 29!). Think of it like this. Solomon says, "I haven't found a good woman, not one." The men shake their heads in agreement, and

---

14. Fox, *Ecclesiastes*, 51.

15. Philip Graham Ryken, *Ecclesiastes: Why Everything Matters*, ed. R. Kent Hughes, Preaching the Word (Wheaton, IL: Crossway, 2010), 177.

they look to each other: "Hey, this guy knows what he is talking about." Then with verse 29, he wallops them all over the head. *No one* is upright! Alternatively, he could be referencing the seductresses of the immediate context, in verse 26. That is, among that type of woman he found only fools. Finally, he could be sharing from personal experience, referring literally to his harem.[16] In 9:9 he will exhort the God-fearing husband to "enjoy life with the wife whom you love." Not all the women in the world are bad, but his story was different. He married a thousand women (2:8; cf. 1 Kings 11:3), all of whom worshiped other gods. Together they "turned away his heart after [those] other gods" (1 Kings 11:4; cf. Neh. 13:26). Compared to those thousand, the percentages of good men in his court were just a touch higher: one-tenth of 1 percent better! Not an overly impressive number.

However we add up these numbers, the equation is virtually the same: original righteousness is found in no one. We all get a zero on the Creator-like test, and 100 percent on the rebellious-creatures test. In fact, the sons of Adam and Lady Folly are closer to each other than they are to God. That is certainly what is said in Ecclesiastes 7:29, but perhaps also in verses 27–28a: "Behold, this is what I found, says the Preacher, while adding one thing to another to find the scheme of things—which my soul has sought repeatedly, but I have not found." Paradoxically, Solomon's intense and thorough search concluded with the discovery that we can learn only so much about our fallen nature.[17] But we can know, and should acknowledge, that we are the problem, not God. God is not to blame for this crooked world, for he created us "neither sinful, nor neutral, but upright."[18] The finger-pointing should not go upward but inward and outward. As Bernard of Clairvaux wrote:

What Thou, my Lord, hast suffered was all for sinners' gain;
Mine, mine was the transgression, but Thine the deadly pain.[19]

---

16. In a similar vein, perhaps Solomon is echoing Proverbs' realism: "An excellent wife who can find?" (Prov. 31:10). In a thousand tries, he *never* found even one precious jewel!

17. Jeffrey Meyers, *A Table in the Mist: Meditations on Ecclesiastes*, Through New Eyes Bible Commentary (Monroe, LA: Athanasius Press, 2006), 154.

18. Ibid.

19. From the hymn attributed to Bernard of Clairvaux, "O Sacred Head, Now Wounded," trans. Paul Gerhardt (1656).

We can't always or often explain why bad things happen to good people or good things happen to bad people. It's a crooked world! It's a crooked world filled with guilty and scheming sinners.

God's Answer to the Scheme of Things

In his famous *Pensées*, Blaise Pascal often addresses the paradoxical nature of the human condition—how our wretchedness and our greatness are weaved together within us.[20] For example, he exclaims, "What sort of freak then is man! How novel, how monstrous . . . . Judge of all things, feeble earthworm, repository of truth, sink of doubt and error, glory and refuse of the universe!" Pascal counsels, "Know then, proud man, what a paradox you are to yourself. Be humble, impotent reason! Be silent, feeble nature! . . . Hear from your master your true condition . . . . Listen to God."[21]

One of my favorite Pascal quotes, which serves as an excellent summary and final application of our text, goes like this:

Knowing God without knowing our own wretchedness makes for pride.
Knowing our own wretchedness without knowing God makes for despair.
Knowing Jesus Christ strikes the balance because he shows us both God and our own wretchedness.[22]

In Ecclesiastes 7:15–29, Solomon discovered that it is a crooked world filled with sinners (vv. 15–18)—even the wise (vv. 19–24), but also the fools (vv. 25–29). Thankfully, Ecclesiastes 7:29 is not the final word in the Bible. Christ Jesus came into the world! Christ has died. Christ has risen. Christ will come again. The cross covers our sin, the Spirit raises us to new life, and the Lord of all wisdom will come again in glory to judge the wicked and grant the righteous long, long life ("eternal life," John 10:28). Jesus Christ is God's answer to the scheme of things.

---

20. Thomas V. Morris, *Making Sense of It All: Pascal and the Meaning of Life* (Grand Rapids: Eerdmans, 1993), 137.
21. Blaise Pascal, quoted in ibid.
22. Pascal, quoted in ibid., 104.

13

LIVING WITHIN THE LIMITS
TO THE LIMIT

Ecclesiastes 8:1—15

*Then I saw all the work of God, that man cannot find out the
work that is done under the sun. However much man may
toil in seeking, he will not find it out. Even though a wise man
claims to know, he cannot find it out. (Eccl. 8:17)*

My family enjoys visiting friends in Clear Lake, Iowa. My
children are so sheltered from worldly amusements that
they actually view northern Iowa as a vacation destina-
tion. While there, we amuse ourselves in the pool and on the lake, which in
spite of its name is *not* clear. One of our other amusing activities is to walk
through Fort Custer Maze. Some creative entrepreneur took thousands of
wooden crates and arranged them creatively to create a multiacre maze.

When considered from the perspective of ground level, that maze, like any
other good maze, seems impossible to make your way through (especially in
under thirty minutes, which is the goal). You run into an unexpected wall.
You turn down a dead end. You stop to reprimand your skinny children
for trying to sneak under the walls. But if you get above ground level—to

the tower at the end, or even highway I-35 that runs close above it—you can clearly see which path is the right one to take.

Politics is one of the many mazes that we have to walk through. We might be (and should be) thankful for our system of government and even for its governors. In the United States, we are not up against a tyrannical dictator, a military junta, or a bunch of lawless bandits. We are not living in Libya, Egypt, Somalia, or North Korea. We are not dealing with genocide or civil war. We are not plagued by extreme poverty or millions dying of preventable diseases. We do not have to call Caesar "Lord" or the chancellor "Führer" upon penalty of death. And we have a peaceful transfer of power. Praise God! Like wanderers through Fort Custer Maze, however, we are challenged by our own flawed leaders and laws. What Winston Churchill said of Russia in 1939, we might say of American politics today: It is a riddle wrapped in a mystery inside an enigma. What are we to make of gay marriage, legalized marijuana, and our taxes' going to support abortion? How are we to deal with politicians who end their speeches with "God bless America," but promote policies that clearly do not have God's blessing? How are we to work our way through the current political maze? Ecclesiastes 8:1–15 helps us through by giving us a higher view.[1]

The Maze

In this fallen world always and everywhere, the political maze is not only difficult, but also dark. Imagine navigating through Fort Custer Maze at night. Ecclesiastes 8:1–15 paints a bleak portrait of politics and people. The picture of the king in verses 2–4 is dim. "He does whatever he pleases" (v. 3), even if his power sustains or promotes "evil," and even if his power hurts others (v. 9). Nor does he seem to be open to suggestions or corrections (v. 4). But the picture of his subjects isn't much brighter. In verse 10 we read that "the wicked . . . used to go in and out of the holy place *and* were praised [!] in the city where they had done such things." It is bad enough that "the wicked" exist in a society (they are mentioned four times in our text, five times if we include the term "sinner," v. 12), but it is horrendous when the wicked go to

1. For the outline of this chapter, I am indebted to Brandon Levering, "The Political Maze and the Perspective of God," a sermon on Ecclesiastes 8:1–17, preached at Westgate Church (Weston, MA), September 16, 2012.

church and a society praises their wickedness inside and outside the church. In his book *God in the Wasteland: The Reality of Truth in a World of Fading Dreams*, David Wells laments how our culture makes "sin look normal and righteousness seem strange."[2] When a suburban neighbor in an affluent, educated, and generally conservative city calls me a bigot for believing that sodomy is sin, we know not only that the times they are a changin', but also that the devil is as sly as a snake. Up is down and down is up; right is wrong and wrong is right. There is a "face-off between Christian faith and our morally disintegrating culture."[3] And the puck has been dropped.

If our government is corrupt, or at least under the control of the curse, and if the culture generally approves of such rule, how are we to navigate our way through the darkness? Wisdom! We need wisdom. This is where Pastor Solomon starts: "Who is like the wise? And who knows the interpretation of a thing? A man's wisdom makes his face shine, and the hardness of his face is changed" (Eccl. 8:1). Like Joseph, who trusted God to grant him the interpretation of Pharaoh's dreams, we must ask God to help us interpret the times we live in. We do so not only because wisdom will light the path we are to walk on, but also because wisdom changes our outlook on life. As coffee in the morning invigorates my body and brain, so wisdom turns a hard face (i.e., a frowning face) into a cheerful one ("wisdom makes his face shine"; cf. Prov. 15:13).

When I was a sophomore in college, I lived with six Christian guys in a campus house. I was a new Christian. I had just started devouring the Bible. So one night I asked my roommate what his favorite book of the Bible was. He replied, "James." I asked him why, and his reason was that it was so practical. The next day, when I did my morning devotions, I turned to James and began to read. When I came to James 1:5–6 (obviously, not very far into the book), my eyes came across this:

> If any of you lacks wisdom, let him ask God, who gives generously to all without reproach, and it will be given him. But let him ask in faith, with no doubting, for the one who doubts is like a wave of the sea that is driven and tossed by the wind.

2. As summarized in David F. Wells, *Losing Our Virtue: Why the Church Must Recover Its Moral Vision* (Grand Rapids: Eerdmans, 1999), 4.
3. Ibid., 1.

I closed my Bible and did precisely what it said. I unwaveringly asked God for wisdom. "Give me wisdom, Lord." It was that simple and that sincere. It is a prayer I still pray, just about every day. We need God's perspective, as much as he will give (what we can know is limited; see Ecclesiastes 8:16–17), to direct our way through the maze. Do you pray for wisdom? If not, why not? As you pray for your daily provision of bread, pray also for your daily dose of wisdom.

THREE COUNTERINTUITIVE TURNS

So, then, with the light of wisdom guiding our way for the remainder of our journey (Eccl. 8:2–15), Pastor Solomon provides us with three counterintuitive turns to take. In Fort Custer Maze, whenever my children said, "Dad, *look*! This *looks* like the right way," I would first examine the path. If it looked too long and too straight, I thought it must be a trap. I was almost always right. In a similar way, the Bible takes us on the seemingly crazy yet completely correct route through life.

Submit to Authority

The first counterintuitive turn is to submit to authority. This submission shows itself in obedience ("I say: Keep the king's command," Eccl. 8:2; cf. v. 5), loyalty ("Do not take your stand in an evil cause," v. 3b—likely referring to a rebellion), and basic protocol and prudence ("Be not hasty to go from his presence," v. 3a; cf. v. 4). If the government you serve is like the king described here (e.g., its unpredictable power is "sometimes used to perpetrate rather than punish injustice"),[4] the temptation would be to take the path of revolution, insurrection, or at least grumbling-between-your-teeth personal rebellion. God's wisdom counsels us not to. Why? What tempers that temptation?

Three reasons are given. The first reason is God's oath. We are commanded to "keep the king's command, *because* of God's oath to him" (Eccl. 8:2). If the king here was an Israelite king, this could refer to God's promise to King David (2 Sam. 7; Ps. 110:1). In light of that messianic promise of an

---

4. Richard Schultz, "Ecclesiastes," in *Baker Commentary on the Bible*, ed. Gary M. Burge and Andrew E. Hill, 2nd ed. (Grand Rapids: Baker, 2011), 597.

heir, God's people were to tread lightly. But the oath here could refer to a human pledge of allegiance, as the alternative ESV reading gives, "because of *your* oath to God." Either way, a high view of providence is in mind. The God who controls the times (Eccl. 3:1–15) also controls the reign of kings: "The king's heart is a stream of water in the hand of the LORD; he turns it wherever he will" (Prov. 21:1; cf. 16:9; Eccl. 9:1).

We must trust that the world isn't "aimlessly whirled about,"[5] but that the "Creator of all" also "sustains, nourishes, and cares for, everything he has made, even to the least sparrow."[6] Everything is directed by "the secret stirring of God's hand."[7] So, then, insubordination to those in authority over you—teachers, parents, bosses, presidents, and others—shows an attitude of ingratitude and a mistrust in God. Be like Daniel instead. Do not compromise, but be discreet, respectful, loyal, diligent, and willing to suffer through wrongdoing. In other words, "be wise as serpents and innocent as doves" (Matt. 10:16) as you serve your "earthly masters," knowing that "you are serving the Lord Christ" (Col. 3:22, 24; cf. Eph. 6:7–8).

When the Pharisees attempted to trick Jesus by asking, "Is it lawful to pay taxes to Caesar, or not?" (Matt. 22:17), our Lord replied, "Render to Caesar the things that are Caesar's" (22:21). To Jesus, "respect for government is an important form of respect for God."[8] This does not mean, of course, that "if Caesar coins a new Gospel,"[9] he is to be obeyed. If the government outlaws Christian faith and practice, we must revolt against such rules, and pay the price of the revolution. Read the story of Peter and John in Acts 4 (cf. 5:29). Read the book of Revelation (esp. Rev. 13 and 18). Read the lives of the early-church martyrs. Jesus, not Caesar, is Lord! We'd better believe that and live that out. And die for it, if necessary. Yet it does mean submission and honor:

5. Augustine, *De diversis quaestionibus*, quoted in John Calvin, *Institutes of the Christian Religion*, ed. John T. McNeill, trans. Ford Lewis Battles, 2 vols., Library of Christian Classics 20–21 (Philadelphia: Westminster, 1960), 1.16.8.

6. Calvin, *Institutes*, 1.16.1.

7. Ibid., 1.16.9. "Ignorance of providence is the ultimate of all miseries; the highest blessedness lies in the knowledge of it" (1.17.11).

8. Frederick Dale Bruner, *The Churchbook: Matthew 13–28*, 2nd rev. ed. (Grand Rapids: Eerdmans, 2004), 399.

9. J. C. Ryle, *Matthew: Expository Thoughts on the Gospels*, Crossway Classic Commentaries (Wheaton, IL: Crossway, 1993), 207.

> Be subject *for the Lord's sake* to every human institution, whether it be to the
> emperor as supreme, or to governors as sent by him to punish those who do
> evil and to praise those who do good. . . . Honor everyone. Love the broth-
> erhood. Fear God. Honor the emperor. (1 Peter 2:13–14, 17; cf. Titus 3:1–2)

Some of us wrongly think that to freely serve God, we must be free from
the yoke of any godless government. Christ was not completely opposed to
Caesar. Even Rome would play its part in the Christian drama—in the spread
of the gospel to Asia Minor and southern Europe through Roman roads,
and through the spread of salvation to the world by that old rugged *Roman*
cross. God is not opposed to government, for even ungodly governments
can be used as his servants for the church's good (Rom. 13:4).

Whatever government God has given us to rule over us, we are to respect
it and (as we can) submit to it. In this era of exile (1 Peter 1:1), as we long for
the city of God (cf. Heb. 11:10), Christians seek the welfare of the city (Jer.
29:7) as we spread the gospel of God (Mark 1:14; Rom. 1:1).

The second reason for submitting to authority is God's reward. If God provi-
dentially rules the world—even over and through bad rulers—then we can trust
what he says in Ecclesiastes 8:5: "Whoever keeps a command will know no evil
thing." Generally speaking, it is in our own best interest to keep the laws of the
land. While we might be tempted to refuse to pay our taxes if some of them go
to immoral organizations and support evil ideas, the counsel here is to keep the
big picture in mind. This is not capitulation but common sense. If we can stay
out of harm's way, we should do so. Moreover, it is evangelistically savvy. In
1 Timothy 2:1–6, Paul puts our political duties under God's evangelistic agenda:

> First of all, then, I urge that supplications, prayers, intercessions, and thanks-
> givings be made for all people, for kings and all who are in high positions,
> [why?] that we may lead a peaceful and quiet life, godly and dignified in
> every way. [To what end?] This is good, and it is pleasing in the sight of God
> our Savior, who desires all people to be saved and to come to the knowledge
> of the truth. For there is one God, and there is one mediator between God
> and men, the man Christ Jesus, who gave himself as a ransom for all, which
> is the testimony given at the proper time.

The third reason for submitting to authority is God's rule. We should
submit to those in authority because we grasp that wickedness ultimately

does not work (Eccl. 8:8; cf. v. 10) and that everyone eventually dies (v. 8). There is no discharge from death: "No man has power to retain the spirit [*ruah*]" (v. 8). Even the most powerful king cannot catch the spirit (*ruah*) as it leaves his body. Death sucks the breath (*ruah*) out of every earthly authority! Where is Caligula? Dead! Genghis Khan? Dead! Henry VIII? Dead! Ivan the Terrible? Dead! Hitler? Dead! Stalin? Dead! Pol Pot? Dead! Kim Jong-il? Dead! While it is true that absolute power corrupts absolutely, know this: even absolute power has absolutely no power over death.

An ancient rabbi once observed that David was "called 'King David' fifty-two times, but in 1 Kings 2:1, when David's life is drawing to a close, he is called simply 'David,' for on that day he has no more authority."[10] At King James I's funeral, John Donne gave the eulogy. In it, he bemoaned the frailty of the earth's most powerful king:

> That hand that ballanced his *owne three Kingdomes* so equally, . . . and carried the *Keyes* of all the Christian world, and locked up, and let out *Armies* in their due season, Dead; how poore, how faint, how pale, how momentary, how transitory, how empty, how frivolous, how Dead things, must you necessarily thinke *Titles*, and *Possessions*, and *Favours*, and all, when you see that Hand, which was the *hand of Destinie*, of *Christian Destinie*, of the *Almighty God*, lie dead?[11]

Only the everlasting God rules forever!

Fear God

The first counterintuitive turn is to submit to authority. This turn is reasonable because of God's oath, reward, and rule. The second counterintuitive turn is to fear God. To fear God is certainly not counterintuitive to Ecclesiastes or to the rest of the wisdom literature of the Bible, but it is counterintuitive to the way we are wired as devolved Adam. If our government is not godly, the temptation is to forget God. Why? We can forget God because, obviously, he is indifferent, impotent, or inactive. Or if he is

10. Rabbi Levi (Koh. R), in Michael V. Fox, *Ecclesiastes*, JPS Bible Commentary (Philadelphia: Jewish Publication Society, 2004), 56.

11. John Donne, *The Sermons on John Donne*, ed. Evelyn R. Simpson and George R. Potter, 10 vols. (Berkeley, CA: University of California Press, 1953), 6:290.

at all active, he is far too slow! So, then, if change is going to happen, let us mobilize first and pray second, or mobilize first and pray never.

At first this sentiment seems sane, as Ecclesiastes 8:11 and 14 attest. Verse 11 reads, "Because the sentence against an evil deed is not executed speedily, the heart of the children of man is fully set to do evil." The slower the legal system moves, the quicker the crime rate rises. To this evil, verse 14 adds another: "There is a vanity that takes place on earth, that there are righteous people to whom it happens according to the deeds of the wicked, and there are wicked people to whom it happens according to the deeds of the righteous. I said that this also is vanity [i.e., it makes no sense]." If the bad guys seem to be winning (8:14) and the good guys have little or no power to change things, then what are we to do? We are not told to *do* anything. Instead, we are told to know something and to trust in someone. Wisdom cautions and promises:

> Though a sinner does evil a hundred times and prolongs his life, yet I know that it will be well with those who *fear* God, because they *fear* before him. But it will not be well with the wicked, neither will he prolong his days like a shadow, because he does not *fear* before God. (Eccl. 8:12–13)

Empirical observation gets us only so far. We must trust in God and his Word. We must believe that ultimately it will go well with those who *fear* God (Eccl. 8:12), and badly for those who don't (vv. 10, 13). We must trust God's timing and be certain of his coming judgment.

Ray Bradbury's novel *Fahrenheit 451* describes a future America where firemen are commissioned to burn any house that contains books. Bradbury's novel was an attack on the television culture of the late 1940s and how it was destroying the interest in books and reading. In the story, a secret society forms for the purpose of remembering great works of literature. To join, you must have memorized a certain classic. The protagonist, Guy Montag, is accepted into this society because he knows Ecclesiastes and Revelation by heart. After a nuclear bomb destroys his city, the final page records Montag's musings:

> To everything there is a season. Yes. A time to break down, and a time to build up. Yes. A time to keep silence and a time to speak. Yes, all that. But what else. What else? Something, something . . . .

And on either side of the river was there a tree of life, which bare twelve manner of fruits, and yielded her fruit every month; And the leaves of the tree were for the healing of the nations.[12]

Oh, that we would memorize Ecclesiastes and Revelation together, for those two books instruct us to see the larger picture and to wait for the victory of the final judgment. Do not trivialize the cosmic conflict at hand. But dismiss the entitlement complex, close your ears to the scoffers, and hasten for the "coming . . . day of God" (2 Peter 3:12).

The just shall live by faith; and the faithful shall fear God.

Be Joyful!

The final counterintuitive turn is to be joyful. What!? Be joyful? Yes, be joyful! While we live in a crooked world filled with sinners and corrupt governments, the temptation would be to wait it out with as much bitterness and dourness as we can muster. Yet Pastor Solomon recommends an odd alternative: "And I commend joy, for man has no good thing under the sun but to eat and drink and be joyful, for this will go with him in his toil through the days of his life that God has given him under the sun" (Eccl. 8:15). Douglas Wilson asks, "What should a man do in a world of powerful kings and wicked men who look as though they got away with it? He should prepare to make merry."[13]

While the wicked scheme against God, his church, and each other, the righteous are to sit down together and praise God from whom all blessings flow. We are to say grace and eat up. We are to gather to *celebrate* the Lord's death ("For Christ, our Passover lamb, has been sacrificed. Let us therefore celebrate the festival," 1 Cor. 5:7–8).[14] We are to gather to rejoice in the death of God's saints (Ps. 116:15). We are to host countercultural party after countercultural party. Hallelujah! You don't take the Christian life to be like sitting on a block of ice drinking sour milk as you wait for the 5 AM train, do you? I hope not.

12. Ray Bradbury, *Fahrenheit 451* (1950; repr., New York: Simon & Schuster, 2012), 158.

13. Douglas Wilson, *Joy at the End of the Tether: The Inscrutable Wisdom of Ecclesiastes* (Moscow, ID: Canon Press, 1999), 95–96.

14. Here I follow Augustine, who saw this verse as an allusion to the partaking of the Lord's Supper—"to the participation of this table which the Mediator of the New Testament Himself, the Priest after the order of Melchizedek, furnishes with His own body and blood." *City of God* 17:20, in *Nicene and Post-Nicene Fathers*, ed. Philip Schaff, vol. 2 (Peabody, MA: Hendrickson, 1995), 358.

Certainly not! To me, as it should be to you, the Christian life is gathering together one day in seven (at the very least) to delight in pre-fall fun in light of resurrection realities. "Count it *all* joy" (James 1:2) is our wisdom slogan.

Solomon's odd exhortation to enjoy life seems out of place because "the world is ungrateful," as Martin Luther put it, "always looking elsewhere and becoming bored with the things that are present, no matter how good they are."[15] Do not underestimate your daily bread and drink. Do not belittle your weekly work. Thank God for such gifts. What is more, this "shalom consolation,"[16] as Daniel Fredericks calls Ecclesiastes 8:15, follows a list of other consolations. In verse 5 we are told how "wisdom can deliver from tragedy"; in verse 8 how "the wicked will not be delivered by their wickedness"; in verse 10 how "the wicked are buried and forgotten"; in verses 12–13 how "justice will come to the wicked" and how "it will be well for those fearing God"; and in verse 14 how "injustice is temporary."[17] So after all those comforts, is it really strange to be told in verse 15 to "enjoy life, for God ultimately determines the days"?[18] We should have seen it coming! But so often we fail to see it coming because we refuse to let God be God,[19] and because we do not look out, down, around, and up and see all that God gives.

With wisdom as our heavenly light, we are to take the seemingly crazy yet completely correct route through the political maze. We are to submit to authority, fear God, and be joyful.

"Ah, How You Will Enchant the Angels"

I remember London's Dick Lucas beginning a sermon by saying something about a Spurgeon illustration that he had been dying to use for months but that never fit the Bible texts he was preaching on. Yet he had been holding

---

15. Martin Luther, "Notes on Ecclesiastes," in *Luther's Works*, trans. and ed. Jaroslav Pelikan, 56 vols. (St. Louis: Concordia, 1972), 15:142. Earlier in his commentary, Luther summarizes: "The point and purpose of this book is to instruct us, so that with thanksgiving we may use the things that are present and the creatures of God that are generously given to us and conferred upon us by the blessing of God" (15:10).

16. Daniel C. Fredericks, "Ecclesiastes," in Daniel C. Fredericks and Daniel J. Estes, *Ecclesiastes and the Song of Songs*, Apollos Old Testament Commentary 16 (Downers Grove, IL: InterVarsity Press, 2010), 198.

17. Ibid.

18. Ibid.

19. "Embracing joy frees him to let God be God." Ellen F. Davis, *Proverbs, Ecclesiastes, and the Song of Songs* (Louisville, KY: Westminster John Knox, 2000), 210.

on to it for so long that he was going to use it in his introduction that day whether it aligned with the text or not! I have felt that same way about Isak Dinesen's short story *Babette's Feast*.[20] I saw that movie years ago and read the book shortly before I preached Ecclesiastes. With every message, I have been waiting to use it, but the text or the timing was never just right. Now the text and timing feel right, but even if they aren't, hear the story as my conclusion anyway.

A long time ago in Norway there lived two elderly ladies. They were tall, slender, graceful, and once extraordinarily beautiful, but "they had never possessed any article of fashion; they had dressed demurely in gray or black all their lives." Their names were Martine and Philippa, after Martin Luther and Philipp Melanchthon. Their father had founded a Christian sect whose "members renounced the pleasures of this world, for the earth and all that it held to them was but a kind of illusion, and the true reality was the New Jerusalem toward which they were longing." For this reason, these women renounced marriage and lived very modestly. Living with them, however, was Babette, who served as their maid. Babette had come to their door "as a friendless fugitive, almost mad with grief and fear." In Christian charity, they took her in. For twelve years she served them faithfully without ever revealing her true identity. Near the end of the story we learn that she had been a Parisian gourmet chef at the Café Anglais. During a time of political upheaval (a civil war), she was forced to flee France. The first day Babette was in their service, the sisters explained to her "that they were poor and that to them luxurious fare was sinful. Their own food must be plain as possible." Babette complied.

Throughout these years a friend in Paris continued to renew Babette's lottery ticket. One day in the mail Babette learned that she had won the French lottery. The prize was ten thousand francs! In that time and place, she was rich.

After much effort, Babette convinced the sisters to allow her to cook them a real French meal. Babette returned to France in order to handpick exotic ingredients and expensive wines (including a Clos Vougeot 1846 from Philippe in Rue Montorgueil!), which were eventually shipped to Norway. The meal was exquisite. The sisters and their guests had certainly never tasted anything like it. The author herself describes it as a taste of heaven,

---

20. Isak Dinesen (Karen Blixen), *Babette's Feast*, Modern Classics (New York: Penguin, 2001). The quotes, in order, are from the following pages: 1, 1–2, 3, 16, 46, 44, 49, 49–50, and 54.

of having been given "one hour of the millennium." At one moment during the meal, one of the guests, General Loewenhielm,[21] gave a speech. A line in that speech summarizes well the author's theology—borrowed, I believe, from Ecclesiastes: "Grace, my friends, demands nothing from us but that we shall await it in gratitude."

After the meal, as Babette was "surrounded by more black and greasy pots and pans than her mistresses had even seen in their life," this conversation follows:

> Martine said again: "They all thought that it was a nice dinner . . . . We will all remember this evening when you have gone back to Paris, Babette."
> Babette said: "I am not going back to Paris."
> "You are not going back to Paris?" Martine exclaimed.
> "No," said Babette. "What will I do in Paris? . . . And how would I go back to Paris, Mesdames? I have no money."
> "No money?" the sisters cried as with one mouth.
> "No," said Babette.
> "But the ten thousand francs?" the sisters asked in a horrified gasp.
> "The ten thousand francs have been spent, Mesdames," said Babette.

She had used all her winnings to serve that one meal.

The story ends with Philippa putting her arms around Babette and whispering to her:

> "Yet this is not the end! I feel, Babette, that this is not the end. In Paradise you will be the great artist that God meant you to be! Ah!" she added, the tears streaming down her cheeks, "Ah, how you will enchant the angels."

As Babette illustrates, we are to enjoy God's good gifts. There is even a place for extravagant feasting! And as Pastor Solomon teaches, we are to enjoy life (go ahead and serve your friends *and your pastor* a million-dollar dinner today!) because we can trust in God's good governance in a world that we know is unwisely governed. By submitting to authority, fearing God, and embracing joy, we are to live within the limits to the limit!

---

21. For another interesting "Ecclesiastes" moment, read the general's pre-dinner address to himself before a full-length mirror; for example, "He looked into the mirror, examined the row of decorations on his breast and sighed to himself: 'Vanity, vanity, all is vanity.'" Ibid., 35.

14

WHAT TO KNOW ABOUT
KNOWING NOTHING

Ecclesiastes 8:16—9:12

*When I applied my heart to know wisdom, and to see the busi-
ness that is done on earth, how neither day nor night do one's
eyes see sleep, then I saw all the work of God, that man cannot
find out the work that is done under the sun. However much
man may toil in seeking, he will not find it out. Even though a
wise man claims to know, he cannot find it out. (Eccl. 8:16–17)*

’ve been reading a diet book. Though, let it be noted, I haven't
traded reading meaty tomes for faddish paperbacks on fat reduc-
tion. The book is by Richard Watson, who is emeritus professor of philosophy at Washington University in St. Louis. It is entitled *The
Philosopher's Diet: How to Lose Weight and Change the World*. It is a real
diet book. The first chapter is called "Fat," and it begins: "Fat. I presume
you want to get rid of it. Then quit eating so much."[1]

What is unique about the book (besides its brutal honesty) is its philosophical outlook. For example, in the introduction, Watson states his purpose:

1. Richard Watson, *The Philosopher's Diet: How to Lose Weight and Change the World* (Boston:
Godine, 1998), 3.

"In this book I tell how to take off weight and keep it off. The book also embodies a philosophy of life. The weight program is the content of the book, the philosophy of life is its form."[2] While I admire Watson's approach, I don't highly recommend the book because it didn't work for me. But I do recommend some of his philosophical statements. The one I like best is this: "Why *don't* philosophers tell you what it all means? The answer is simple. They don't *know*."[3]

In the information age—where we can get the weather in some remote village in Cameroon, learn who ruled the Ming Dynasty while misspelling "Ming" and "Dynasty," and get a million other factoids on a million other subjects, all in the palm of our hand and all with the slide of a finger—not knowing the answers seems almost sinful. "Let me Google it" has become our international motto. But here in Ecclesiastes, Pastor Solomon starts where Professor Watson did—admitting the limits to human wisdom. Wisdom is valuable but also vulnerable. Wisdom is not immune to "the hebel-ness of life."[4]

Not Know

In Ecclesiastes 8:16–17 and 9:1, as well as 9:12, this theme of not knowing is noted.[5] In 9:12, Solomon speaks of not knowing the "time" of death. Death might happen as suddenly as fish caught in a net or birds in a snare. In 9:1, he speaks of good people ("the righteous and the wise") who do not know whether the bad things that happen to them arise from God's "love or hate." That is, the equation from experience can't be that health and wealth equal God's love and sickness and poverty his hatred. And yet, like Job, the wise wonder whether the awful outward circumstances are for our testing (under God's loving pleasure) or our punishment (under God's disapproving displeasure).[6] We don't always know.

Then, in Ecclesiastes 8:16–17, Solomon introduces and summarizes the lack-of-information situation:

2. Ibid., xiii.

3. Ibid.

4. Jeffrey Meyers, *A Table in the Mist: Meditations on Ecclesiastes*, Through New Eyes Bible Commentary (Monroe, LA: Athanasius Press, 2006), 181–82.

5. Most commentators, because of its inclusio (Eccl. 8:1a/17b), select 8:1–17 as a pericope. But I see 8:16–17 as a "double inclusio," if you will. That is, it serves as the ending inclusio to 8:1 and the beginning inclusio for 9:12. In this pericope, our lack of knowledge is mentioned seven times (8:16, 17 [2×]; 9:1, 5, 10, 12).

6. See Jerome, *Commentary on Ecclesiastes*, trans. Richard J. Goodrich and David J. D. Miller, Ancient Christian Writers 66 (New York: Newman, 2012), 100.

When I applied my heart to know wisdom, and to see the business that is done on earth, how neither day nor night do one's eyes see sleep, then I saw all the work of God, that man cannot find out the work that is done under the sun. However much man may toil in seeking, he will not find it out. Even though a wise man claims to know, he cannot find it out.

Note the threefold repetition of the "cannot find it out" motif. Our major trouble is not that we cannot predict the future or absolutely control the present; it is rather that we cannot completely fathom how God works—"His governance of *our* lives *here* and *now*."[7] "God moves in a mysterious way," and we want to be able to follow; God's wisdom is "deep in unfathomable mines," and we want to bring to the surface all the treasures.[8] But it is not to be. God's greatness is unsearchable (Ps. 145:3). As Zophar rightly tells Job:

Can you find out	the deep things	of God?
Can you find out	the limit	of the Almighty?
It is higher	than heaven	—what can you do?
Deeper	than Sheol	—what can you know? (Job 11:7–8)

The Bible is clear that there are certain pieces of information that only God knows ("the secret things belong to the LORD our God," Deut. 29:29), and there are other bits of information that he shares with us ("but the things that are revealed belong to us and to our children," v. 29). As our Lord Jesus taught, sometimes the Father hides certain knowledge from the wise and reveals it to little children (see Matt. 11:25–26). Well, in Ecclesiastes 8:16–9:12, what God has revealed to the wise children of Adam is that *we are to enjoy life all the days of our vain life.*

Vain Life

One thing we can know is that our life is vain. It is "vain" in the sense of being short-lived. Put more negatively, we can and should know something

7. See Douglas Wilson, *Joy at the End of the Tether: The Inscrutable Wisdom of Ecclesiastes* (Moscow, ID: Canon Press, 1999), 98.
8. Those two lines come from William Cowper, "God Moves in a Mysterious Way" (1774).

about death, since it is alluded to and named nine times: "the same event" (Eccl. 9:2, 3), "dead" (vv. 3, 4, 5), "die" (v. 5), "Sheol" (v. 10; i.e., "the chambers of death," Prov. 7:27), "his time" (Eccl. 9:11), and "it" (v. 12). What should we know? In 9:1–6, 11–12, we are reminded of what we already know but often suppress: that death is certain (vv. 2–3), sad (vv. 4–6), and potentially sudden (vv. 11–12).

Death Is Certain

The certainty of death is addressed in Ecclesiastes 9:2–3. In verse 2, we read that "the same event," namely, death, happens to everyone—the good and the bad:
It is the same for all, since the same event happens

to the righteous	and the wicked,
to the good	and the evil,
to the clean	and the unclean,
to him who sacrifices	and him who does not sacrifice.
As the good one is,	so is the sinner, and
he who swears	is as he who shuns an oath.

Morality is no protection against mortality. Keeping God's law (the ritual washings, sacrifices, oaths, etc.) cannot keep you from Adam's curse. As the poet John Donne wrote:

Earth is the womb from whence all living came,
So is't the tomb, all go unto the same.[9]

Then in Ecclesiastes 9:3, we read that death is an "evil" earthly event: "This is an evil in all that is done under the sun, that the same event happens to all." To the Preacher, "death is not a 'natural' phenomenon . . . but an invincible evil."[10] Death is like a demon-possessed scorpion—it has an unethical edge to its sting.

Finally, at the end of verse 3, we read that death is a deserved event:

9. John Donne, quoted in Eric S. Christianson, *Ecclesiastes through the Centuries*, Blackwell Bible Commentaries (Malden, MA: Blackwell, 2007), 116.
10. Michael A. Eaton, *Ecclesiastes: An Introduction and Commentary*, Tyndale Old Testament Commentaries 16 (Downers Grove, IL: InterVarsity Press, 1983), 125.

Also, the hearts of the children of man are full of evil,
>   and madness is in their hearts while they live,
>   and after that they go to the dead.

Ecclesiastes 9:3 is a further exposition of the beginning of the Bible. In Genesis, Adam sins. In Adam, all the "children of man [*adam*]" spiritually and physically die. And between being born in sin and dying in our sin, we sin. As it was in the days of Noah, so it is now: our "hearts . . . are full of evil" or "madness." This is not merely an outward problem, but an inward one—at the core of our beings (our "hearts"). As the result of Adam's sin *and* our own evil inclinations and actions, death is certain. "For the wages of sin is death" (Rom. 6:23).

Death Is Sad

Beyond the certainty of death is the sadness of death. This also we should *know*. After Pastor Solomon has us drink a "dose of our own dust-to-dustness,"[11] next he puts a bitter cup to our parched lips. In Ecclesiastes 9:4–6, what begins sweetly ends sourly. See how it tastes!

> But he who is joined with all the living has hope, for a living dog is better than a dead lion. For the living know that they will die, but the dead know nothing, and they have no more reward, for the memory of them is forgotten. Their love and their hate and their envy have already perished, and forever they have no more share in all that is done under the sun.

Here, "the traits of the dead are morbidly catalogued. They have no knowledge, no wages, no memory, no emotion (love, hate, envy), and no portion"[12] in this world ("all that is done under the sun," Eccl. 9:6). While in 12:7 Solomon will speak of the return of the human spirit to God (seemingly hinting at an afterlife), here in 9:5–6 as well as 9:10 ("there is no work or thought or knowledge or wisdom in Sheol, to which you are going") death is not viewed as the door to immortality but rather as a sealed-shut tomb. This is why even the most-loathed creature in

11. Daphne Merkin, quoted in Christianson, *Ecclesiastes through the Centuries*, 13.
12. Ibid., 207.

ancient Israel (a dog) is better off than the most lauded (a lion) *if* the dog "ain't dead."

In the *Peanuts* cartoon "Theology and the Dog," Snoopy is atop his dog-house, typing away. Charlie Brown arrives on the scene and is handed what Snoopy has written. It reads, "As it says in the ninth chapter of Ecclesiastes, 'a living dog is better than a dead lion.'" Charlie Brown gives the paper back and asks, "What does *that* mean?" Snoopy examines it and replies, "I don't know, but I agree with it."[13] While I will admit that Snoopy's got smarts, nevertheless my wisdom (and thorough study on the matter) exceeds that of a make-believe dog. I *do* know what it means, and I also agree with it. It means that a miserable existence, like that of an alley cat or a sewer rat, is better than a king's situation in his coffin.

When human beings—the pinnacle of God's creation—die, it is a sad, sad business.

Death Is Sudden

In case we are not yet thoroughly depressed, Solomon invites us to take one more sip of the sourness. Death is certain, sad, and potentially sudden:

> Again I saw that under the sun [i.e., on earth] the race is not to the swift, nor the battle to the strong, nor bread to the wise, nor riches to the intelligent, nor favor to those with knowledge, but time and chance [i.e., bad luck—or, more piously, bitter providence; cf. Ruth 1:20] happen to them all. For man does not know his time [death]. Like fish that are taken in an evil net, and like birds that are caught in a snare, so the children of man are snared at an evil time, when it [death] suddenly falls upon them. (Eccl. 9:11–12)

Just as life is sometimes unpredictable (e.g., the swiftest runner loses the race, the strongest warrior dies in the fight, the highly educated man ends up poor, hungry, and despised),[14] so the day of death is potentially unpredictable and abrupt, and certainly inescapable.

---

13. See ibid., 210 (plate 12).

14. As Walter C. Kaiser illustrates from the Old Testament: "Who was swifter than Asahel, who fell needlessly, smitten by the butt end of Abner's spear (2 Sam. 2:22–23)? Who was stronger than Samson, but who was weaker before women (Judg. 16:19)? Who was wiser than Solomon, but who was more indulgent in sin (1 Kings 11:1–25)? Who was more discerning than Ahithophel, but who was so easily supplanted by Hushai and his foolish counsel (2 Sam. 16:23; 17:5–14)? Who was more

Two everyday snapshots are given. The first picture is that of fish caught in a net. Picture a fisherman's round net tossed into the air. Suddenly it strikes the water; and as the fisherman quickly pulls the net out of the water and into the boat, that school of fish so freely swimming a second ago is caught and killed. The second picture is of birds pecking on the ground for food, when they suddenly walk into a snare—think of a rope tied in a circle on the ground or a metal trap. The trap is pulled or snaps and the birds are caught and killed, or killed when caught.

The application to those images is this: While the children of Adam aren't "gullible, ignorant creatures"[15] like fish and birds, nevertheless we must be aware that life is not only like a vapor, quickly dissolving into the air (see James 4:14), but potentially like a candle snuffed out with a gust of wind. Who knows when it's your time to go? It might be today. It might even be now!

Do you think the Illinois lottery winner who was poisoned the day after he won the million-dollar jackpot thought that day would be his last?[16] I know of a young woman in Chicago who was hit by a bus a week before her wedding. I know of a boy who drowned last summer in Clear Lake, Iowa. I know that two children were stabbed in their home a few days ago in my hometown. The stories are endless. Do you think you are immune to such oddities?

Death is certain, sad, and potentially sudden.

ENJOY LIFE . . . ALL THE DAYS OF YOUR VAIN LIFE

In *Calvin and Hobbes*, I found the most serious comic strip that I have ever come across. Calvin (the boy) and Hobbes (his stuffed tiger who comes to life in his imagination) find a baby raccoon that is barely alive. Calvin runs to get his mom. Hobbes says, "I sure hope she can help." Calvin, now running away from Hobbes, yells back, "Of course she can! You don't get to be Mom if you can't fix everything just right." When Mom gets there,

---

learned in all the ways of the Egyptians than Moses, yet who also preempted every agency of justice in rushing into murder (Exod. 2:11–15; Acts 7:22)?" *Ecclesiastes: Total Life*, Everyman's Bible Commentary (Chicago: Moody, 1979), 103.

15. Michael V. Fox, *Ecclesiastes*, JPS Bible Commentary (Philadelphia: Jewish Publication Society, 2004), 65.

16. On Urooj Khan's murder, see http://www.huffingtonpost.com/2013/03/01/urooj-khan-autopsy-chicag_n_2790667.html, accessed on May 19, 2013.

however, she realizes that the raccoon is likely to die. Nevertheless, she puts the poor creature in a box and brings him home. They keep him in the garage and bring him food and water. Even Calvin puts on the generous spirit. "Chances are, I'll be happy to donate most of my dinner," he tells his mom. She replies, "Calvin, you don't even know what we're having." Before Calvin and Hobbes go to bed, the boy peers over the lid of the box, with a sad expression on his face, "Don't die, little raccoon." In the morning, as Calvin is running to the garage, he is met by his dad. "Dad, did you check on the little raccoon this morning?" "Yes, Calvin . . . . I'm afraid he died." Calvin cries and cries—"WAAHHHH! WAHHAAHH!" After they bury the little raccoon under a tree, Calvin says, "I didn't even know he existed a few days ago and now he's gone forever." The strip ends with Calvin's back to the reader, leaning over to Hobbes and saying, "What a stupid world."[17] Is the world stupid or senseless? And is that the reason Pastor Solomon has had us taste our dust-to-dustness and sip the sour cup of death? No. No, it's not!

In another *Calvin and Hobbes* cartoon, Watterson gets closer to the truth. This time the boy and his tiger are sitting on the ground with their backs to a tree. In the first frame, Calvin leans forward and says, "I don't understand this business about death." In the second frame, the drawing focuses entirely on him. With his arms stretched out horizontally, he asks, "If we're just going to die, what's the point of living?" The third frame shows them staring straight at the reader with baffled looks on their faces. They are silent. Finally, in the fourth and final frame, an answer comes from hungry Hobbes. He says, "Well, there's seafood . . ."[18]

Pastor Solomon hasn't reminded us what we already know about death for the sake of stupidity or seafood, but the enjoyment-of-seafood answer gets us closer to where he takes us next. What is the purpose of all this *memento mori*? The purpose is to reinforce the fact that we are not in control. God is. And if God is in control of life *and death*, then we should walk the way of wisdom, which for Pastor Solomon is also the journey of joy. In Ecclesiastes

17. Bill Watterson, *The Essential Calvin and Hobbes: A Calvin and Hobbes Treasury* (Kansas City, MO: Universal Press Syndicate, 1988), 223–25.

18. Ibid., 161. In the final frame, Calvin is not amused. He looks down with an angry expression on his face and says, "I don't know why I even *talk* to you before dinner."

9:7–10, the dark cloud of despair moves past and the bright light of God's love shines on the righteous:

> Go, eat your bread with joy, and drink your wine with a merry heart, for God has already approved what you do.
>   Let your garments be always white. Let not oil be lacking on your head.
>   Enjoy life with the wife whom you love, all the days of your vain life that he has given you under the sun, because that is your portion in life and in your toil at which you toil under the sun. Whatever your hand finds to do, do it with your might, for there is no work or thought or knowledge or wisdom in Sheol, to which you are going.

This is the sixth enjoyment exhortation in Ecclesiastes. Once again, it comes unexpectedly. Moreover, it comes more emphatically than ever! Pastor Solomon has "recommended enjoyment before (2:24–26; 3:12–13, 22; 5:18–20; 8:15, and will do so once more in 11:7–9) but never in such strong terms . . . and so elaborately . . . as in this passage."[19] As Daniel Fredericks notes:

> This rendition of the shalom refrain is unique in intensity in two ways. First, these are refreshing elaborations of what was becoming very formulaic. These recommendations are interesting in their detail and enhancements of the previous refrains. Secondly, Qoheleth has turned from mere comparative statements to imperatives in order to express what Brown describes as the "moral urgency" of pursuing enjoyment.[20]

The center of our text is the centerpiece for our table in the mist. There are five imperatives to feast on: go, eat, drink, enjoy, and do. The central command is "enjoy life." How so? Here are three possible (not exhaustive) ways: Enjoy your wine, wife, and work. Don't worry; I won't leave out the husband, the clothing, the bread, and the oil on the head. They'll all get squeezed under the three Ws—*wine, wife,* and *work*.

The first imperative is to enjoy your wine: "Go, eat your bread with joy, and drink your wine with a merry heart, for God has already approved what

19. Sidney Greidanus, *Preaching Christ from Ecclesiastes: Foundations for Expository Sermons* (Grand Rapids: Eerdmans, 2010), 221.
20. Daniel C. Fredericks, "Ecclesiastes," in Daniel C. Fredericks and Daniel J. Estes, *Ecclesiastes and the Song of Songs*, Apollos Old Testament Commentary 16 (Downers Grove, IL: InterVarsity Press, 2010), 208.

you do" (Eccl. 9:7). The command "go" is a "wake up call."[21] Stop bemoaning death's certainty. Stop lamenting over death's sadness. Stop stressing about death's suddenness. Get over it and "go." Go out for dinner, or at least go to the dinner table:

Eat your bread with joy, and
Drink your wine with a merry heart.

In ancient Israel, bread and wine were the staples of daily existence. Here Solomon is saying that when you eat and drink what you normally eat and drink, do so with a happy heart. Why? "For God has already approved what you do." This motive is a historical flashback to the garden of Eden, where the trees and plants were ripe for the picking ("You may surely eat of every tree of the garden" but one, Gen. 2:16–17). It is also a theological fast-forward to justification by faith in Christ.[22] We can eat and drink because we already have God's approval. We do not have to work to earn God's favor. We are already favored. We say grace before the meal because of the grace already given. We can eat up and drink up because Jesus was raised up for us. He died for us! The early church models this for us in Acts 2:46–47: "And day by day, attending the temple together and breaking bread in their homes, *they received their food with glad and generous hearts*, praising God and having favor with all the people." Eugene Peterson's paraphrase of Ecclesiastes 9:7 summarizes the first application well: "Seize life! Eat bread with gusto, Drink wine with a robust heart. Oh yes—God takes pleasure in your pleasure!" (*The Message*).

Second, enjoy your wife:

Let your garments be always white. Let not oil be lacking on your head.
    Enjoy life with the wife whom you love [the one woman you have covenanted with], all the days of your vain life that he has given you under the sun, because that is your portion in life and in your toil at which you toil under the sun. (Eccl. 9:8–9)

It is difficult to know whether the command about the garments and oil in Ecclesiastes 9:8 is separate from the command to "enjoy life with the wife

---

21. Greidanus, *Preaching Christ from Ecclesiastes*, 232.
22. "The basis of contentment is that God has already approved what you do. This almost Pauline touch is the nearest the Preacher came to a doctrine of justification by faith." Eaton, *Ecclesiastes*, 127.

whom you love" (v. 9) or whether they are to be taken together. Verse 8 might also go best with verse 7—that is, festal garments for a feast! (cf. Esth. 8:15). I think verses 8–9 do go together, and the movement is from the kitchen to the bedroom, so to speak. Perhaps my persistent reading of the Song of Songs—with its blend of the metaphors of wine, oils, and clothing—has blurred my judgment. If I'm correct, however, and these verses go together, then the command is commonplace. Most adults in the world, certainly in the ancient world, are or will be married sometime in their lives. The command is to smell good and look good in the bedroom.[23]

Of course, married love is much broader than the bedroom, and that is certainly implied here: "Enjoy *life*" (all of it!) with your spouse "all the days" of your God-appointed, brief life. Marriage is for life. Marriage is for mutual lifelong enjoyment. Marriage is not made *for* heaven (see Matt. 22:30), but that does not mean your marriage isn't *of* heaven and can't be heavenly.

If you prefer to apply smelling good and looking good to other contexts, be my guest. Don't wear sackcloth to work. Buy a white dress. Splash on a dash of cologne. Shampoo and rinse. I'll let you expand the applications from there. However we are to apply Ecclesiastes 9:8–9, we are not to apply it with "monkish fanaticism," as Martin Luther so often put it. That is, we are to avoid asceticism for asceticism's sake—or, worse, to gain God's approval. True spirituality has "honest delight" in lawful pleasures.[24] In Christ, and as a taste of the new earth, we can and should find pure pleasure in eating, drinking, marriage, and work (see Gen. 2:15–25). We can "rejoice always," knowing that "this is the will of God in Christ Jesus for you" (1 Thess. 5:16, 18). In the Bible, both oil and white clothing symbolize joy (e.g., Ps. 45:7; Rev. 7:9). By what you wear, how you smell, and whom you love, let the world know that you have the joy of Jesus!

Third, enjoy your work. "At the end of the day, Ecclesiastes is a lecture on the theology of work, not on the meaning of life,"[25] and it echoes God's first command to man to subdue and have dominion over the earth (see Gen. 1:28).

23. "The admonition is comparable to that of Proverbs 5:15–19, which is designed to (re)kindle the flame of marital passion." William P. Brown, *Ecclesiastes*, Interpretation (Louisville, KY: Westminster John Knox, 2000), 93–94.

24. The phrase "honest delight" comes from the Reformer Theodore Beza and "lawful pleasures" from the Puritan Henry Smith ("a lawfull pleasure in earthly things"), both quoted in Christianson, *Ecclesiastes through the Centuries*, 212 and 108, respectively.

25. Fredericks, "Ecclesiastes," 215.

As Ecclesiastes 9:10 says: "Whatever your hand finds to do, do it with your might, for there is no work or thought or knowledge or wisdom in Sheol, to which you are going." *Sheol* is the place of the dead, although sometimes the word simply symbolizes death itself (e.g., Ps. 116:3—"the snares of death" parallels "the pangs of Sheol"). In light of death, if you have the opportunity to work at something, work hard at it. You only live once; make it count! Nike's slogan *Just Do It* is close to the sentiment expressed here. But Paul's saying in Colossians 3:23 is better: "Work hard and cheerfully at whatever you do" (NLT).

There is much that we cannot know. But we do know that death is certain, sad, and potentially sudden. We also know that in light of that terrible reality, we are called to enjoy life. Enjoy your wine, wife, and work. Enjoy all the days of your vain life!

EAT OF IT AND NOT DIE

In traditional Judaism, the command "eat your bread with joy" (Eccl. 9:7) is read aloud at the end of Yom Kippur (the Day of Atonement), "when the time has come for celebrating."[26] I advocate that as Christians who believe that Jesus Christ has fulfilled the Day of Atonement in his death on the cross, we read Ecclesiastes 9:7 (along with verses 8, 9, and 10) on Good Friday (the Day of Atonement) *and* Easter (the Day of Resurrection). According to Pastor Solomon, we should enjoy life because of our impending death. "Seize the day before death seizes the self."[27] According to Jesus, however, we should enjoy life because of the hope of everlasting life. "For the wages of sin is death, *but the free gift of God is eternal life in Christ Jesus our Lord*" (Rom. 6:23).

Through Jesus we have eternal life. In John 6:48–51, Jesus made a most astonishing announcement. He said:

> I am the bread of life. Your fathers ate the manna in the wilderness, and *they died*. This is the bread that comes down from heaven, so that one may eat of it and *not die*. I am the living bread that came down from heaven. If anyone eats of this bread, he will *live forever*.

26. Christianson, *Ecclesiastes through the Centuries*, 211.
27. Brown, *Ecclesiastes*, 93.

As Christians, we can "rejoice in the Lord *always*" (Phil. 4:4)—even when we walk through the valley of the shadow of death—because though we die, yet we will live! At the marriage of the Lamb, as we will be clothed in immortality, we will join in the thundering voice from the throne: "Praise our God, . . . you who fear him . . . . Hallelujah! For the Lord our God the Almighty reigns" (Rev. 19:5–6). And we will sit at table as our Good Shepherd anoints our heads with oil, as our cup overflows, and as goodness and mercy follow us all the days of our lives and we dwell in the house of the Lord forever (see Ps. 23:5–6).

15

DEAD FLIES, A SERPENT'S BITE, AND TWITTER

Ecclesiastes 9:13–10:20

> *But I say that wisdom is better than might, though the poor*
> *man's wisdom is despised and his words are not heard. The*
> *words of the wise heard in quiet are better than the shouting of*
> *a ruler among fools. Wisdom is better than weapons of war, but*
> *one sinner destroys much good.* (Eccl. 9:16–18)

arl Trueman's book *Fools Rush In Where Monkeys Fear to Tread* references the classic 1960s short video *Powers of Ten*. Shortly after I read Trueman's book, a man from my congregation told me about the film as well. Then in the winter edition of my college's alumni magazine, a professor's article mentioned it yet again. I saw this threefold cord to be strong enough proof of divine guidance to necessitate a description of that video as my introduction. Professor Burden summarizes:

The film opens, focusing on a one-square meter blanket near the Chicago lakefront. Hovering over a couple enjoying a picnic, the camera pans back, increasing the viewing area ten-fold every ten seconds. Like a harbinger of

Google Earth, many powers of ten are quickly surpassed, and you are soon looking at planet Earth from outer space, followed by the Milky Way, then neighboring galaxies. The expansion stops at the edges of the known universe, leaving viewers dizzied by the enormity. The view quickly returns to the blanket and begins a descent onto the hand of the sleeping man. As the scale shrinks one power of ten every ten seconds, a small hair on the man's hand grows as large as the screen. Skin and blood cells quickly balloon outside of view. Inside the cell, small organelles are surpassed, and large molecules can be seen performing their various functions. Eventually, the scene plunges into the subatomic underworld, continuing to shrink through seven more powers of ten before coming to a close.[1]

In Ecclesiastes, the camera lens rarely moves above the sun. It scans over creation—the rivers, vineyards, parks, trees, ponds, flocks, herds, dogs, lions, horses, birds, fish, flies, and grasshoppers—as it settles on the human hands and eventually goes deep down into our hearts. In 9:13–10:20, the focus settles again on the topics of wisdom, folly, and government. The repetition of certain key words—*wise/wisdom* (11×), *fool/fools/folly/foolishness* (10×), and *king* (4×) and *ruler* (3×)—makes it easy to see that these three topics are the focus here. What is not easy, however, is finding the flow of thought and the overarching theme of this text. Commentators join hands in holding up hands in bewilderment. Martin Luther observed, "Solomon really makes some harsh transitions!"[2] Indeed. We jump back and forth between a short story, a proverb, a case study, a comparison, a saying, and a command. And as we do so, we wonder, "Where is all this going?" Not that Pastor Solomon has given us linear, logical arguments in each section, but we see here, as Peter Enns expresses it, "a scattered, perhaps even frantic, effort to express himself."[3] But through it all, a clear contrast does emerge. There are two ways to live: like the wise or like the fool.[4] One way

---

1. Daniel Burden, "From Cells to Atoms: How Does the Nanoscale Invite Discovery, Invention, and Reflection?," *Wheaton Alumni Magazine* (Winter 2012): 60.

2. Martin Luther, "Notes on Ecclesiastes," in *Luther's Works*, trans. and ed. Jaroslav Pelikan, 56 vols. (St. Louis: Concordia, 1972), 15:156.

3. Peter Enns, *Ecclesiastes*, Two Horizons Old Testament Commentary (Grand Rapids: Eerdmans, 2011), 98.

4. In Stephen Brown's chiastic structure of Ecclesiastes 9:13–10:20, he sees 10:2–3 (the contrast of folly and wisdom) as the center. "The Structure of Ecclesiastes," *Evangelical Review of Theology* 14, 3 (1990): 204. While I agree with Sidney Greidanus that this "suggested chiasm seems rather strained" (*Preaching Christ from Ecclesiastes: Foundations for Expository Sermons* [Grand Rapids: Eerdmans,

to further divide that division is by focusing on the superiority of wisdom over folly—that is, wisdom is better than might even if a little folly spoils wisdom's gain (9:13–10:1); wisdom is better than folly even if folly sometimes sits in high places (10:2–20). Another more creative way to divide the two paths is by the unique illustrations of the three small creatures mentioned: the fly (10:1), the snake (vv. 8, 11), and the bird (v. 20).

THE SERPENT'S BITE

Since Solomon's thought seems all over the place, we may join him in his disorganization and organize our thoughts by starting first with the serpent, whom we find in the middle. Ecclesiastes 10:8 talks about the snake's bite. Moreover, verse 11 reads, "If the serpent bites before it is charmed, there is no advantage to the charmer."

But before explaining these verses, we should look first at Ecclesiastes 10:2:

> A wise man's heart   inclines him   to the right,
>   but a fool's heart   to the left.

In Ecclesiastes 10:2–11, the actions of the fool are set in contrast to those of the wise. The first contrast involves holiness and the lack thereof. Verse 2 can work as a nice proof text for right-wing politics. Yet its original intention involves right living: "A wise man's heart inclines him to the right" ("the right" connotes "moral goodness"[5]), while "a fool's heart" does the opposite.

Next, in Ecclesiastes 10:3, we move from the fool's attitude and inclinations (his "heart") to his actions (his "walk"). The fool's walk shows that he lacks common sense: "Even when the fool walks on the road, he lacks sense, and he says to everyone that he is a fool." We have all done foolish things—in the sense of lacking common sense. When I was in Ireland recently, I went to a car-rental place to pick up a car. The only car they had left was a stick shift. In Ireland you drive on the opposite side of the road, and thus the stick is on the opposite side of the driver. "No problem," I said as I bravely

---

2010], 240–41), nevertheless, it hits the bull's-eye of the thematic center. As Greidanus summarizes: "The focus of this passage is on the contrast between wise and foolish inclinations, words, and actions, particularly in the area of politics" (246).

5. James L. Crenshaw, *Ecclesiastes: A Commentary*, Old Testament Library (Philadelphia: Westminster John Knox, 1987), 169.

signed the paperwork. Needless to say, getting out of the airport I looked like quite the fool. (Mind you, I did get the hang of it; I got into only *one* accident on the trip.)

The fool in our text gets into one accident after another because "he lacks sense." His heart has gone in the wrong direction, and his head is turned around. The illustrations of such folly are provided in Ecclesiastes 10:8–11 (which is where the snake's fangs come in):

He who digs   a pit will fall into it, and a serpent will bite
him who breaks   through a wall.
He who quarries   stones is hurt by them, and
he who splits logs is endangered by them.
If the iron is blunt, and one does not sharpen the edge,
    he must use more strength, but wisdom helps one to succeed.
If the serpent bites before it is charmed, there is no advantage to the charmer.

Ecclesiastes 10:8–9 mentions four accidents. These are accidents that could happen to anyone, whether he is a fool or not. Even the wisest man could dig a pit and cover it in order to capture an animal and mistakenly walk right over it and down into it. The same is true of knocking down a wall that just happens to have a snake housed in it—a snake that isn't happy with your work![6] Likewise, in moving heavy stones you could throw out your back, and in splitting a log the ax head could fly off and hit your head. "Stuff happens"—even to the wise.

The wise, by contrast, do not do the dumb things mentioned in Ecclesiastes 10:10–11. "The wise do everything in its proper time,"[7] and they rely on the brain, not just brawn. Instead of first sharpening the iron blade to cut a log, the fool takes a dull blade and works tirelessly, trying to cut his way through (and perhaps swings so hard that he hits himself in the head, v. 9). Instead of first charming a snake, the fool approaches this dangerous

---

6. Michael V. Fox notes: "When dismantling a stone wall, a person may get bitten by a poisonous snake that was nesting in it. This is a real danger in the land of Israel, where there are quite a few poisonous serpents (currently some twenty species)." *Ecclesiastes*, JPS Bible Commentary (Philadelphia: Jewish Publication Society, 2004), 69.

7. Ovid, quoted in Philip Graham Ryken, *Ecclesiastes: Why Everything Matters*, ed. R. Kent Hughes, Preaching the Word (Wheaton, IL: Crossway, 2010), 239. "Timing is everything in applied wisdom." Fredericks, "Ecclesiastes," 236.

creature as he would a pet rabbit. The unmesmerized serpent is not amused. He strikes the stupid man!

So, then, the fool lacks holiness (Eccl. 10:2) and common sense (vv. 3, 8–11). Nevertheless (guess what?), sometimes fools rule over us. In Ecclesiastes, "the fool loves rowdy songs (7:5) and noisy, shallow laughter (7:6); he is lazy (4:5), garrulous (5:3; 10:12), irascible (7:9), unreceptive to advice (9:17), morally blind (2:14), with a fatal malady at heart (10:2) and disapproved by God (5:4). [Yet] he may be found in any section of society, even in the temple (5:1) or on a throne (4:13)."[8] Well, in verses 4–7 it is King Folly who sits on the throne:

> If the anger of *the ruler* rises against you, do not leave your place,
>   for calmness will lay great offenses to rest.

>> There is an evil that I have seen under the sun, as it were an error proceeding from *the ruler*: folly is set in many high places, and *the rich sit in a low place*. I have seen slaves on horses, and princes walking on the ground like slaves.

The world is a topsy-turvy place. Sometimes the highest ruler in the land makes great errors in judgment (no kidding). And sometimes the normal (seemingly God-ordained; cf. Prov. 30:21–22) ordering of things is upside down. What is a lowly slave doing riding on a high horse while a rich prince sits on the ground? It is one thing for a drunk to stumble into town not knowing where he is going, but quite another thing for a king to act so incompetent.

A fool dressed in rags, while not acceptable, is expected; but a fool dressed in royal robes makes us want to rend our garments. Yet the advice given here is to take a deep breath, hold your ground, and wait out the ruler's rising temper: "If the anger of the ruler rises against you, do not leave your place,[9] for calmness will lay great offenses to rest" (Eccl. 10:4).

---

8. Michael A. Eaton, *Ecclesiastes: An Introduction and Commentary*, Tyndale Old Testament Commentaries 16 (Downers Grove, IL: InterVarsity Press, 1983), 134.

9. "The courtier is not to leave because his calm demeanor will soothe the king. Apparently, if he left the scene, the king could suspect him even more, and his anger would increase." Tremper Longman III, *The Book of Ecclesiastes*, New International Commentary on the Old Testament (Grand Rapids: Eerdmans, 1998), 241.

In other words, don't fight folly with folly. Let a cool and kind tongue kick down the door. "With patience a ruler may be persuaded, and a soft tongue will break a bone" (Prov. 25:15). In politics, as in all of life, do not underestimate the persuasive power of a calm demeanor and a soft word (cf. Prov. 15:1).

TWITTER

Let's stay on this political theme, but move from the snake's bite to the bird's whisper. Ecclesiastes 10:20 reads:

Even	in your thoughts,	do not curse the king,	
nor	in your bedroom	curse the rich,	
for a bird of the air		will carry	your voice, or
or some winged creature		tell	the matter.

The lesson of this verse is the lesson of verses 12–20 as a whole, namely, that the wise person knows how to use the tongue, especially in relation to bad government.

The use of the tongue is the number-one topic in Proverbs. The tongue is discussed in every chapter, and words such as *tongue, mouth(s),* and *lips* total nearly a hundred uses! In Ecclesiastes, the tongue is an important topic as well, especially here in 10:12–20 (cf. 9:16–17). By the use of contrast, verse 12 gives the main thesis:

The words	of a wise man's mouth	win him favor, but
the lips	of a fool	consume him.

An illustration of such consumption is given in Ecclesiastes 10:13–15:

The beginning of the words of his mouth is foolishness,
   and the end of his talk is evil madness.
A fool multiplies words,
   though no man knows what is to be,
   and who can tell him what will be after him?
The toil [i.e., excessive talking] of a fool wearies him,
   for he does not know the way to the city.

187

When the fool misses the obvious exit ramp to the big city, he journeys on, wearing himself (and certainly others) out with his chatting on about nothing (see Eccl. 10:15). When he starts to speak, he does not know where he is going ("his mouth is foolishness," v. 13); when he finally stops, he has made it nowhere ("his talk is evil madness," v. 13), and in between starting and stopping, he jabbers on ("multiplies words") about future events of which he cannot possibly know the outcome (v. 14).

Three times in Ecclesiastes Pastor Solomon has said that no one can know the future ("who knows . . . ?"—3:21; 6:12; cf. 8:7), but apparently this fool never got the memo. He is like the man described in James 4:13–15 who thinks he knows what the next day will bring: "Tomorrow we will go into such and such a town and spend a year there and trade and make a profit" (v. 13). He is like Job's friends, who were certain that God would soon vindicate their judgment of Job, when instead God judged their judgment—their false testimony (Job 42:7–8). Plato once said, "Wise men speak because they have something to say; fools because they have to say something."[10] To borrow a phrase from Shakespeare, the fool is "full of sound and fury," and he "signif[ies] nothing."[11]

So on one hand we have the fool. His words are self-cannibalistic: by his own endless talking he devours or swallows himself up. On the other hand, Ecclesiastes 10:16–20 illustrates how the wise win favor through the taming of the tongue. Before the tongue ("your voice") is mentioned in verse 20, however, first we read about how the rhythm of healthy government is replaced by role reversals and revelry (note below the extensive varieties of parallelisms):

> Woe to you, O land, when your king is a child,
> and your princes feast in the morning!
> Happy are you, O land, when your king is the son of the nobility,
> and your princes feast at the proper time,
> for strength, and not for drunkenness!

> Through sloth the roof sinks in, and
> through indolence the house leaks.

10. Plato, quoted in Ryken, *Ecclesiastes*, 246.
11. William Shakespeare, *Macbeth*, act 5, scene 5.

Bread is made	for	laughter, and
wine gladdens		life, and
money answers		everything. (Eccl. 10:16–19)

These verses contrast two kings and two kingdoms—one wise and the other foolish. The wise kingdom is run by "the son of the nobility" (Eccl. 10:17), not "a child" (v. 16). It is ruled by moderation and self-control ("your princes feast at the proper time [i.e., dinnertime]," v. 17c; "for strength," v. 17d), not excess and self-indulgence ("your princes feast in the morning [i.e., they party late into the night]," v. 16c; "for drunkenness," v. 17d). Such licentiousness—failing to eat at the appropriate time and to drink only the proper amount of wine—has terrible consequences. As the lazy leaders sing their self-indulgent song ("Bread is made for laughter, and wine gladdens life, and money answers everything," v. 19),[12] "the roof sinks in, . . . the house leaks" (v. 18). The White House has become the Wet House; Number 10 Downing Street has become Number 10 Drowning Street. Bad government has disastrous consequences.

Now, if we find ourselves under the reign of such a foolish government, what is the wise thing to do? Shouldn't we curse the king and his cronies? If that is what we think, then we might not like Solomon's suggestion. In fact, we might be ready to write him off when it comes to his political advice. "Stick with the pithy proverbs," we might say to Solomon the sage, "and let someone else handle political affairs." For in Ecclesiastes 10:20 we read, "Even in your thoughts, do not curse the king, nor in your bedroom curse the rich, for a bird of the air will carry your voice, or some winged creature tell the matter." Here is George Sandys 1632 paraphrase:

Curse not thy Rulers though with vices fraught;
Not in thy Bed-Chamber, nor in thy thought:
For Birds will beare thy whisperings on their wings,
To the wide ears of Death-inflicting Kings.[13]

---

12. Choon-Leong Seow notes that perhaps this was a line from a drinking song. *Ecclesiastes*, Anchor Bible 18C (New York: Doubleday, 1997), 332. Greidanus adds: "They are totally focused on the good times they can have for themselves. They like their feasts, their wine, and use the public purse for their partying: 'Money meets every need.'" *Preaching Christ from Ecclesiastes*, 257.

13. George Sandys, quoted in Eric S. Christianson, *Ecclesiastes through the Centuries*, Blackwell Bible Commentaries (Malden, MA: Blackwell, 2007), 219.

In view here is total self-restraint. The natural reaction to the situation would be to think and talk about the terrible government. But here we are told to guard our *thoughts* and close our mouths, even in our *bedrooms*.

The negative motivation is that we might get caught and presumably punished; the positive motivation is to gain "favor" (Eccl. 10:12). More on "favor" in a moment. First, let's take a look at the negative motivation. Our political situation might well be different from the one described here. We might not be under a monarchy or have reason to fear spies, the secret police, or the death penalty for speaking our minds. Yet even if we live in a democratic republic, where free speech is a protected right, unrestrained speech (even in the privacy of our own homes) can still lead to our ruin. These days our rooms aren't bugged, but many are *birded*.

To see what I mean, consider the popular microblogging service Twitter, which ironically has a little blue bird for its icon. With one "tweeted" line, that little blue bird has been the downfall of politicians, professional athletes, celebrities,[14] and the regular employee at the regular job. In our culture, not only do we still use the expression "a little bird told me," but we actually send that little birdie to the Internet to share each thoughtful and thoughtless thought that comes to mind. As I was typing my notes for the sermon that became this chapter, I was listening to the North Carolina/North Carolina State basketball game. As the announcers highlighted one of the stars, they discussed the trouble that he had gotten into because of a recent tweet. One of the announcers summarized the situation like this: "So much trouble for one press on a smartphone."

Jesus never tweeted, of course, but he was well aware of the danger pervading our society and discussed in Ecclesiastes 10:20. In Luke 12:2–3, commenting on the Pharisees' hypocrisy, he said, "Nothing is covered up that will not be revealed, or hidden that will not be known. Therefore whatever you have said in the dark shall be heard in the light, and what you have whispered in private rooms shall be proclaimed on the housetops." A large part of wisdom is mouth-management! Luther said, "A wise man teaches with few words and says what he feels with brevity . . . . Fools, on the other

---

14. For example, comedian Gilbert Gottfried, the voice of the Aflac insurance company's "duck," tweeted about the 2011 Japanese tsunami: "Japan is really advanced. They don't go to the beach. The beach comes to them." Aflac happens to be the largest insurance company in Japan, and needless to say, Gottfried was fired.

hand, spill over with words, and cannot be restrained or put down with words so that they will keep quiet, but will answer one word with a thousand."[15] Of course, there are exceptions to the rule. I hope the four-thousand-plus words that I use to speak on Sundays fall under the "wisdom" category. God help me if they don't! Whether we speak for a living or live to speak, we all must understand that "talk is the acid test of wisdom,"[16] for as our Lord taught, "out of the abundance of the heart the mouth speaks" (Matt. 12:34) (and the fingers "tweet").

If the negative motivation is that you can get caught and presumably punished, the positive motivation is to gain "favor"—"The words of a wise man's mouth win him favor [hen]" (Eccl. 10:12a). "Favor" might mean protection from persecution, or it might mean winning a hearing. Either way, it is a good outcome.

The book of Esther is an extended treatise on this subject. The actions of Esther that are connected to the word *favor* [hen] are especially interesting. The book begins by highlighting the power and wealth of King Ahasuerus. As the book goes on, we quickly learn that King Ahasuerus acts precisely like the king mentioned in Ecclesiastes 9:13–10:20. He is arrogant, is easily angered, drinks too much, and makes rash, foolish decisions. One of his decisions is to get rid of Queen Vashti because she didn't come when she was called (Esth. 1:12). Soon thereafter, beautiful Esther replaces beautiful Vashti. In Esther 2:15 we read of the new queen, "Now Esther was winning *favor* [hen] in the eyes of all who saw her," and in Esther 2:17 we read that "she won grace and *favor* [hen] in [the king's] sight." In chapter 3, the king (not even knowing that Esther is a Jew) signs an edict that would "annihilate all Jews" (3:13). Esther's uncle Mordecai asks her to help. But helping wasn't so easy. Upon penalty of death (4:11), no one—not even the queen—could enter the king's inner court without an invitation. Time was ticking. No invitation came. So Esther decided to risk her life and see the king. Chapter 5 begins:

> On the third day Esther put on her royal robes and stood in the inner court of the king's palace, in front of the king's quarters, while the king was sitting on his royal throne inside the throne room opposite the entrance to the palace. And when the king saw Queen Esther standing in the court [oh, dear,

---

15. Luther, "Notes on Ecclesiastes," 15:164.
16. Eaton, *Ecclesiastes*, 136.

what will happen next?], she won *favor* [*hen*] in his sight, and he held out to Esther the golden scepter that was in his hand. Then Esther approached and touched the tip of the scepter. And the king said to her, "What is it, Queen Esther? What is your request? It shall be given you, even to the half of my kingdom." (Esth. 5:1–3)

Needless to say, the risk paid off! The king not only spared Esther's life, but also opened his heart and kingdom to her. She saved the day.

Fast-forward through the rest of the story (Esth. 6–10), and the king's ears open even wider to Esther's will. Based on her word, the evildoers are exposed and judged (see 9:12–15). The book closes with a eulogy for Esther's uncle Mordecai: "Mordecai the Jew was second in rank to King Ahasuerus, and he was great among the Jews and popular with the multitude of his brothers, for he sought the welfare of his people and spoke peace to all his people" (10:3).

Sometimes God's people change the world, as Esther and Mordecai did, with slow, careful, prayerful actions and "speech . . . seasoned with salt" (Col. 4:6). What if Christians were known for our quietness rather than our venomous attacks, or for our kindness rather than our inflammatory tempers? What if Christians conducted themselves "in wisdom toward outsiders" (4:5), as Paul called the non-Christians in his days? Maybe we would gain the ear of the king and of the culture. Maybe our calm, careful, clear, and concise words would "open to us a door for the word, to declare the mystery of Christ" (4:3). Maybe. Shall we give God's truth a try?

THE DEAD FLIES

Beyond the serpent and the bird are the bugs: "Dead flies make the perfumer's ointment give off a stench; so a little folly outweighs wisdom and honor" (Eccl. 10:1). The link between the three creatures is their size and disproportionate danger. All three small creatures can potentially cause great damage: "little snakes can kill a big person; and a little bird can tell the king your secret thoughts and get you into trouble"; and "dead flies spoil a lot of precious ointment."[17] The image, in case we don't see (or smell!) it, is that of an expensive batch of perfume attracting a few flies. Some of these

---

17. Greidanus, *Preaching Christ from Ecclesiastes*, 258.

insects, unknown to the owner or maker, die and fall into the ointment (or perhaps die because they come too close and sniff). Over time, the sweet, seductive smell is replaced by a putrid, rancid one. The whole batch is ruined because of a few little bugs.

The lesson from the flies is that as valuable as wisdom is (and as much as we hope it will be preserved), nevertheless a small amount of folly—for example, the verbosity of a fool or one awful politician—can ruin what wisdom has accomplished. That lesson is stated through an analogy in Ecclesiastes 10:1, three "better than" proverbs in 9:16–18, and a story in 9:13–15. Here is the story:

> I have also seen this example of wisdom under the sun, and it seemed great to me [i.e., it left a "big impression" or had a "large impact"].[18] There was a little city with few men in it, and a great king came against it and besieged it, building great siegeworks against it. But there was found in it a poor, wise man, and he by his wisdom delivered the city. Yet no one remembered that poor man. (Eccl. 9:13–15)

The story starts with striking contrasts. There once was "a great king" who came to conquer "a little city with few men" (Eccl. 9:14). This king likely had a great army; he certainly had superior military technology—"great siegeworks" (v. 14). But he underestimated one poor man and the power of his wisdom. In verse 11, Pastor Solomon mentally prepared us for unpredictable outcomes—"the battle" doesn't always go "to the strong." Here in verse 15, wisdom wins the day. We are not told how; we are given only a hint. The wisdom had something to do with the poor man's words and obviously with people's heeding them. In verse 16 "the poor man's wisdom" is equated with "his words," and in verse 17 the contrast is made between the king's shouts (yelling out orders?) and the wise man's sharing of his secret plan to a few good men who listen carefully:

> The words of the wise heard in *quiet* are better than the *shouting* of a ruler among fools.

But there is one final twist to the story. When the war was won, did the city make this man mayor? No. Did they rename the city after him?

18. Longman, *The Book of Ecclesiastes*, 234.

193

No again. What about build a statue of him and set it in the center of town? Wrong again. Instead, we are told that "no one remembered that poor man" (Eccl. 9:15).[19] Jerome laments: "Alas for men's ingratitude and forgetfulness!"[20] In our world, we must recognize "that wisdom is better than might," even though wisdom is often "despised"—that is, it goes unappreciated and unrewarded.

DIVINE RESOLUTION

Our text ends with an unresolved tension (Eccl. 10:1). To use a musical analogy, it is like an unresolved seventh. For the key of C, the dominant seventh chord goes from G to B to D to F. Then the F should resolve down a step to form a C-major chord. A chord is unresolved when this doesn't happen, and listeners are left waiting for a sound that they never get.[21] While that effect is inspiring musically, it is disconcerting theologically. I want to know how the notes *wisdom, folly,* and *king* get resolved. It is good to learn to expect flawed rulers in a fallen world. It is helpful to be reminded to be patient and prayerful, and to tame my thinking and talking. This practical advice is useful as far as it goes, but there must be something more.

The resolution, if there is one, must involve God. But where is he? God isn't even mentioned in these twenty-six verses. What about joy, then? We have learned to expect happiness to pop up in unexpected places. Again, there is no ode to joy here. Of course, in Ecclesiastes 11 and 12 we will be exhorted to remember God and rejoice. But here the lack of resolution is disturbing, especially when the one person the world longs for—whether we are under a relatively stable and ethical government or a volatile and wicked one—is a wise ruler to govern wisely.

19. "The wise man who saved the city was forgotten—his deed was remembered, but his name was lost. We can compare the two women who saved their cities but whose names and identities go unmentioned: the woman of Tebez (Judg. 9:52–55) and the wise woman of Abel Beth Maacah (2 Sam. 20:14–22)." Fox, *Ecclesiastes*, 66.

20. Jerome, *Commentary on Ecclesiastes*, trans. Richard J. Goodrich and David J. D. Miller, Ancient Christian Writers 66 (New York: Newman, 2012), 108.

21. After preaching from this passage, I received the following letter from a member of the congregation: "Doug, your sermon illustration yesterday of the unresolved seventh made me think of this piece [he included the sheet music], Messiaen's 'Le Banquet Céleste,' which ends on the unstable dominant seventh chord, held for a seemingly interminable 30–40 seconds. This final chord is likely supposed to represent our eternal remaining in him (John 6:56)." Letter from Russell Callender, February 4, 2013.

When Jesus died on the cross, the notice above his head read, "This is Jesus, the King of the Jews" (Matt. 27:37). These words were written in mockery. As Jesus died, the world laughed. Yet we know that that poor man from Nazareth saved the world through the wisdom of the cross. Even the Lord of the Flies could not spoil the work of this anointed King! "Christ crucified" (1 Cor. 1:23) "is folly to those who are perishing, but to us who are being saved it is the power of God" (v. 18). Jesus *is* the divine resolution. He is the righteous King who conquered all unrighteousness by the "folly" of the cross. And to those who bow the knee before him in silent adoration, he is our "wisdom from God, righteousness and sanctification and redemption" (v. 30). Yes, to those who acknowledge that God has placed "the government . . . upon his shoulder" (Isa. 9:6)—an everlasting rule of justice and righteousness (v. 7)—there is now life and hope and joy under his dominion.

16

BEFORE THE EVIL DAYS COME

Ecclesiastes 11:1–12:8

*Rejoice, O young man, in your youth, and let your heart cheer
you in the days of your youth. Walk in the ways of your heart and
the sight of your eyes. But know that for all these things God will
bring you into judgment. Remove vexation from your heart, and
put away pain from your body, for youth and the dawn of life are
vanity. Remember also your Creator in the days of your youth,
before the evil days come and the years draw near of which you
will say, "I have no pleasure in them." (Eccl. 11:9–12:1)*

*T*hroughout the ages, people have had strong reactions to Ecclesiastes. The poet A. M. Klein began his poem "Koheleth" about Pastor Solomon's work, saying, "Take your black quill, O Scribe, and write in wormwood and with gall." Louise Erdrich wrote that "Ecclesiastes speaks to people in tough binds, people with vendettas, a bone to pick, no dog to kick, the sour-grapers, the hurt, those who've never shucked off their adolescent angst."[1] Herman Melville had a more balanced reaction. In his classic novel *Moby Dick*, he wrote: "The truest of all men was the Man of Sorrows,

---

1. Louise Erdrich, "The Preacher," in *Out of the Garden: Women Writers on the Bible*, ed. C. Büchmann and C. Spiegel (London: Pandora, 1995), 235.

and the truest of all books is Solomon's, and Ecclesiastes is the fine hammered steel of woe." Moving in a much more positive direction, Thomas Wolfe said:

> Of all that I have ever seen cr learned, that book seems to me the noblest, the wisest, and the most powerful expression of man's life upon this earth—and also earth's highest flower of poetry, eloquence, and truth. I am not given to dogmatic judgments in the matter of literary creation, but if I had to make one I could only say that Ecclesiastes is the greatest single piece of writing I have ever known, and the wisdom expressed in it the most lasting and profound.[2]

In this chapter we come again, for the second-to-last time, to Solomon's woeful, wormwood wisdom, his literary masterpiece that still "shakes the world in pieces."[3] Open Ecclesiastes 11:1–12:8, and Pastor Solomon will shake your soul.

THE EVIL DAYS AHEAD

Unlike the previous text (which was as awkward as a little bird trying to fit a python into its mouth with three flies hovering above its beak), the structure and theme of this text is as straight and as sharp as a razor blade. Put simply, it is this: While you are still young (Eccl. 12:1–8), fear God (11:7–10) and serve others (11:1–6). Put more precisely, it is this:

> 12:1–8: Before the impending "evil days" of old age and death strike you like
> a cosmic thunderstorm (i.e., while you are still young),
> 11:1–6: work hard in order to give generously to others and
> 11:7–10: enjoy life in light of your Creator and Judge.

Since our passage begins with a lengthy description of our "end," we will do the same. Hear Pastor Solomon's words:

---

2. Klein, Erdrich, Melville, and Wolfe, quoted in Eric S. Christianson, *Ecclesiastes through the Centuries*, Blackwell Bible Commentaries (Malden, MA: Blackwell, 2007), 71, 13–14, 128, 70, respectively.
3. In his sermon on Ecclesiastes 5:13–14, John Donne preached: "Solomon shakes the world in pieces, he dissects it, and cuts it up before thee, that so thou mayest the better see how poor a thing, that particular is, whatsoever it be, that thou settest thy love upon in this world. He threads a string of the best stones, of the best jewels in this world . . . and then he shows you an *ire*, a flaw, a cloud in all these stones; he lays this infancy upon them all, vanity, and vexation of spirit." Quoted in ibid., 122.

Remember also your Creator in the days of your youth, before the evil days come and the years draw near of which you will say, "I have no pleasure in them"; before the sun and the light and the moon and the stars are darkened and the clouds return after the rain, in the day when the keepers of the house tremble, and the strong men are bent, and the grinders cease because they are few, and those who look through the windows are dimmed, and the doors on the street are shut—when the sound of the grinding is low, and one rises up at the sound of a bird, and all the daughters of song are brought low—they are afraid also of what is high, and terrors are in the way; the almond tree blossoms, the grasshopper drags itself along, and desire fails, because man is going to his eternal home, and the mourners go about the streets—before the silver cord is snapped, or the golden bowl is broken, or the pitcher is shattered at the fountain, or the wheel broken at the cistern, and the dust returns to the earth as it was, and the spirit returns to God who gave it. (Eccl. 12:1–7)

This lengthy poetic sentence is filled with beautiful imagery about a harsh reality. The intention of the imagery is emotional engagement. Instead of merely stating that "everyone gets old and dies, and it ain't fun," Pastor Solomon employs images to get us to see, hear, smell, taste, and touch the depressing decay.

He starts his "delicately sketched vignettes of old age" with the image of an impending and vicious storm[4]—"before the sun and the light and the moon and the stars are darkened and the clouds return after the rain" (Eccl. 12:2). The sun has been mentioned thirty-four times in Ecclesiastes. Now, in its final scene, as a dark curtain covers the stage, the sun, along with the other celestial lights, takes a bow. It is pitch-black. Using apocalyptic imagery that is strikingly similar to the prophets' description of the last days,[5] Solomon heightens the personal tragedy of the reader's death by comparing it to the great day of God's cosmic judgment. As at the end of the world creation will be unmade, so at the end of human life we are all unmade as well. Our end time is like *the* end time. "When you die, a world *is* ending—*yours*."[6]

4. Robert Davidson, *Ecclesiastes and the Song of Solomon*, Daily Study Bible Series 5 (Philadelphia: Westminster, 1986), 85.

5. See Isa. 13:9–10; Ezek. 30:3; 32:7–8; Joel 2:2, 10; Amos 5:18, 20; Zeph. 1:15; cf. Matt. 24:29; Mark 13:24–25.

6. Michael V. Fox, *Ecclesiastes*, JPS Bible Commentary (Philadelphia: Jewish Publication Society, 2004), 76.

From the black sky in Ecclesiastes 12:2 the imagery descends to earth in verses 3–6, describing "the haunting effects of death."[7] While "there are almost as many opinions as there are people,"[8] as Jerome comments, the interpretation of the imagery is obvious enough. This is not an allegory of the deterioration of the church before the Reformation, but rather the decline of an old man before death. It is Solomon's version of Ingrid Michaelson's "Breakable" or Sting's "Fragile."

Ecclesiastes 12:7 summarizes the sad situation. We will all die:

and the dust returns	to the earth as it was,
and the spirit returns	to God who gave it.

But before death happens, bodily frailties accumulate as we age. Like a once-vibrant but now-unattended estate, our hands, legs, teeth, eyes, ears, vocal cords, and hair slowly decay. Our hands, which once provided a living and protection, now shake ("in the day when the keepers of the house tremble"), our legs can't support the weight of our bodies for long ("and the strong men are bent"), our remaining molars can't chew food like they used to ("the grinders cease because they are few"), and our vision declines ("those who look through the windows are dimmed," Eccl. 12:3).

And if all that were not bad enough, other awful issues accompany old age. When we want our ears to work well, they don't (we can't even hear ourselves chew: "and the doors on the street are shut—when the sound of the grinding is low"), but when we would be fine with deafness, our ears work too well ("and one rises up at the sound of a bird," Eccl. 12:4). Moreover, we cannot sing like we used to. Our vocal cords "no longer have the elastic strength to make sweet music"[9] ("and all the daughters of song are brought low," v. 4b).

Finally, before we die (go to our "eternal home") and people grieve our passing ("and the mourners go about the streets"), our hair turns gray or

---

7. Christianson, *Ecclesiastes through the Centuries*, 226.

8. Jerome, *Commentary on Ecclesiastes*, trans. Richard J. Goodrich and David J. D. Miller, Ancient Christian Writers 66 (New York: Newman, 2012), 124. For example, Fox notes: "This is the most difficult section of the book. Its Hebrew is difficult, sometimes obscure, and its imagery is enigmatic." *Ecclesiastes*, 76.

9. Philip Graham Ryken, *Ecclesiastes: Why Everything Matters*, ed. R. Kent Hughes, Preaching the Word (Wheaton, IL: Crossway, 2010), 270.

white ("the almond tree blossoms"),[10] we lose our mobility and get around painfully ("the grasshopper drags itself along"), our motivation to work, our appetite for food, and our sex drive diminish ("desire fails"), and a fear of falling and of other dangers increases ("they are afraid also of what is high, and terrors are in the way," Eccl. 12:5). And then the moment comes! What was once beautiful, precious, useful, and life-giving is destroyed ("the silver cord is snapped, or the golden bowl is broken, or the pitcher is shattered at the fountain, or the wheel broken at the cistern," v. 6). Light crashes to the ground and life spills out like water. "Life is broken beyond repair. Death is final and irreversible."[11]

A Look at Death

Jane Yolen wrote forty-three sonnets—a poem a day—when her husband underwent chemotherapy for brain cancer. She entitled the collection of poems *The Radiation Sonnets: For My Love, in Sickness and in Health*. In her poem "Words" for day 38, she wrote of death as the "single syllable too awful to be said." Yet, she ends that poem knowing that the "subject" and "object" of their speech—"Death"—is "the one true word that lies within our reach."[12] It is difficult for everyone, even those dying or losing a loved one, to look death in the eyes.

In the 1936 movie *Rembrandt*, Ecclesiastes is featured in the film's final two scenes. The movie "follows the artist's life from 1642, a time of his considerable wealth and established reputation to his final years in, as the film has it, relative obscurity (c. 1668–9)."[13] Rembrandt has lost his wife, his fortune, and much of his fame. In the penultimate scene, he enters a tavern. After the young men offer their toasts ("To beauty! To woman! To youth! To love! To money!"), they turn to the artist and ask, "What about you, grandpa? You haven't given us your toast!" (They don't even recognize him.)

---

10. As Anne Bradstreet paraphrases: "My Almond-tree (gray hairs) doth flourish now, / And back, once straight, begins apace to bow." From "The Four Ages of Man," quoted in Christianson, *Ecclesiastes through the Centuries*, 236.

11. Sidney Greidanus, *Preaching Christ from Ecclesiastes: Foundations for Expository Sermons* (Grand Rapids: Eerdmans, 2010), 293.

12. Jane Yolen, *The Radiation Sonnets: For My Love, in Sickness and in Health* (Chapel Hill, NC: Algonquin Books of Chapel Hill, 2003), 75.

13. Christianson, *Ecclesiastes through the Centuries*, 138. My description of the movie follows Christianson's.

He responds, "I can't think of a toast." The crowd insists, for they had seen him "mumble something" into his glass. Rembrandt replies, "That wasn't a toast, and they weren't my words. They were the words of King Solomon. They are the best words I know!" He then quotes four different verses from Ecclesiastes (1:14, 18; 3:22), including 12:8, "Vanity of vanities . . . ; all is vanity" (cf. 1:2). The tavern erupts in laughter.

The final scene depicts Rembrandt alone in his studio. He is completing his self-portrait by looking into a cracked mirror. Through the mirror, the camera focuses on his face. He pauses, stares at himself, and utters the film's last words, "Vanity of vanities. All is vanity."

In my upstairs bathroom there is a *vanity* mirror. It has three planes of glass, two of which are on the sides, which you can open to get a full view of your face. Ecclesiastes 12:1–8 is like those two side mirrors. On one side we are to see the utter fleetingness of life, on the other side our reflection of the image of God. The first perspective comes post-poem. After that brilliant and exquisite seven-verse sentence (12:1–7), we have the book's bleak ending: "Vanity of vanities, says the Preacher; all is vanity" (12:8). This is the final time that *vanity* is used—the last of thirty-eight times—and it echoes the introduction in 1:2: "Vanity of vanities, says the Preacher, vanity of vanities! All is vanity." In light of the description of old age and death in 12:1–7, the sense of *vanity* here is fleetingness (i.e., the end of life comes too soon). Whatever mist we have to walk through to see this point of the poem, "when we peer through the murk of the images, metaphors, and symbols, we realize with a shudder that we are describing our own obliteration."[14] To borrow a phrase from Shakespeare, "Youth's a stuff will not endure."[15]

The second perspective comes pre-poem. Notice the repetition of the word *before*—"before the evil days come" (Eccl. 12:1), "before the sun" is "darkened" (v. 2), and "before the silver cord is snapped" (v. 6). These three *befores* push our eyes back to what comes before the *befores*, namely, the imperative in 12:1: "Remember also your Creator in the days of your youth." The term *youth* is defined by what comes after it—which is a description of old age and death. Thus, *youth* (which is used four times in our text; cf. *young man*, used once) is not exclusively teenagers but inclusively everyone—everyone who isn't dead or dying. So for the most part I agree with Daniel Fredericks that

14. Fox, *Ecclesiastes*, 77.
15. The line is from a song in William Shakespeare's *Twelfth Night*, act 2, scene 3.

"Qoheleth's audience probably included officials of every adult age, young and old. The 'youth' he is talking about is not pre-adulthood or adolescence; rather, it is the time of life when one is not considered 'old.'"[16] Meditation on our end should bring us to "in the beginning, God" (Gen. 1:1)! The other perspective, then, is to "remember" (consider, know, trust, obey) "your Creator" (the One who made you and continually gives you good gifts) "in the days of your youth" (before most or all of your vitality has left you).

INDUSTRY FOR OTHERS

How, then, do we remember our Creator? We do so by keeping God's commandments (Eccl. 12:13), especially "the great commandment" (Matt. 22:36, 38)—loving God and loving others. As Jesus said, "You shall love the Lord your God with all your heart and with all your soul and with all your mind" and "You shall love your neighbor as yourself" (vv. 37, 39). Pastor Solomon gives a similar summary. He exhorts us to work hard in order to give generously to others (Eccl. 11:1–6) and enjoy life in light of our Creator and Judge (11:7–10). Let's look first at his exhortation to remember our Creator by working hard so that we can be generous:

> *Cast your bread* upon the waters,
>   for you will find it after many days.
> *Give a portion* to seven, or even to eight,
>   for you know not what disaster may happen on earth.
> If the clouds are full of rain,
>   they empty themselves on the earth,
> and if a tree falls to the south or to the north,
>   in the place where the tree falls, there it will lie.
> He who observes the wind will not sow,
>   and he who regards the clouds will not reap.
>
> As you do not know the way the spirit comes to the bones in the womb
> of a woman with child, so you do not know the work of God who
> makes everything.

16. Daniel C. Fredericks, "Ecclesiastes," in Daniel C. Fredericks and Daniel J. Estes, *Ecclesiastes and the Song of Songs*, Apollos Old Testament Commentary 16 (Downers Grove, IL: InterVarsity Press, 2010), 237.

In the morning *sow your seed*, and at evening *withhold not your hand*, for you do not know which will prosper, this or that, or whether both alike will be good. (Eccl. 11:1–6)

As David Hubbard rightly notes, "Ours may be the first generation in civilized times that has not raised its young on proverbs."[17] Because of this unfortunate reality, the proverbs contained in these verses perhaps sound strange to many of us. To make sense of them, start by making some simple observations. First, notice the four commands (italicized above): "cast your bread" (Eccl. 11:1), "give a portion" (v. 2), "sow your seed" (v. 6a), and "withhold not your hand" (v. 6b).

Second, notice the phrase "you do not know," which is repeated four times (in Eccl. 11:2, 5 [2×], and 6). Admittedly, we know something about precipitation and gravity: "If the clouds are full of rain, they empty themselves on the earth, and if a tree falls to the south or to the north, in the place where the tree falls, there it will lie" (v. 3). Isn't that impressive knowledge! Yet there are some limitations to our knowledge. Three limitations are listed. Two have to do with the future: we don't know when disaster might strike (v. 2) or whether we will be prosperous (v. 6). The other limitation has to do with God: just as we do not understand perfectly how a baby is formed within a woman's womb, so we cannot comprehend everything that God does (v. 5).

When my youngest son, Simeon, was seven years old, we went to visit my oldest son, Sean, in college. When we visited Sean, we stayed in the old, refurbished granary on the farm belonging to our friends Sharon and Peter Taylor. At night, I made a fire and we warmed ourselves. Around the cast-iron wood-burning stove, we had a fireside chat. I don't know how the conversation got to the topic of heaven and hell, but it did. (Stranger things happen when you hang out with me.) Simeon asked, "What happens to babies who die in a mommy's tummy?" The question took me by surprise—not in the sense that I hadn't heard it before, but because it was coming from my seven-year-old son. I fumbled around and said something to this effect: "Whatever happens, remember that God is merciful." Simeon replied, "Yeah, maybe he brings them to heaven." He shrugged his shoulders and said, "Who knows?"

17. David Hubbard, *Ecclesiastes, Song of Solomon*, Mastering the Old Testament 15B (Dallas: Word, 1991), 223.

Wise people learn to say "who knows?" in response to a lot of questions. But wise people also learn to labor diligently in spite of their lack of knowledge. If we put together the commands to work ("cast," "give," "sow," and "withhold not your hand") with the statements of ignorance ("you do not know"), we get this: *work diligently in spite of your lack of knowledge.* Put differently, let God take care of his mysteries and let us take care of our work. The surprise is that our limitations should not lead us to despair or sloth, but rather to investment and industry. Ecclesiastes 11:4 and 6 especially touch on this theme. Verse 4 reads:

He who observes	the wind	will not sow, and
he who regards	the clouds	will not reap.

Someone who watches ("observes," "regards") the Weather Channel all day waiting for the perfect weather (no "wind" or "clouds") for planting crops might never leave the sofa. So stop the sloth. Put off the procrastinating. Ignorance is no excuse for idleness. Trust God, get off your duff, and obey verse 6:

In the morning	sow your seed, and
at evening	withhold not your hand.

Work all day. Put in a full workweek (not 24/7, but 12/6). Why? "For you do not know which will prosper, this or that, or whether both alike will be good" (Eccl. 11:6). We cannot know all the works of God (see v. 5)—"The wind blows where it wishes" (John 3:8)—but we can know that our sovereign God wants us to work. So let's work!

The wisdom literature appeals to the individual to be industrious. It persistently rolls us out of bed and pushes us off the sofa. Yet biblical industry is not industriousness for mere self-improvement. Rather, our work is to center on others for the benefit of others. This is what is taught in Ecclesiastes 11:1–2—God's goads to get us to give generously:

Cast your bread upon the waters,	for you will find it after many days.
Give a portion to seven, or even to eight,	for you know not what disaster may happen on earth.

The images are of "fearless generosity."[18] The casting of bread upon the waters is an image of complete commitment and courage. It is likely that the image of tossing a stale-hard, easy-to-float piece of pita bread in a river is not that of a careless risk but a calculated one. Notice the confidence expressed in the phrase "you will find it after many days." Many commentators (and I agree with them) see the bread image as representative of ancient sea trade. For example, to sail a few ships from Palestine to Italy and back was a perilous but profitable enterprise. Even if one of three ships made it to port, sold its cargo, and received more goods to travel back and trade, the whole venture was worth it. The profit was enormous (cf. 1 Kings 10:22). The point of Ecclesiastes 11:1, then, is "nothing ventured, nothing gained," to borrow a traditional investment slogan.

Ecclesiastes 11:2 follows: "Give a portion to seven, or even to eight, for you know not what disaster may happen on earth." This verse might speak of spreading the risk (i.e., don't just send the *Santa Maria*, but also the *Niña* and the *Pinta*). But more likely, it deals with diversifying earnings rather than investments. I say this because of the imperative *give*. We are to "give a portion to seven, or even to eight" (v. 2). If we gain from a courageous investment, we are to give just as courageously. Why? "For you know not what disaster may happen on earth" (v. 2). The parable of the rich fool should come to mind. Instead of making money so as to hoard it, we are to spend it on others, because we never know whether this very night our soul might be required of us (see Luke 12:20). Do not lay up treasure for yourself; instead, be "rich toward God" (v. 21) by richly giving to others. Before it is too late, divide your earnings "seven"—no, make it *"eight"*!—ways. This is the *better than perfect* way to live . . . and give.

According to Pastor Solomon, there are lots of things we don't know ("You do not know. You do not know. You do not know."). But as Christians, we do know this: "You know the grace of our Lord Jesus Christ, that though he was rich, yet for your sake he became poor, so that you by his poverty might become rich" (2 Cor. 8:9). So as our humble Creator/Savior (Col. 1:13–20) humbly served us through the sacrifice of the cross (cf. Phil. 2:6–8), let us be of the same "mind" (v. 5). Let us put first "the interests of others" (v. 4). Do not be a "wicked and slothful servant" (Matt. 25:26), but a "good and

---

18. Richard Schultz, "Ecclesiastes," in *Baker Commentary on the Bible*, ed. Gary M. Burge and Andrew E. Hill, 2nd ed. (Grand Rapids: Baker, 2011), 601.

faithful servant" (v. 23) who serves others by sharing what God has entrusted to you. As Phil Ryken observes, "God invites us to be venture capitalists for the kingdom of God."[19] Amen! As John Wesley preached, "Having, First, gained all you can, and, Secondly, saved all you can, Then give all you can."[20] Let us sow "bountifully" (2 Cor. 9:6) in order to "give . . . freely" (Deut. 15:10). Let us do "honest work with [our] own hands, so that [we] may have something to share with anyone in need" (Eph. 4:28).

Enjoyment under God

Added to our industry is our enjoyment. For the seventh and final time in Ecclesiastes, enjoyment is commanded (11:7–8).[21] Verse 7 says, "Light is sweet, and it is pleasant for the eyes to see the sun." That is, it's good to be alive! Verse 8 continues, "So if a person lives many years, *let him rejoice* in them all; but *let him remember* that the days of darkness[22] will be many. All that comes is vanity [breath]." Even in light of death, it is good to rejoice every day.

That theme of rejoicing continues into Ecclesiastes 11:9–10. I'll also add 12:1 because it continues with the themes of youth and enjoyment or pleasure (in this case, "no pleasure"):

> *Rejoice*, O young man, in your youth, and let your heart cheer you in the days of your youth. Walk in the ways of your heart and the sight of your eyes. But know that for all these things God will bring you into judgment.
>
> *Remove* vexation from your heart, and put away pain from your body, for youth and the dawn of life are vanity.
>
> *Remember* also your Creator in the days of your youth, before the evil days come and the years draw near of which you will say, "I have no pleasure in them." (Eccl. 11:9–12:1)

19. Ryken, *Ecclesiastes*, 256.
20. From Wesley's sermon "The Use of Money," in *The Works of John Wesley*, 14 vols. (1872; repr., Grand Rapids: Baker, 2007), 6:133.
21. "Cheerfulness, here, is not merely permitted; it is commanded, and represented as an essential element of piety." Ernst Hengstenberg, quoted in Michael A. Eaton, *Ecclesiastes: An Introduction and Commentary*, Tyndale Old Testament Commentaries 16 (Downers Grove, IL: InterVarsity Press, 1983), 145.
22. Those dark days refer to old age and death (cf. Eccl. 12:1–7, esp. "evil days").

We could summarize this section with three Rs—*rejoice, remove,* and *remember*. (That'll preach!) Yet all those commands teach the same truth, namely, to *enjoy life in light of your Creator and Judge*.

The "enjoy life" part comes in a number of phrases. Even the final phrase in Ecclesiastes 12:1 implies that we should have pleasure in the days of our youth. The most obvious admonition comes from 11:9: "rejoice" and "let your heart cheer you." It also comes from the two negative admonitions in verse 10: "Remove vexation [i.e., sorrow or unhappiness] from your heart" and "put away pain from your body." The parallelism of "your heart" and "your body" could be antithetical (i.e., your soul and body) or synonymous (heart = body). I think they mean the same thing and that the command here is a rhetorical merism—that our total self should rejoice.

What motives are given? Again, the motive of time is mentioned at the end of Ecclesiastes 11:10. We should "remove vexation" because "youth" (i.e., "the dawn of life") is "vanity" (i.e., short-lived). The new and central motivation, though, is God.[23] God is our Creator (12:1), but also our Judge (11:9). Think Genesis. Think Revelation.

Let me take you to this motive by walking you through the three parts of Ecclesiastes 11:9. First, we should rejoice while we can: "Rejoice . . . in your youth" (v. 9). Second, we even have the freedom to do what we want:

Walk in the ways of your heart and the sight of your eyes. (Eccl. 11:9)

Finally, "but know that for all these things God will bring you into judgment" (v. 9). This could refer to the judgment of death. But since there is a definite article in the Hebrew—"*the* judgment"—more likely it envisions "the day of judgment" (e.g., Matt. 11:22, 24; 12:36, 41, 42). This reading certainly

---

23. Fredericks ("Ecclesiastes," 232) also sees this phrase *at the center*:

```
11:3    A—clouds and rain
7          B—light and sun
8              C—consider dark days
                  D—all that comes is breath
9                      E—enjoy your youth
                          F—know that God will judge
10                     E'—enjoy your youth
                      D'—youth is breath
12:1              C'—consider God before dark days
2          B'—sun and light
       A'—clouds and rain
```

fits with the apocalyptic tone of Ecclesiastes 12:2, as well as the next time judgment is mentioned in 12:14. So "the judgment" refers to "that day," as Jesus calls it in the Sermon on the Mount, when everyone will stand before him (see Matt. 7:21–23), when even our secret thoughts, words, and actions will be evaluated (see Rom. 2:16; cf. Eccl. 12:14).

Some people think that the coming judgment stifles and chokes our freedom and fun. But this is precisely the opposite of the way Solomon sees it. It is rather due to God's judgment that we can "live life fully to the end."[24] *Because* we are marching toward old age, death, and the judgment, we are able to "drink wine (9:7), enjoy food (2:25), be sensual (9:9), seek the sun (11:7), enjoy a rest (4:6), clean up (9:8), pursue dancing, embracing, peace, laughter and love (3:4–5, 8), appreciate money (7:11–12), [and] take pleasure in gardens and music (2:5, 8)."[25] Put differently, *because* we are marching toward God, we can rejoice responsibly.[26] We can pursue with all our hearts attitudes and actions—such as "righteousness, faith, love, and peace" (2 Tim. 2:22)—that bring along with them genuine joy. Holiness leads to happiness. Aimless indulgence leads to endless misery. "Walk in the ways of your heart" (Eccl. 11:9) is not Romanticism but Biblicism. To neglect God is to neglect joy. God has designed us for pleasure, to enjoy all the pleasures that come from being faithful to him and his rules.

Remember him. Fear him. And watch the freedom and fun follow.

Breath

In 1969 the Irish playwright Samuel Beckett wrote the play *Breath*. It is unusually terse, lasting only about thirty-five seconds! Ryken describes it:

> As the curtain opens, there is a pile of rubbish on the stage, illuminated by a single light. The light dims and then brightens a little before going com-

---

24. Fox, *Ecclesiastes*, 74. Fox uses this phrase in light of death, not the judgment day, as I see it.

25. Fredericks, "Ecclesiastes," 237.

26. "Doesn't his reminder of God's judgment put a damper on our rejoicing? The answer is, No . . . . In other words, the Teacher commands 'responsible pleasure, not license to exploit others or squander our own bodies and abilities.'" Ellen F. Davis, *Proverbs, Ecclesiastes, and the Song of Songs* (Louisville, KY: Westminster John Knox, 2000), 222, quoted in Greidanus, *Preaching Christ from Ecclesiastes*, 287. Fox notes: "Some early readers worried that the advice here to follow one's desires might be conducive to hedonism or heresy (see Koh. R. 1:3). As a precaution, some manuscripts of the Septuagint add 'innocently' after 'your heart' in verse 9." *Ecclesiastes*, 75. Whether we add that protective measure to our translation or not, the sense is correct.

pletely out. There are no words or actors in the drama, only a sound track with a human cry, followed by an inhaled breath, an exhaled breath, and another cry.[27]

If Beckett's play comes to your city, you might want to pass on it, since the plot has been given away. But please don't pass on this point: Whether you are a modernist who dislikes Christianity (like Beckett) or a postmodernist who likes Christianity (whoever and whatever you are), the dark days are coming. Life will be gone sooner than you ever imagined. It will seem like a thirty-five-second breath of air. 34, 33, 32 . . . 10, 9, 8 . . . 3, 2, 1.

Zero.

So, then, what are we to do? Put on this lasting and profound wisdom: Before the impending "evil days" of old age and death strike you like a cosmic thunderstorm (i.e., while you are still "young"), work hard in order to give generously to others and enjoy life in light of your Creator and Judge.

---

27. Ryken, *Ecclesiastes*, 274. For Beckett's one-page script, see http://www.bradcolbourne.com /breath.txt.

17

Repining Restlessness

Ecclesiastes 12:9–14

The end of the matter; all has been heard. Fear God and keep
his commandments, for this is the whole duty of man. For God
will bring every deed into judgment, with every secret thing,
whether good or evil. (Eccl. 12:13–14)

Can any praise be worthy of the Lord's majesty? How magnificent his strength! How inscrutable his wisdom! Man is one of your creatures, Lord, and his instinct is to praise you. He bears about him the mark of death, the sign of his own sin, to remind him that you thwart the proud. But still, since he is part of your creation, he wishes to praise you. The thought of you stirs him so deeply that he cannot be content unless he praises you, because you made us for yourself and our hearts find no peace until they rest in you.[1]

Above is the famous opening prayer of Augustine's *Confessions*, his autobiography of sorts, wherein he testifies to God and his readers how his restless heart found rest in Christ. Augustine confesses how, after three decades of drinking the desiccated dregs of sexual immorality and sipping from this

1. Augustine, *Confessions*, trans. R. S. Pine-Coffin (New York: Penguin, 1961), 21.

world's parched philosophies, he quenched his impoverished soul with the living waters of Jesus Christ. He confesses how he gave up feasting on nature's appetites—drunkenness, lust, anger, and jealousy (Rom. 13:13)—and came instead to feed on the Bread of Life (John 6:35, 48).

In Ecclesiastes 12:9–14, we come to the climax of Solomon's *Confessions*. Like Augustine, Pastor Solomon throughout Ecclesiastes has confessed his failings as well as his findings. Now in the final verses he announces his ultimate discovery: God's remedy for what the poet George Herbert called our "repining restlessness" (our God-given yearning for ultimate rest).[2]

A Word on the Words of the Wise

Before we unravel Solomon's remedy, look first at his word on the words of the wise. We should be glad that the final word in this book is not Ecclesiastes 12:8: "Vanity of vanities, says the Preacher; all is vanity." Instead, verses 9–14 sound like an editorial appendix or epilogue, but also so much more:

> Besides being wise, the Preacher also taught the people knowledge, weighing and studying and arranging many proverbs with great care. The Preacher sought to find words of delight, and uprightly he wrote words of truth.
>
> The words of the wise are like goads, and like nails firmly fixed are the collected sayings; they are given by one Shepherd. My son, beware of anything beyond these. Of making many books there is no end, and much study is a weariness of the flesh.
>
> The end of the matter; all has been heard. Fear God and keep his commandments, for this is the whole duty of man. For God will bring every deed into judgment, with every secret thing, whether good or evil.

Two mistakes are often made when reading these verses. The first is to assume that because "the Preacher" (*Pastor Solomon*, as I have been calling him) is referred to in the past tense, these verses must have been written by another author, usually called a *frame narrator*. This may be, but is not necessarily the case. Pastor Solomon could have created this frame narrator

---

2. "Yet let him keep the rest, / But keep them with repining restlessness: / Let him be rich and weary, that at least, / If goodness lead him not, yet weariness / May toss him to my breast." From the last stanza of George Herbert's "The Pulley," in *The Complete English Works*, Everyman's Library 204 (New York: Knopf, 1995), 156.

as a character, as is still done in books today. For this book to end with such artistic flair would be fitting. Another option is that Solomon is speaking about himself by using another voice. Jesus sometimes did this: "And as Jesus was going up to Jerusalem, he took the twelve disciples aside, and on the way he said to them, 'See, we are going up to Jerusalem. And the Son of Man will be delivered over,'" and so on (Matt. 20:17–18). Jesus is talking about himself! Therefore, my educated assumption is that Pastor Solomon wrote everything in Ecclesiastes, even the ending. As an author today might be asked to write a brief biography and book summary for the back of his own book, so Solomon gives an honest appraisal of himself and his work.

The second mistake is to view Ecclesiastes 12:9–14 as an orthodox corrective of 1:2–12:8, the sense being this: "Forget everything the Preacher has preached and remember the heart of the Torah: fear God and obey his law." This view is absolutely wrong. There is no thematic disconnect between the final verses and the rest of the book. These verses affirm what was "affirmed previously: (1) the value of revering God (3:14; 5:7; 7:18; 8:12–13), (2) the need to obey God's commands (e.g., 5:4–6, which cites Deut. 23:21–23 regarding vows; cf. also 8:5, literally, 'a command-keeper'), and (3) the certainty of divine judgment, either under the sun or after death (3:15, 17; 5:6; 7:17; 8:12–13; 11:9; possibly 8:5–6)."[3] Thus, I agree with Richard Schultz that "at the core [the Preacher] has not strayed from the central convictions of the Israelite faith."[4] Better yet, Daniel Fredericks writes that the summary ending "is not 'changing the subject'; it *is* the subject of Ecclesiastes."[5] Indeed! The ending is the rudder that steers the ship. Without verses 9–14 (esp. vv. 13–14) to guide, we would easily read Ecclesiastes wrongly.

Having avoided these potential mistakes, we are ready to move on to the end of the matter, starting with Ecclesiastes 12:9–10:

> Besides being wise, the Preacher also taught the people knowledge, weighing and studying and arranging many proverbs with great care. The Preacher sought to find words of delight, and uprightly he wrote words of truth.

3. Richard Schultz, "Ecclesiastes," in *Baker Commentary on the Bible*, ed. Gary M. Burge and Andrew E. Hill, 2nd ed. (Grand Rapids: Baker, 2011), 606.
4. Ibid.
5. Daniel C. Fredericks, "Ecclesiastes," in Daniel C. Fredericks and Daniel J. Estes, *Ecclesiastes and the Song of Songs*, Apollos Old Testament Commentary 16 (Downers Grove, IL: InterVarsity Press, 2010), 251.

As we learned in the previous passage about courageous generosity in relation to money, so here generosity relates to wisdom. Pastor Solomon didn't hoard his learning. He collected knowledge in order to give it away. And he still gives it away! As elastic Ecclesiastes has stretched around the world for the past three thousand years, Solomon has distributed his always-contemporary wisdom to billions of people.

Furthermore, Solomon gave his wisdom away as a labor of love. When it came to teaching, he made it easy on the ears. What Jonathan Edwards once wrote about his own aims summarizes well Pastor Solomon's teaching ministry: "I should think myself in the way of my duty to raise the affections of my hearers as high as I possibly can provided that they are affected by nothing but the truth."[6] Solomon considered and studied a matter. Then he arranged what he had learned with great care.[7] Finally, he found a way to communicate those truths clearly and interestingly. For example, he didn't just write, "Community is important"; instead, he said it this way: "A threefold cord is not quickly broken" (Eccl. 4:12). Isn't that more beautiful, memorable, and compelling? He didn't just write, "Don't think that life is about possessing every earthly pleasure that money can buy"; instead, he said that pursuing such pleasures is like "striving after wind" (2:11). Isn't that intangible image so tangible?

Carefully evaluating, skillfully arranging, and then artistically delivering "words of delight" (Eccl. 12:10) is part of the preacher's calling. If I am at a pastor's conference and I hear a sermon that lacks "logical clarity, literary artistry, and intellectual integrity,"[8] I leave the room, if able. Don't waste my time, preacher. The dark days are coming soon. I've got better things to do than to hear you make the Bible boring. As Ambrose taught: "Therefore let your sermons be flowing, let them be clear and lucid so that by suitable disputation you may pour sweetness into the ears of the people and by the grace of your words may persuade

---

6. Jonathan Edwards, *The Works of Jonathan Edwards*, ed. Edward Hickman, 2 vols. (Carlisle, PA: Banner of Truth, 1992), 1:391.

7. And artistry as well! "The real artistry of this brilliant little scroll [Ecclesiastes] lies in its thematic assembly." Eric S. Christianson, *Ecclesiastes through the Centuries*, Blackwell Bible Commentaries (Malden, MA: Blackwell, 2007), 258.

8. Philip Graham Ryken, *Ecclesiastes: Why Everything Matters*, ed. R. Kent Hughes, Preaching the Word (Wheaton, IL: Crossway, 2010), 276.

the crowd to follow willingly where you lead."[9] The preacher's job is not to tickle ears but to open them.

The reason our ears are to be opened is so that wisdom might be poured in! Words of wisdom effect change. Or, to switch the metaphor from wisdom poured into our ears to sharp spurs pushed into our sides, Solomon writes:

> The words of the wise are like goads, and like nails firmly fixed are the collected sayings; they are given by one Shepherd. My son, beware of anything beyond these. Of making many books there is no end, and much study is a weariness of the flesh. (Eccl. 12:11–12)

Genuine words of wisdom are sufficient, God-given truths that sting and stabilize us.[10] The sufficiency comes from Ecclesiastes 12:12, where the reader is addressed as "my son," a personal, familiar way in wisdom literature of speaking to those under a sage's tutelage. And here, as students, we are warned to rest in this written revelation. There is no need to look to other books in the hope of gaining better answers. Study the topics of work, time, death, companionship, wisdom, injustice, worship, and politics all you like—it will amount to nothing more than what is essentially taught here. The book of Ecclesiastes is sufficient to instruct us how to walk in wisdom while living east of Eden. What is required is not more books for more study, but more obedience to what has already been revealed.

Moreover, God's revelation is sufficient because it is God-given: "The words of the wise . . . are given by one Shepherd" (Eccl. 12:11). In many Bible translations, *Shepherd* is capitalized because the translators, or at least the pious publishers, think the word symbolizes God. Indeed it does. Praise God for pious publishers! In Isaiah (e.g., Isa. 40:11) and the Psalms (e.g., Ps. 80:1), God is called a shepherd; and in Ezekiel, the Messiah—"the coming Davidic shepherd king"—is called the "one shepherd" (Ezek. 34:23; 37:24), which Jesus in turn calls himself in John 10:16.[11] Moreover, in the wisdom

---

9. Ambrose, "Letter 15, to Constantius," in *Proverbs, Ecclesiastes, Song of Solomon*, ed. J. Robert Wright and Thomas C. Oden, Ancient Christian Commentary on Scripture 9 (Downers Grove, IL: InterVarsity Press, 2005), 282.

10. Brandon Levering, "The End of the Matter," a sermon on Ecclesiastes 12:8–14, preached at Westgate Church (Weston, MA), November 11, 2012.

11. Sidney Greidanus, *Preaching Christ from Ecclesiastes: Foundations for Expository Sermons* (Grand Rapids: Eerdmans, 2010), 302. Cf. Nicholas Perrin, "Messianism in the Narrative Frame of Ecclesiastes?," *Revue Biblique* 108 (2001): 51–57.

literature God is clearly seen as the source of wisdom (cf. Job 28:12, 23; Prov. 2:6). Therefore, I agree with the traditional reading. Capitalize the *S*! The "one Shepherd" is "the good shepherd" (John 10:11). Our Lord's breath comes through these words (even through the "breath of breaths" parts).

What, then, is the purpose of these inspired, sufficient words? Their purpose is "for reproof, for correction, and for training in righteousness" (2 Tim. 3:16)—or, following the imagery here, to sting and stabilize us. The "sting" comes from the goad analogy. A goad is a long staff with a sharp nail embedded into it. If needed, a shepherd would use it to move his sheep in the right direction and away from danger. Sometimes God's wisdom is painful but necessary to receive. Without the pain, there is no gain; without the prodding, we would walk in the wrong direction or down a perilous path. This is true of Ecclesiastes. Has it pricked your conscience? Driven you to repentance? Pushed you forward in faith? If so, God's goad has been for your good (cf. Acts 26:13–14).

Ecclesiastes stings! But it also stabilizes. Its wisdom is "like nails firmly fixed." This image could be synonymous with that of the goads, yet it seems to symbolize stability. Think of it this way. You are like a piece of driftwood that has finally floated to shore. Wisdom is the carpenter who comes along, picks you up, sets you against a safe and straight wall, and hammers a few nails through you to keep you in place. Or consider a more inviting image. You are like a tent, and wisdom is like four tent pegs. Wisdom puts you in your place and protects you from being blown away by the wicked wind. Genuine words of wisdom are sufficient, God-given truths that sting and stabilize us.

THE DARK DESCENT

God's Word stings and stabilizes us one final time in Ecclesiastes' final few lines. Like Virgil in Dante's *Inferno*, Solomon has taken us on a tour—not of damned people but of a cursed world. In this dark descent we have seen the unbearable brevity of our labors. "What has been done is what will be done" (Eccl. 1:9); "There is no remembrance of former things" (v. 11). All our work eventually goes up in smoke. We have also seen the limit and limitations of human wisdom. What we can know (2:14; 3:12, 14; 9:5; 11:9) is often eclipsed by what we can't know (3:21; 6:12; 7:24; 8:17; 9:1, 12). "You know not" (11:2), Solomon says. "You do not know" (v. 6). "You do not know . . . you do not know" (v. 5).

Moreover, we have journeyed through the house of hedonism only to find it hollow. It is empty of genuine meaning and lasting happiness, yet full of the God-ordained bitter aftertaste: those unexpected, unavoidable, and awful consequences of sin. Finally, whether it was the vanity of our worldly work, wisdom, pleasures, or whatever else Solomon has shown us, the days of darkness and death consume us all. The tick and tock of time hangs over our heads, while the trapdoor of death lies beneath our feet.

But unlike Dante's *Inferno*, where at the entrance we read, "Abandon all hope, ye who enter here," the exit of Ecclesiastes reads, "Abandon all hopelessness." Leave behind the idea that there is no cure to the *dis-ease* of our *disease*, no answer to our repining restlessness. Here is the answer! Consider the cure: "The end of the matter; all has been heard. Fear God and keep [or *obey*] his commandments, for this is the whole duty of man" (Eccl. 12:13).

So much for human autonomy! Solomon crushes that cult under his heel. Here he calls all the children of "man" (Eccl. 12:13), not just one "son" (v. 12) or a few students, to listen to his clearest and perhaps most convicting command. He claims that the fundamental reason we have been created is to be in relationship with our Creator (v. 1), a relationship in which we reverently acknowledge God as King and seek in humble submission to heed all his commands (cf. Matt. 28:18–20). This is the answer. This is the end of the matter.

One day I was listening to a classical music station whose program host read an advertisement for a retirement home that had as its slogan: "Life on Your Own Terms." I had to laugh as I heard this slogan because if anyone would know the vanity of attempting to live life on one's own terms, it would be those who have most experienced what life has to offer. From reading Ecclesiastes, I believe Solomon would have reacted just as I did. He would have laughed, if not cried, at such foolishness. Solomon had lived "Life on His Own Terms" and found that such living was not a genuine retirement from restlessness. The real retirement from restlessness came only when he began to live "Life on God's Terms," the terms written in Ecclesiastes 12:13.

Perhaps the terms *fear* and *obey* are not the terms that we either expected or wanted to read at the end of Ecclesiastes. Modern people tend to find the words *freedom* (instead of *fear*) and *independence* (instead of *obedience*) much easier to swallow. The words *fear* and *obey* sound so constricting. After all, we live and breathe and move and have our being in a made-to-order, drive-thru culture. We like things done our way and done fast: fat to skinny, dumb to smart, sad to happy, godless to godly, all with the snap of a finger, the push of a button, or the dial of a phone—God in our hearts, fast and easy! But the Word of God corrects our consumer Christianity and spoiled spirituality. The words *fear* and *obey* are the precise words that God wants us to reflect on and heed. Fearing God and obeying his commands are his solution—the only solution that truly satisfies.

To fear God (i.e., Yahweh)[12] is the central concept of the wisdom literature of the Bible. It refers simply to an attitude of submission to, respect for, dependence on, and worship of the Lord (see Eccl. 5:1–7)—*trembling trust*, as I have summarized it before. "Serve the LORD with fear," wrote the psalmist, "and rejoice with trembling" (Ps. 2:11). To fear God embodies faith and hope in God, as well as a genuine love for him. And when, by the gift of God, someone possesses the fear of God, sin loses its sweetness and strength. Obedience to the Word of God follows naturally because it becomes the delight of the soul. In the language of the Westminster Shorter Catechism, this "new obedience" (Q. 87) to "the word of God" (Q. 2) for the glory of God (Q. 1) flows from faith in Christ, wherein we "rest upon Him alone for salvation" (Q. 86). Therefore, the fear of God and obedience to his revelation are (in both Old and New Testaments) the two inseparable components of genuine faith—"the obedience of faith" (Rom. 1:5; 16:26). For this reason, some scholars use the terms *fear* and *faith* interchangeably,[13] and others go so far as to say that Solomon "has

12. Some scholars make too much of Ecclesiastes' use of "fear God" instead of "the fear of the Lord." Such language, while uncommon, is not unprecedented (see esp. Gen. 22:12; Job 1:9; cf. Job 40:1–2). Ecclesiastes was written by a Hebrew sage who surely understood "God" as "the LORD"—"the God of Abraham, the God of Isaac, and the God of Jacob" (Ex. 3:6). Moreover, this "God" in Ecclesiastes (named forty times in the book) certainly acts like the God of the Pentateuch (see Eccl. 2:26; 3:9–18; 5:1–7, 18–20; 6:1–2; 7:13–14; 8:16–9:1; 11:5, 9; 12:1, 7). Daniel J. Estes, *Handbook on the Wisdom Books and Psalms: Job, Psalms, Proverbs, Ecclesiastes, Song of Songs* (Grand Rapids: Baker Academic, 2005), 382. Estes argues that the term "fear Elohim" rather than "fear Yahweh" is used in Ecclesiastes because the book was "written to a universal audience" (i.e., not just Israel).

13. Cf. Graeme Goldsworthy, *Gospel and Wisdom: Israel's Wisdom Literature in the Christian Life*, Biblical Classics Library (London: Paternoster, 1995), 157; Michael V. Fox, *Ecclesiastes*, JPS Bible Commentary (Philadelphia: Jewish Publication Society, 2004), ix.

anticipated perhaps the deepest mystery of the gospel: The just shall live by faith (Hab 2:3; Rom 1:16–17; Gal 3:11; Heb 10:38)."[14]

First Motivation: Joy

If we are struggling to embrace the terms *fear* and *keep* (*obey*) as the answer to our emptiness, God graciously provides two motivations. First, there is the motivation of joy.

The Myth of Sisyphus is the legendary Greek tale of King Sisyphus, who was condemned to roll a large rock up a mountain, watch it tumble back down, and bring that boulder back up again—for eternity. With this myth in mind, the philosopher Albert Camus wrote an essay entitled "The Myth of Sisyphus" (1942) wherein he argued for what he called "the philosophy of the absurd." Similar to the tone of Ecclesiastes, he wrote of "man's futile search for meaning . . . in the face of an unintelligible world devoid of God and eternity." But unlike the teaching of Ecclesiastes, Camus argued that our response to this reality should be absurdity. He used the fate of King Sisyphus to illustrate: our lives are like his—we push the rock up and watch it roll down, only to do it again and again. But imagine the struggle itself as being "enough to fill a man's heart." In other words (in Camus' words), "imagine Sisyphus happy."[15] But this is impossible to imagine. The solution is not just an attitude adjustment that turns his frown upside down each time he sees the rock roll back down. No, the solution is not revolution against reality, but rather an embrace of the ultimate reality. It is not rebellion against God, but relationship with him. To expand on this idea: there is no straight line to happiness; one has to go through—and stay with—God to get there.

Here's how it works. If we try to take the straight line from self to happiness, "all the things that we call the 'goods' of life—health, riches, possessions, position, sensual pleasures, honors, and prestige—slip through our hands."[16] But if we go through God (not making idols of creation but living in dependence on the Creator), then whatever we receive from his hand

14. Duane A. Garrett, *Proverbs, Ecclesiastes, Songs of Songs*, New American Commentary 14 (Nashville: Broadman & Holman, 1993), 345.

15. Albert Camus, *The Myth of Sisyphus and Other Essays*, trans. Justin O'Brien (New York: Alfred A. Knopf, 1967), 123.

16. Walter C. Kaiser, *Ecclesiastes: Total Life*, Everyman's Bible Commentary (Chicago: Moody, 1979), 59.

is seen as a gift that brings joy. I pray that we have learned this one, if we have learned any lesson from Ecclesiastes, for seven times we have heard a refrain that reflects this philosophy of holy happiness (Eccl. 2:10, 24–26; 3:12–13; 5:18–19; 8:15; 9:7–9; 11:7–10): "Everyone should eat and drink and take pleasure in all his toil" (3:13). "Enjoy life" (9:9). "Rejoice . . . in your youth" (11:9).

Like dark storm clouds that move across the summer sky until the sun finally strikes through, Ecclesiastes intentionally waits for certain key points in the drama to penetrate the darkness—to shine the sweet light of what life looks like under the reign of God. This stark comparison brings out the beauty of life *under the sun* when directed *by the Son*. When one devotes one's life to the Lord, the mundane march through this passing world becomes a dance of eternal significance. Yet it is not as though this world stops being cursed or becomes a substitute for the world to come. We remain in this fallen world eating, drinking, and working, but we do so to the glory of God and to the satisfaction of our souls.

This is the way God works. He delights in irony. He loves to turn the values of this world on their heads, that is, right side up. Those who labor only for the mouth will not find satisfaction, but those who hunger and thirst after righteousness, as Jesus said, will be filled (Matt. 5:6).

Second Motivation: Judgment

One reason to fear and obey is the positive motivation of joy. But if that is not enough to persuade us to abandon the godless life, God graciously extends another motivation: judgment.[17] This is what we find in Ecclesiastes 12:14. After the decree to fear God and keep his commandments, we read, "For God will bring every deed into judgment, with every secret thing, whether good or evil."

This verse can be read in one of two ways, depending on our relationship with the Lord (or lack thereof). If we have yet to realize that God is in charge of this exceedingly complex universe and therefore that we are not in charge,

---

17. See Choon-Leong Seow, "'Beyond Them, My Son, Be Warned': The Epilogue of Qohelet Revisited," in *Wisdom, You Are My Sister: Studies in Honor of Roland E. Murphy, O.Carm., on the Occasion of His Eightieth Birthday*, ed. Michal L. Barre, Catholic Biblical Quarterly Monograph Series 29 (Washington, DC: Catholic Biblical Association of America, 1997), 139. Seow notes, "It is probable that an eschatological judgment is meant in 12:14."

then the door to the kingdom of God and a meaningful life remains closed. Our self-made keys simply won't fit the lock, no matter how hard and long we try. If this describes you, then this final verse serves as a final warning.

The weight of the warning falls on the words *every* and *secret*. Every secret deed is recorded and will be assessed by God. Think of it this way: on the day you were born, God hit the RECORD button, and on the day you die, he'll hit STOP and REWIND and then PLAY. Each and every thought, word, and action (the emphasis falls on *action*) will be judged by him (cf. Eccl. 11:9–12:7).[18] What a frightening thought! If we will not let joy draw us to a saving relationship with God through faith, then this promise of *judgment*—this "goad"—may still reach us and move us through the narrow gate that leads to life (Matt. 7:13–14). Let this final verse be a gracious invitation, not a sentence of condemnation.[19]

But if you have come to God in faith (or *fear*), and if you are willing to live happily under his reign, then this last verse serves as a reminder of the comfort that will come when God balances the scales of justice at the "judgment" (Eccl. 12:14)—vindicating the righteous and condemning the wicked.

The end of Ecclesiastes brings eschatological hope for those who walk by faith and not by sight.[20] There is no need for despair or pessimism. God will win. The Judge of all will do right. Christ will crush the serpent's head. Soon he will straighten this crooked world. So be not dismayed. Have faith *now* in the *future*. Believe that the Lord will make everything right. Leap off the ash heap. Stand up straight. Walk forward in faith. Obey what God has said. And count it all joy as you do so.

THE *END* OF ECCLESIASTES

Without a doubt, Ecclesiastes is a dark book, and Solomon has taken us to some very dark places. Such darkness—his realistic look at work, wisdom, pleasure, loneliness, old age, death, and so on—can be depressing. In fact, on several occasions when I have read through Ecclesiastes I have actually

18. Cf. WCF 33:1.

19. Fox writes, "In some Masoretic editions, and in public readings, verse 13 is repeated, so that the book not end with a threat." *Ecclesiastes*, 85.

20. I am indebted to Peter J. Leithart for his thoughts on this verse and others like it (e.g., Eccl. 3:16–17; 11:9). See *Solomon among the Postmoderns* (Grand Rapids: Brazos, 2008), esp. 100–101, 163, 166–67.

become depressed. I do not become depressed easily or often, and rarely do I get depressed by simply reading the Bible. Yet it was the Bible that depressed me. Thus, I gladly accepted this depression because I reasoned that it was a crucial part of our Author's intention. It was the way I was supposed to *feel* after reading and thinking about such things.

Our culture, like every other culture that I am aware of, finds no value in depression. We despise it so much that we have taken nearly every medical precaution and treatment available to eliminate it. More and more, our world resembles the imaginary world described in Aldous Huxley's famous novel *Brave New World.* In that "world," the government required all its citizens to consume the drug Soma, which made everyone happy and ensured peace and prosperity. Yet it provided these benefits at the expense of genuine existence. Human beings sacrificed their humanity by eliminating unhappiness.

Depressed into Dependence

Ecclesiastes describes not a brave new world, but a frightening old world still under the curse of Genesis 3. Thus, this book gives no duloxetine for the disenchanted. It provides no Prozac for the pain. It offers no Soma for the sad soul. Rather, God's Word prescribes a seemingly distasteful but effective elixir for any and every child of Adam. If you are a fallen human being living in this fallen world, Ecclesiastes was written to depress you. It was written to depress you into dependence on our joyous God and his blessed will for your life.

This book is God's reminder that if you are attempting to live the "meaningful" secular life—"a life without absolutes, a life lived out of values without reference to God, a life that expects lasting satisfaction from earthbound things"[21]—you are attempting to grasp the unattainable. You are like a foolish child trying to catch the winds of a hurricane within the strands of a butterfly net.

The best remedy for the depression caused by this realistic observation and experience of the world is not to pop pill after pill but rather to digest once and for all the goodness of God. The ultimate remedy to meaninglessness and the depression caused by a godless life is God. The Lord alone can

---

21. Gordon J. Keddie, quoted in T. M. Moore, *Ecclesiastes: Ancient Wisdom When All Else Fails* (Downers Grove, IL: InterVarsity Press, 2001), 91.

fill the void in human hearts. This *end*, or goal, is precisely what we find at the *end* of Ecclesiastes (12:13–14).

"Woe to You . . . Come to Me"

Two scenes in Matthew 11 portray Jesus in the same way that God is depicted at the end of Ecclesiastes. In the first scene Jesus is portrayed as the powerful Judge who denounces those who heard his words of wisdom and saw his mighty deeds, yet rejected him. "Woe to you," he thunders. "I tell you that it will be more tolerable on the day of judgment for the land of Sodom than for you" (Matt. 11:20–24). Jesus himself will bring "every deed"—sins of commission and omission—"into judgment" (Eccl. 12:14).[22] As Paul was later to say, "We must all appear before the judgment seat of Christ, so that each one may receive what is due for what he has done in the body, whether good or evil" (2 Cor. 5:10).

The second scene, which is right next to the first, is quite different. Jesus' fist is no longer clenched, and he has discarded his judicial robes. He opens wide his arms to any and all who would run to him like "little children" (Matt. 11:25): "Come to me, all who labor and are heavy laden, and I will give you rest. Take my yoke upon you, and learn from me, for I am gentle and lowly in heart, and you will find rest for your souls" (vv. 28–29). Here Jesus is certainly not calling us to cease from labor. He is not simply offering us peace of mind. Rather, he is offering us himself. He is offering us our true humanity, which is found only in submission and devotion to him.

In the "one Shepherd" who is both holy Judge and loving Savior, we find the embodiment of divine wisdom (Col. 2:3) and meaningful life (John 10:10). Come to him. Embrace him. For in doing so, you will find rest for your restless soul.

---

22. See Matt. 25:41–46; Rev. 2:23; 22:12; cf. Rom. 2:6–8; 2 Thess. 1:8; 2 Tim. 4:14; 1 Peter 1:17; Rev. 20:12–13, as listed in Bruce K. Waltke, *Book of Proverbs, Chapters 1–15*, New International Commentary on the Old Testament (Grand Rapids: Eerdmans, 2004), 131.

SELECT BIBLIOGRAPHY

Alter, Robert. *The Wisdom Books: Job, Proverbs, and Ecclesiastes: A Transla-tion with Commentary.* New York: W. W. Norton & Co., 2010.

Bartholomew, Craig G. *Ecclesiastes.* Baker Commentary on the Old Testa-ment Wisdom and Psalms. Grand Rapids: Baker Academic, 2009.

Beza, Theodore. *Ecclesiastes, or the Preacher: Solomon's Sermon Made to the People.* Cambridge: John Legatt, 1593.

Brown, William P. *Ecclesiastes.* Interpretation. Louisville, KY: Westminster John Knox, 2000.

Bullock, C. Hassell. *An Introduction to the Old Testament Poetic Books.* Chicago: Moody, 1988.

Christianson, Eric S. *Ecclesiastes through the Centuries.* Blackwell Bible Commentaries. Malden, MA: Blackwell, 2007.

Crenshaw, James L. *Ecclesiastes: A Commentary.* Old Testament Library. Philadelphia: Westminster John Knox, 1987.

Eaton, Michael A. *Ecclesiastes: An Introduction and Commentary.* Tyndale Old Testament Commentaries 16. Downers Grove, IL: InterVarsity Press, 1983.

Estes, Daniel J. *Handbook on the Wisdom Books and Psalms: Job, Psalms, Proverbs, Ecclesiastes, Song of Songs.* Grand Rapids: Baker Academic, 2005.

Fox, Michael V. *Ecclesiastes.* JPS Bible Commentary. Philadelphia: Jewish Publication Society, 2004.

———. *A Time to Tear Down and a Time to Build Up: A Rereading of Eccle-siastes.* Grand Rapids: Eerdmans, 1999.

Fredericks, Daniel C., and Daniel J. Estes. *Ecclesiastes and the Songs of Songs.* Apollos Old Testament Commentary 16. Downers Grove, IL: Inter-Varsity Press, 2010.

Garrett, Duane A. "Preaching Wisdom." In *Reclaiming the Prophetic Mantle: Preaching the Old Testament Faithfully*, edited by George L. Klein. Nashville: Broadman & Holman, 1992.

———. *Proverbs, Ecclesiastes, Song of Songs*. New American Commentary 14. Nashville: Broadman, 1993.

Goldsworthy, Graeme. *Gospel and Wisdom: Israel's Wisdom Literature in the Christian Life*. Biblical Classics Library. London: Paternoster, 1995.

Greidanus, Sidney. *Preaching Christ from Ecclesiastes: Foundations for Expository Sermons*. Grand Rapids: Eerdmans, 2010.

Hengstenberg, Ernst Wilhelm. *A Commentary on Ecclesiastes*. Eugene, OR: Wipf & Stock, 1998.

Hubbard, David. *Ecclesiastes, Song of Solomon*. Mastering the Old Testament 15B. Dallas: Word, 1991.

Jerome, *Commentary on Ecclesiastes*. Translated by Richard J. Goodrich and David J. D. Miller. Ancient Christian Writers 66. New York: Newman, 2012.

Johnston, Robert K. *Useless Beauty: Ecclesiastes through the Lens of Contemporary Film*. Grand Rapids: Baker Academic, 2004.

Kaiser, Walter C. *Ecclesiastes: Total Life*. Everyman's Bible Commentary. Chicago: Moody, 1979.

Kidner, Derek. *The Message of Ecclesiastes: A Time to Mourn, and a Time to Dance*. The Bible Speaks Today. Downers Grove, IL: InterVarsity Press, 1976.

———. *The Wisdom of Proverbs, Job and Ecclesiastes: An Introduction to Wisdom Literature*. Downers Grove, IL: InterVarsity Press, 1985.

Krüger, Thomas. *Qoheleth*. Edited by Klaus Baltzer. Translated by O. C. Dean Jr. Hermeneia. Minneapolis: Fortress, 2004.

Leithart, Peter J. *Solomon among the Postmoderns*. Grand Rapids: Brazos, 2008.

Leupold, H. C. *Exposition of Ecclesiastes*. Grand Rapids: Baker, 1952.

Limburg, James. *Encountering Ecclesiastes: A Book for Our Time*. Grand Rapids: Eerdmans, 2006.

Loader, J. A. *Ecclesiastes: A Practical Commentary*. Text and Interpretation. Grand Rapids: Eerdmans, 1986.

Longman, Tremper, III. *The Book of Ecclesiastes*. New International Commentary on the Old Testament. Grand Rapids: Eerdmans, 1998.

———. *Ecclesiastes & Song of Songs*. Cornerstone Biblical Commentary 6. Carol Stream, IL: Tyndale, 2006.

Luther, Martin. *Ecclesiastes, Song of Solomon, Last Words of David, 2 Samuel 23:1–7*. Vol. 15 of *Luther's Works*. St. Louis: Concordia, 1972.

Meyers, Jeffrey. *A Table in the Mist: Meditations on Ecclesiastes*. Through New Eyes Bible Commentary. Monroe, LA: Athanasius Press, 2006.

Moore, T. M. *Ecclesiastes: Ancient Wisdom When All Else Fails*. Downers Grove, IL: InterVarsity Press, 2001.

Murphy, Roland E. *Ecclesiastes*. Word Biblical Commentary 23A. Nashville: Thomas Nelson, 1992.

———. *The Tree of Life: An Exploration of Biblical Wisdom Literature*. Anchor Bible Reference Library. New York: Doubleday, 1990.

O'Donnell, Douglas Sean. *The Beginning and End of Wisdom: Preaching Christ from the First and Last Chapters of Proverbs, Ecclesiastes, and Job*. Wheaton, IL: Crossway, 2011.

———. "Ecclesiastes." In *The ESV Gospel Transformation Bible*. Edited by Bryan Chapell. Wheaton, IL: Crossway, 2013.

Ogden, Graham S. *Qoheleth*. 2nd ed. Readings: A New Biblical Commentary. Sheffield, UK: Sheffield Phoenix Press, 2007.

Provan, Iain. *Ecclesiastes/Song of Songs*. NIV Application Commentary. Grand Rapids: Zondervan, 2001.

Ryken, Leland. *Words of Delight: A Literary Introduction to the Bible*. 2nd ed. Grand Rapids: Baker, 1992.

Ryken, Philip Graham. *Ecclesiastes: Why Everything Matters*. Edited by R. Kent Hughes. Preaching the Word. Wheaton, IL: Crossway, 2010.

Schultz, Richard. "Ecclesiastes." In *Baker Commentary on the Bible*. Edited by Gary M. Burge and Andrew E. Hill. 2nd ed. Grand Rapids: Baker, 2011.

Seow, Choon-Leong. *Ecclesiastes*. Anchor Bible 18C. New York: Doubleday, 1997.

Webb, Barry G. *Five Festal Garments: Christian Reflections on the Song of Songs, Ruth, Lamentations, Ecclesiastes, and Esther*. New Studies in Biblical Theology 10. Downers Grove, IL: InterVarsity Press, 2000.

Whybray, R. N. *Ecclesiastes*. Old Testament Guides. Sheffield, UK: JSOT Press, 1989.

———. "Qoheleth, Preacher of Joy." *Journal for the Study of the Old Testament* 7, 23 (1982): 87–98.

Wilson, Douglas. *Joy at the End of the Tether: The Inscrutable Wisdom of Ecclesiastes.* Moscow, ID: Canon Press, 1999.

Wright, J. Robert, and Thomas C. Oden, eds. *Proverbs, Ecclesiastes, Song of Solomon.* Ancient Christian Commentary on Scripture 9. Downers Grove, IL: InterVarsity Press, 2005.

INDEX OF SCRIPTURE

Genesis
1–3—153
1:1—36, 202
1:7—46n5
1:11–12—46n5
1:16—46n5
1:25–26—46n5
1:27–30—86
1:28—179
1:29—46n5
1:31—46n5, 153
2—46
2:2–4—46n5
2:5–6—46n5
2:8—46n5
2:8–10—46n5
2:9—46n5
2:15–16—46n5, 64
2:15–17—55
2:15–25—179
2:16–17—46n5, 178
2:17—40
2:18—46n5, 94
2:20—154
2:23–25—49
3—56
3:4—55
3:5—154
3:14–19—9
3:17b–19—17
3:19—85n6
4:8—7, 56
4:12—94
5:1—56

5:5—56
5:8—56
5:11—56
5:14—56
5:17—56
5:20—56
5:24—55
5:27—56
5:31—56
6:11—154
9:29—56
11:4—154
12:5—52
13:2—52
19:17—49
19:26—50
22:12—217n12
25:8—56
28:20–22—116n15
38—153
39—153
50:16—56
50:26—56

Exodus
1:8—104
2:11–15—175n14
3:5—114
3:6—217n12
20:2–3—53
20:12—148

Leviticus
6:2–5—95

10:1–3—110
15:24—72n6
15:31—110
19:18—97, 124
27:1–25—116

Numbers
15:30–31—116

Deuteronomy
4:39—110
6:4—115
6:4–5—130
15:10—206
23:21—116
23:21–23—212
29:29—75, 171

Judges
9:52–55—194n19
11:29–40—118
16:19—174n14

Ruth
1:20—174

1 Samuel
1–2—116
6:19–20—110

2 Samuel
2:22–23—174n14
7—160
16:23—174n14
17:5–14—174n14

1 Kings
2:1—163
3:12—5n6, 34
3:13—52
4:22–23—47
4:29–34—5, 34

5:12—5n6
7:1—46n6
8:1—6
8:27—110
8:46—149
9:10—46n6
10—48
10:14–29—47
10:17—46n6
10:22—205
10:23–24—34
11—48
11:1a–3a—48
11:1–25—174n14
11:3—155
11:4—155
11:14–12:24—59

1 Chronicles
27:29–31—47
29:25—5n6

2 Chronicles
1:11–12—129
1:12—5n6
5:2—6
6:23—84n3
9:25–27—47
19:6–7—84n3

Nehemiah
13:26—155

Esther
1:12—191
2:15—191
2:17—191
3:13—191
4:11—191
5:1–3—191–92
6–10—192
7:10—63

8:15—179
9:12–15—192
10:3—192

Job
1–2—143
1:9—217n12
1:13–19—126
1:20—95
1:21—126, 129, 143
2:10—143
2:11–13—95
3:3—96
10:1—61
11:7–8—171
16:2—95
27:16–17—63
28:8—63
28:12—215
28:23—215
36:27–28—20
37:14—142
38–41—142
40:1–2—217n12
40:4—80
42—142
42:3–5—142
42:7–8—188

Psalms
2:11—217
4:2—84
8:5–8—86
9:8—83
16:11—54
18—51
23:4–5—66
23:5–6—181
31:15—75
36:1—118
45:7—179
49:12—87

49:17—127
50:1–4—111
50:16—117
55:23—148
73—19
73:17—96
75:2—83
76:11—118
80:1—214
90:12—139
110:1—160
116:3—180
116:15—165
132:2–5—116n15
143:2—149
144:4—8, 133
145:3—171

Proverbs
1:1—5
1:7—78
1:10–19—95
1:20–33—152
1:29—111n5
2:5—111n5
2:6—215
3:1–2—148
3:13–18—152–53
4:5–13—152–53
5:1–14—153
5:15–19—179n23
6:9–11—98
7:4—152–53
7:5—153
7:11—153
7:21—153
7:27—172
8:13—110n5
9:10—111n5
9:18—153
10:27—111n5
10:30—148

12:1—139
13:22—63
14:3—117
14:26—111n5
14:27a—111n5
14:29—140
14:30—97
15:1—187
15:13—159
15:16—110n5
15:28—117
15:33—111n5
16:6—110n5
17:10—139
17:15—84n3
19:23—111n5
20:9—149
20:25—117
21:1—161
22:1—134
22:22–23—83n3
23:17—110n5
24:23–25—83n3
24:28–29—83n3
25:11—73
25:15—187
26:18–19—45
30:21–22—186
31—72
31:10—155n16

Ecclesiastes
1–3—88
1–4—109
1:1—5, 17
1:1–2—3
1:1–11—56
1:1–4:16—112
1:2—8, 9, 18, 201
1:2–12:8—212
1:3—10, 15, 17, 18, 32
1:3–11—17, 27

1:4—20, 23n10, 201
1:4–8—19
1:4–11—18
1:5–7—37, 70
1:6—20n6
1:7—20
1:8—20
1:9—215
1:9–10—18
1:11—21, 40, 215
1:12—5, 32, 33, 34, 34n7
1:12–13—33
1:12–15—33
1:12–18—32, 40, 56
1:12–2:26—32, 61
1:13—32, 35, 36
1:13–14—33
1:13–15—33, 35
1:13–18—70
1:14—8, 32, 35, 36, 82
1:14–15—35
1:15—33, 36
1:16—32, 34
1:16–17—33
1:16–18—33, 38
1:17—32, 39, 40
1:17–18—31
1:18—33, 40, 201
2:1—8, 32, 42, 44, 51
2:1–2—50
2:1–3—44
2:1–11—26, 39, 43, 52, 64, 65, 66, 127
2:1–26—40
2:2—44, 45, 139
2:3—23, 32, 57
2:4—46n5, 51
2:4–7—45, 46, 51
2:4–8—57
2:5—46n5, 208
2:5–6—46n5
2:6—46n5
2:7—44

2:8—44, 47, 48, 155, 208
2:9–11—50
2:10—219
2:11—8, 32, 213
2:12—57
2:12–14—56, 57
2:12–26—56, 66
2:13—18n4, 57, 82
2:14—186, 215
2:14–17—58
2:14–18—23n10
2:15—8
2:17—8, 32, 58, 61
2:18—32, 61
2:18–19—18
2:18–23—59
2:19—8, 32
2:20—32, 61
2:20–21—23n10
2:21—8, 57
2:22—32
2:23—18, 32, 61
2:24—9n20, 32n2, 52, 64, 82
2:24–25—64, 109, 129
2:24–26—40, 55, 62, 66, 88, 177, 219
2:25—208
2:26—8, 32, 40, 63, 64, 217n12
3–4—82
3:1—70, 85
3:1–8—69–70, 74
3:1–15—79, 112, 144n15, 161
3:1–22—85n6
3:2—23n10, 71, 72n6
3:2–8—70
3:4—87
3:4–5—208
3:5—72n6
3:6—72n6
3:7—72n6
3:8—72n6, 208
3:9—17, 72, 73, 79
3:9–11—73, 74

3:9–15—73, 74
3:9–18—217n12
3:10—32n3, 73, 82, 109
3:10–15—73, 76
3:10–18—109n4
3:11—79, 84, 109, 143, 144
3:12—52, 73, 82, 88, 215
3:12–13—9n20, 74, 75, 129, 177, 219
3:13—18n4, 76, 79, 109, 219
3:14—9n19, 68, 73, 78, 79, 82, 109, 212, 215
3:14–15—77
3:15—78, 79, 82, 109, 212
3:16—83, 84n5, 94
3:16–17—81, 82, 85, 220n20
3:16–22—91, 112
3:17—82, 83, 84, 85n6, 86, 96, 109, 212
3:17–19—87
3:18—87
3:18–22—85
3:19—8, 85n6
3:19–20—86
3:19–21—86
3:19–22—23n10, 45n3
3:20—86
3:21—86, 188, 215
3:22—9n20, 18n4, 87, 89, 90, 97, 177, 201
4—95, 109
4:1—32n3, 82, 94
4:1–2—100n14
4:1–3—45n3, 51n14, 94, 97, 99, 100, 103
4:1–12—100n14
4:2–3—23n10, 96
4:3—100n14, 104
4:4—8, 18, 82
4:4–5—100n14
4:4–6—94, 97, 99, 103
4:5—23, 98, 186
4:5–6—97
4:6—100n14, 104, 208
4:7—82
4:7–12—94, 103

4:7–8—8, 99, 100, 101
4:8—99
4:9—99, 100, 104
4:9–10—93
4:9–12—100, 101
4:10—99, 100
4:10–12a—100n14
4:11—99, 101
4:12—99, 100n14, 101, 103, 213
4:13—186
4:13–16—103, 104
4:15—82
4:16—8, 23n10, 105
5:1—96, 107, 108, 109, 110, 113, 186
5:1–3—113–14
5:1–7—108, 109, 111, 118, 217
5:2—17, 73, 83, 110, 112
5:2–7—113
5:3—108, 112, 117, 186
5:4—108, 109, 112, 116, 117, 186
5:4–6—212
5:4–7—116
5:5—112, 116
5:6—110, 112, 117, 212
5:7—9n19, 79, 107, 108, 110, 112, 113, 117, 212
5:8—96, 124
5:8–9—96n6
5:8–12—122, 123, 124
5:8–17—129
5:8–6:9—121, 123
5:9—124
5:10—7, 8, 121, 123, 124
5:11—121, 125
5:12—18, 32n3, 121, 124, 126
5:13–14—197n2
5:13–17—122, 123, 126
5:15–16—23, 127
5:16—17
5:17—127, 128
5:18—9n20, 18n4, 129
5:18–19—120, 122, 219
5:18–20—88, 123, 129, 177, 217n12

5:18–6:2—109n4
5:19—129, 130
5:20—23n10, 122, 129
6:1—32n3
6:1–2—122, 217n12
6:1–6—126, 127, 129
6:2—8, 127
6:3—23n10, 128
6:3–6—122, 123
6:4—8, 128
6:5–6—128
6:7—23, 122
6:7–9—122, 123
6:8—17
6:9—8
6:10—133, 144
6:10–7:14—132
6:11—17, 133
6:11–12—133
6:12—7, 8, 23n10, 133, 188, 215
7:1—134, 137, 139n8
7:1–2—23n10
7:1–4—133–34, 138
7:1–12—133, 141
7:1–14—144n15
7:2—138, 139n8
7:4—137, 138, 139n8
7:5—138, 139, 186
7:5–12—137, 138, 139
7:6—8, 139n8, 186
7:7—140
7:7–10—139–40
7:8—139n8, 140
7:9—140, 186
7:10—140
7:11—139n8
7:11–12—18n4, 141, 208
7:12—57, 139n8, 149
7:13—26, 36, 142, 143
7:13–14—132, 133, 141, 217n12
7:14—23n10, 143
7:14–22—146

7:15—8, 32n3, 146, 148, 150, 152n12
7:15–18—146, 149, 151, 156
7:15–29—156
7:16—147, 148, 149
7:16–17—147
7:17—147, 150, 212
7:18—9n19, 79, 148, 212
7:19—57, 149
7:19–20—149
7:19–22—151
7:19–24—149, 151, 156
7:19–29—147
7:20—149, 150, 154
7:21—149
7:21–22—149, 150
7:22—150
7:23—57, 152n12
7:23–24—151
7:24—215
7:25—39n14, 150, 152
7:25–29—152, 156
7:26—150, 152, 153, 155
7:27—152n12, 153
7:27–28—154, 155
7:27–29—150
7:28—152, 154
7:29—38, 145, 152n12, 153, 154, 155, 156
8:1—57, 159, 170n5
8:1–15—158
8:1–17—158n1, 170n5
8:2—32n3, 160
8:2–4—158
8:2–15—160
8:3—158, 160
8:4—34n6, 158, 160
8:5—160, 162, 166, 212
8:5–6—212
8:7—188
8:8—23n10, 163, 166
8:9—158
8:10—8, 23n10, 158, 163, 164, 166
8:11—164

8:12—158, 164
8:12–13—9n19, 79, 164, 166, 212
8:12–17—109n4
8:13—23n10, 164
8:14—8, 164
8:15—9n20, 88, 165, 166, 177, 219
8:16—170n5
8:16–17—160, 169, 170, 170n5
8:16–9:1—217n12
8:16–9:12—171
8:17—26, 143, 157, 170n5, 215
9:1—32n3, 161, 170, 215
9:1–6—172
9:2—172
9:2–3—172
9:3—39, 172, 173
9:3–5—23n10
9:4—172
9:4–6—172, 173
9:5—170n5, 172, 215
9:5–6—173
9:6—173
9:7—178, 179, 180, 208
9:7–9—9n20, 88, 219
9:7–10—177
9:8—178, 208
9:8–9—178, 179
9:8–10—180
9:9—8, 155, 179, 208, 219
9:10—23n10, 172, 173, 180
9:11—7, 172, 193
9:11–12—172, 174
9:12—170, 172, 215
9:13–15—193
9:13–10:1—184
9:13–10:20—183, 191
9:14—193
9:15—57, 193, 194
9:16—57, 193
9:16–17—187
9:16–18—182
9:17—186, 193

10:1—184, 192, 193
10:2—184, 186
10:2-3—183n4
10:2-11—184
10:2-20—184
10:3—184, 186
10:4-7—186
10:5—32n3
10:8—184
10:8-9—185
10:8-11—185, 186
10:9—185
10:10—18n4
10:10-11—185
10:11—184
10:12—186, 187, 190, 191
10:12-20—187
10:13—188
10:13-15—187
10:14—188
10:15—188
10:16—189
10:16-19—188-89
10:16-20—188
10:17—189
10:18—189
10:19—7, 189
10:20—34n6, 184, 187, 188, 189, 190
11—32n3, 194
11:1—203, 205
11:1-2—204
11:1-6—197, 202-3
11:1-12:8—197
11:2—203, 205, 216
11:3—203, 207n22
11:4—204
11:5—26, 143, 203, 204, 216, 217n12
11:6—203, 204, 216
11:7—206, 207n22, 208
11:7-8—206
11:7-9—177
11:7-10—88, 197, 202, 219

11:8—8, 23n10, 206, 207n22
11:9—78, 207, 208, 212, 215, 217n12, 219, 220n20
11:9-10—206
11:9-12:1—196, 206
11:9-12:7—9n20, 220
11:10—8, 207
12—194
12:1—32n3, 36, 201, 206, 207, 216, 217n12
12:1-5—34n7
12:1-7—23n10, 198, 201, 206n21
12:1-8—197, 201
12:2—198, 199, 207n22, 208
12:3—7, 199
12:3-6—199
12:4—199
12:5—200
12:6—200, 201
12:7—136, 173, 199, 217n12
12:8—8, 201, 211
12:8-14—214n10
12:9-10—212
12:9-14—211, 212
12:10—213
12:11—214
12:11-12—214
12:12—214, 216
12:13—9n19, 11, 64, 79, 202, 216, 220n19
12:13-14—112, 210, 212, 222
12:14—78, 86, 136, 208, 219, 219n17, 220, 222

Song of Songs
1:1—5
7:6-7—48n11

Isaiah
5:22-23—84n3
6:1—110
6:3—110
6:5—79
9:6—195
9:7—195

13:9–10—198n4
22:13—25
29:13—108
29:14—40
40:11—214
45:7—143
46:10—77
53:3—143
55:9—151
57:15—119

Jeremiah
2:13—43
20:14—61
20:18—96
22:17—95
29:7—162

Lamentations
3:38—143

Ezekiel
21:7–8—198n4
22:1–29—95
22:6–7—95
22:7—95
22:12—95
22:29—95
30:3—198n4
34:23—214
37:24—214

Daniel
2:21—77
7:12—77

Hosea
11:9—110

Joel
2:2—198n4
2:10—198n4

Amos
4:1—95
5:12—83n3
5:18—198n4
5:20—198n4

Micah
2:1–2—95
7:3—84n3

Habakkuk
2:3—218

Zephaniah
1:15—198n4

Malachi
1:14—108

Matthew
4:1–11—53
5:6—219
6:7—114
6:9—17, 114
6:12–13—115
6:19–33—130
6:24—130
6:33—26
7:13–14—220
7:21–23—208
7:24—138
7:26—138
8–9—27n16
9:10–15—67
9:35–36—97
10:16—161
10:28—79
10:29—76
10:37—130
10:42—28
11—222
11:2—27n16

11:5—27n16

11:19—27n16

11:20–24—222

11:22—207

11:24—207

11:25—222

11:25–26—171

11:28–29—222

11:28–30—27n16

12:6—115

12:34—191

12:36—207

12:36–37—150

12:41—207

12:42—207

13:22—128, 130

13:36—73

14:14–21—67

15:32–38—67

16:15—132

16:21–23—53

18:18–20—102

19:3–6—49

19:19—124

19:22–24—130

20:17–18—212

21:13—115

21:28–30—118

22:17—161

22:21—161

22:30—179

22:36—105, 202

22:37—50, 130, 202

22:37–39—105

22:38—202

22:39—50, 97, 202

23:16–22—117

23:38—115

24:2—115

24:29—198n4

25—29

25:23—54, 206

25:26—205

25:34–40—97

25:40—29

25:41–46—84n4, 222n22

26—29

26:10–13—29

26:24—96

26:26–29—67

26:35—117

26:61—115

26:70—117

26:72—117

26:74—117

27:37—195

27:40—115

27:46—61, 106

27:51—115

28:18–20—216

Mark

1:14—162

1:15—75

6:3—27

6:7—102

7:20–23—150

8:31—75

8:36—54, 132

10:17–22—100

10:18—83

11:15—95

12:30—130

13:24–25—198n4

Luke

2:49—27

5:8—79

6:25—139

6:39—101

10:27—130

10:30—101

10:42—129

12:2–3—190

12:15—65, 130
12:16–20—130
12:16b–21—65
12:20—205
12:21—130, 205
12:31—130
18:10–12—114
18:13—114
19:8—99
19:26—63
19:27—63
19:45–46—97
23:42–43—28
24:44—11

John
2:1–11—67
2:13–17—108
3:8—204
4:13–14—43
4:23–24—115
4:34—27
5:22—84n4
5:36—27
5:39—11
6:27—131
6:35—211
6:48—211
6:48–51—180
6:56—194n21
7:30—75
9:4—27
10:10—222
10:11—215
10:16—214
10:28—156
10:32ff—27
11:25—90, 136
11:35—95
13:1—75
14:1–3—90
14:6—151

15:11—143
17:4—27
19:30—27

Acts
1:7—75
2:46–47—178
4—161
5:1–11—117
5:29—161
7:22—175n14
17:30–31—84n4
26:13–14—215

Romans
1:1—162
1:5—217
1:16–17—218
2:6–8—222n22
2:16—208
3:9–10—150
3:10—149
3:18—118
3:23—149
4–11—76
5:6—75
5:6–8—150
6:23—173, 180
8:20—37
8:21—37
8:28—75, 143
11:33—80, 151
11:36—80
12:1—76
13:4—162
13:13—211
16:26—217

1 Corinthians
1–2—41
1:18—195
1:18–24—41

1:19—40
1:23—195
1:30—41, 195
2:2—41
2:7—41
3:16—115
3:9–14—29
4:4–5—84n4
5:7–8—165
8:3—28
10:31—66
11:21—108
11:26—67
12:14—102
12:21—102
13:12—77, 142
15:26—136
15:32—25, 62
15:54—67
16:22—130

2 Corinthians
1:3—95
4:16–18—136
5:10—222
5:21—150
7:6—102
8:9—205
9:6—206

Galatians
3:11—218
3:13—13
4:4—75
4:6–9—29
5:22—140

Ephesians
2:13–22—115
2:19–22—115
4:28—206
5:22—28

6:7—28
6:7–8—161

Philippians
1:21—137
1:21–23—90
2:3—53
2:4—205
2:5—205
2:6–8—205
2:7–8—53
2:12—29, 79
2:13—29
3:1—53
4:4—53, 130, 181
4:10—53
4:10–13—130

Colossians
1:13–20—205
2:3—222
3:5—130
3:17—64
3:22—161
3:23—180
3:24—161
4:3—192
4:5—192
4:6—192

1 Thessalonians
5:16—179
5:18—179

2 Thessalonians
1:8—222n22
3:10–12—99

1 Timothy
1:15—150
2:1–6—162
4:4–5—64

6:3—130
6:6—99
6:6–8—65
6:7—65, 127
6:10—131
6:17—131

2 Timothy
1:8—103
1:10—90
2:22—208
3:5—110
3:15—11
3:16—215
4:2—103
4:9—103
4:9–22—103
4:11—103
4:12–13—103
4:14—222n22
4:21—103

Titus
3:1–2—162

Hebrews
4:1—79
4:15—150
7:23–28—115
10:24–25—102
10:38—218
11:5—55
11:6—64n13
11:10—162
12:2—53
12:28—79, 110
13:5—131
13:8—75

James
1:2—166
1:5–6—159

1:19—115
1:27—97
2:2–4—107
3:5–6—149n8
4:13—188
4:13–15—188
4:14—175

1 Peter
1:1—162
1:17—222n22
2:5—115
2:13–14—162
2:17—162
2:21—84
2:22–23—84
4:5—84n4

2 Peter
3:9—86
3:12—165

1 John
2:16—53

Revelation
1:5—119
1:8—75
1:14–16—119
2:23—222n22
6:10—84
7:9—179
13—161
18—161
19:1–3–63–64
19:5–6—181
20:12–13—222n22
21:3–4—72
21:6—75
22—37
22:12—222n22
22:13—75

Index of Subjects and Names

Abel, 56, 67, 94

above the sun, 83, 183

abundance, 12, 48n8

accidents, 185

adam, 17

Adam

    devolution of, 152–55

    sin of, 17, 36–37, 39, 55–56, 94

adultery, 49, 150

affliction, 97

afterlife, 90, 136

alcohol, 45

allegory, 65n14

alliteration, 5

Allen, Woody, 13, 37, 49, 59

alpha and *omega*, 78

Alter, Robert, 8n16, 20n6

ambition, 23

Ambrose, 213–14

anger, 211

Annie Hall (film), 37

antinomianism, 148

antithetical parallelism, 5, 71, 121, 139n8

apocalyptic imagery, 198

arrogance, 148

asceticism, 179

Asperger syndrome, 31

assonance, 5, 87, 138–39

Augustine, 74, 115, 165n14, 210–11

authority, submission to, 160–63

autonomy, 64, 216

babbling, vanity of, 133

Babette's Feast (Dinesen), 167–68

Beatitudes, 138

Beatles, 103–4

Beckett, Samuel, 208–9

behold, 50

Bernard of Clairvaux, 155

"Be Thou My Vision" (hymn), 130

"better than" comparisons, 133, 137–38, 193

Beza, Theodore, 179n24

black sky, 198–99

Bollhagen, James, 5n8

Boston, Thomas, 142

Bradbury, Ray, 164

Bradstreet, Anne, 200n9

Brahms, Johannes, 45

Brave New World (Huxley), 221

bread, 178

breast, 48–49

breath, 8

Breath (Beckett), 208–9

Bridges, Matthew, 74n10

Brown, Stephen, 183n4

Bunyan, John, 50

Burden, Daniel, 182–83

Burns, Robert, 51

Byrds, 69

Caesar, 161–62

Cain, 94

Calvin, John, 151
Calvin and Hobbes (comic strip), 38,
    175–76
Calvinism, 142
Camus, Albert, 218
Canada, Geoffrey, 144
Canterbury Tales (Chaucer), 120–21
carpe diem, 62
Carr, Jimmy, 136
celebration, 165
celebrities, 21–22
Chapel, Bryan, 147
Chapman, Alister, 134
Chaucer, Geoffrey, 120–21
Chesterton, G. K., 151
chiasm, 122, 129
children of man, 36–37, 48n9, 216
Childs, Brevard, 5n8
Christian life, 165–66
Christians, as fools, 41
Christianson, Eric S., 45n3
Christmas Carol (Dickens), 81
church, 6, 36–37
    as community, 102–3
    entertainment in, 107
Churchill, Winston, 158
Collins, Billy, 15, 89
common grace, 51
common sense, 184, 186
community, 102–3
companionship, 100–103
concubines, 48–49
constructive criticism, 139
consumer Christianity, 217
contentment, 12, 65, 98–99
control, 76, 78
coveting, 153
crookedness, 142–43, 151–52
cross, 12, 150–51, 195
    as folly, 41
culture of death, 135
curse, 9, 17–18, 38, 215

Daniel, 161
Dante, 215–16
dark days, 206, 209
darkness, 56–57, 128, 216
David, 163
Davis, Ellen F., 208n25
Day of Atonement, 180
day of judgment, 198, 207–8, 222
dead flies, 192–93
Dead Sea, 20
death, 10, 23, 55–56, 58, 67, 134–37, 180,
    200, 216
    certainty of, 172–73
    as "dark days", 206n21, 208
    preoccupation with, 91
    reality of, 71
    sadness of, 173–74
    suddenness of, 174–75
delight, in God's gifts, 61–62
dependence, 221–22
depravity, 150
depression, 220–21
despair, 156, 220
devolved Adam, 152–55
Dickens, Charles, 43, 62, 81
Dinesen, Isak, 167–68
disgust, 60–62
disillusionment, 50
divine time, 73
divorce, 49
Donne, John, 23n11, 48, 163, 197n2
drinking, 10, 65n14
drug addiction, 153
drunkenness, 211

eating, 10, 65n14, 128
Eaton, Michael, 10, 57
Ecclesiastes, 50
    authorship of, 5–6
    end of, 220–22
    as an enigma, 7
    and Feast of Tabernacles, 87

through the lens of Christ, 11–12
unified message of, 4, 6–11, 12
Edwards, Jonathan, 213
Eichrodt, Walther, 79n14
"Eleanor Rigby" (song), 103–4
Elohim, 36, 217n12
enjoyment, 129–30, 175–80, 209
    under God, 206–8
Enns, Peter, 183
envy, 97–99
Erasmus, 87
Erdrich, Louise, 196
escapism, 23, 24, 38–39
eschatological hope, 220
Estes, Daniel J., 217n12
Esther, 191–92
eternity, in our hearts, 74
evil days, 197–98, 209
evildoing, 150
excess, 189

faith, 144, 220
    and fear, 217–18
fall, 40
fallen world, 17
fame, 23, 42
fatalism, 142
"fearless generosity", 205, 213
fear of God, 9, 10–11, 77, 110, 118–19,
    163–65, 216–17
feasting, 177–79
feasts, 67
felt needs, 109
final judgment, 63, 165. *See also* judgment
fleetingness, 201
folly, 39–40, 148, 183–84
    and darkness, 56–57
    of wisdom of world, 41
food, appetite for, 123
fool, 114, 137, 184–86
fornication, 150
Fort Custer Maze (Iowa), 157–58, 160

Fowler, Gene, 88
Fox, Michael V., 7n13, 51n15, 102, 185n6,
    199n7, 208n25
"frail children of dust", 92, 96
frame narrator, 211
Fredericks, Daniel, 5n8, 6n10, 7, 8n16, 21,
    36, 49n12, 61, 74n10, 84n6, 88, 104,
    152, 166, 177, 201, 212
freedom, 217
funeral, 133–34, 136
futility, 16
future, 188

gambling, 153
garden, 45–46, 52
Garrett, Duanne, 5n8, 6n10, 7n13, 34n7,
    49n13, 58
generosity, 204–5, 209, 213
Gieser, Marge, 12
giving. *See* generosity
God
    character and promises of, 84
    in Ecclesiastes, 36
    as the Gift-Giver, 64–65
    as greatest good, 144
    hears and speaks, 110
    in heaven, 112
    holiness of, 110
    and providence, 77–78
    as source of wisdom, 215
    sovereignty of, 75–77, 129, 142, 176
    and time, 73–75, 80
    transcendence of, 87, 108–9
gold, 47–48
good name, 134
Good Samaritan, 97, 101
Gordis, Robert, 66n15
gossip, 153
Gottfried, Gilbert, 190n14
government, 160–63, 183, 189–90
grace, 168
gratitude, 168

greed, 123, 130–31
Greidanus, Sidney, 10, 71, 122n2, 149n7, 183–84n4, 189n12

Halloween, 91
happiness, 75–76, 208, 218–19
Hawking, Stephen, 35
heart, 110, 137
heaven, 203
hebel, 7–8, 124
Hebrew poetry, 33
hedonism, 23, 25–26, 42–54, 216
hell, 106, 203
Hemingway, Ernest, 87
Hengstenberg, Ernst, 206n20
Henley, William Ernest, 68–69
Herbert, George, 211
hoarding, 126
holiness, 75–76, 114, 186, 208
homosexuality, 49
hope, 37, 85
hopelessness, 85
Horace, 123
house of God, 109, 113
Hubbard, David, 52, 203
Hughes, Kent, 103
Huxley, Aldous, 221
hyperbole, 5
hypocrisy, 108, 190

idleness, 204
idolatry, 43, 49–50, 52–53
idols, 143
image of God, 201
immorality, 83
impatience, 140
incarnation, 106
independence, 217
individualism, 102
indulgence, 208

industriousness, 18n4, 204–6
inheritors, ill-deserved, 59–60
injustice, 37, 82–84, 146–48
inverted parallelism, 5, 71
"Invictus" (Henley), 68–69
irony, 219
isolation, 94–95, 99–103, 106
Israel, in wilderness, 129

Jagger, Mick, 130
jealousy, 211
Jerome, 6n11, 8n15, 20–21, 65n14, 192, 199
Jesus
    abolished death, 90
    as bread of life, 180, 211
    as divine resolution, 195
    forsaken, 106
    justified wisdom, 27n16
    as Lord, 131, 161
    made into our own image, 118
    resurrection of, 13
    satiates the soul, 53
    as shepherd, 222
    transforms world from hopelessness
        to beauty, 27
    work of, 27–28
Job, 19, 62, 142–43, 188
joy, 10, 12, 54, 62, 64–65, 85, 88–89, 128,
    165, 179, 218–19, 220
judgment, 84, 212, 219–20. *See also* day of
    judgment; final judgment
justice, 63, 83–84
justification by faith, 178

Kaiser, Walter C., 5n8, 46n6, 174n14
keeping God's commandments, 202
Keller, Timothy J., 48n8, 126
Kidner, Derek, 11, 45
king, 34
kingdom, 29

Klein, A. M., 196
Krüger, Thomas, 51n14, 84n5
Kushner, Harold, 52

lack of knowledge, 204–5
Lady Folly, 152–53, 155
Lady Justitia, 83
Lady Wisdom, 152
Last Supper, 28, 66–67
laughter, 45, 52
law of end stress, 113
Lazarus, 90
Lee, Peggy, 25
Lennon, John, 21–22
Levering, Brandon, 146, 158n1
Lewis, C. S., 111
life
    in fallen world, 71
    as short-lived, 171
light, 56–57
Lion, the Witch, and the Wardrobe, The
    (Lewis), 111
listening, 112–16, 118–19
living waters, 43, 211
loneliness, 99, 104
Longman, Tremper, III, 5n9, 49n13
Lord's Supper, 28, 67, 165n14
love
    for God, 50, 105, 202
    of money, 121–31
    for neighbor, 50, 105, 124, 202
Love and Death (film), 13
Lucas, Dick, 166
lust, 211
Luther, Martin, xiii, 57n3, 77, 87, 115, 127,
    143, 166, 179, 183, 190–91

Maclaren, Alexander, 113
madness, 39
marriage, 101, 179

marriage of the Lamb, 181
Masoretes, celebrations of, 88
maze, 157–58
meaninglessness, 12, 221
Melville, Herman, 61, 196–97
metaphors, 5
Meyers, Jeffrey, 10, 100
Michaelson, Ingrid, 199
Michel, D., 84n5
Milton, John, 90–91
minor problems, 18
moderation, 189
modernism, 209
Moffatt, James, 139
money, 47, 121–31, 141
monotony, 20
Moody, D. L., 115
Mordecai, 191–92
mortality, and joy, 89–92
mouth of fools, 114
Muggeridge, Malcolm, 42–43
Murphy, Roland E., 58n4, 88n14e
music, 44
Myth of Sisyphus, 218

neighbor, 97–98
"new and improved", 18
new covenant, 28, 115
new life, 28
new work, of Jesus, 27
nihilism, 23–25
Nilsson, Harry, 99n12
Nine Inch Nails, 50
Noah, 56
nonexistence, 96
nostalgia, 140
not knowing, 170–71

oath, to a king, 160–61
obedient trust, 11

obeying God's commands, 212, 216–17
Ogden, Graham S., 72n5, 100n14
ointment, 192–93
old age, 202, 206n21, 208
Oliver, Mary, 15–16, 89
"One" (song), 99n12
onomatopoeia, 138–39
oppression, 37, 94–97, 140
optimism, 62

paradise lost, 72
parallelism, 5, 70–71, 121–22, 139n8, 147, 188
paronomasia, 139n8
Pascal, Blaise, 156
patience, 140
Paul, on companionship, 102–3
peace, 73
Peanuts (cartoon), 174
Percy, Walker, 135–36
pessimism, 220
Peterson, Eugene, 178
Pharisee and tax collector, parable of, 114
Pharisees, 190
Pilgrim's Progress (Bunyan), 50
Piper, John, 109
Plato, 188
pleasure, 10, 43–50
pleasure paradox, 51–52
poetry, 5, 15, 33, 69–71
politics, 157–58
pornography, 49, 153
postmodernism, 209
power, 10, 53, 94–95, 158, 160, 163
Powers of Ten (video), 182
"Preacher", 5
pride, 11, 156
Provan, Iain, 109n2
proverbs, 5, 203
providence, 74n10, 77–78

Qoheleth, 5–6
quietness, 93–94, 98, 113, 192

Rashi, 59
reading Ecclesiastes, 3–4
realism, 149
reality, 85–87
rebuke, 139
rejoicing, 179, 181, 206–7
Rembrandt (film), 200–201
remembering, 202, 206–7
remembrance, 21–23
repentance, 87–88
repetitiveness, of activities, 19
resolution, involves God, 194–95
rest, 128, 222
restlessness, 210–11
Revelation (book), 164–65
revelation, sufficiency of, 214
revering God, 212
riches, 121–31
rich fool, parable of, 65–66
righteous, 149
righteousness, 148
Rossetti, Christina, 53
royal autobiography, 5n9
ruler, 186
Ryken, Philip, 6, 12, 62, 142, 206, 208–9

sacrifices, offered in silence, 114–15
Sandys, George, 189
Sartre, Jean-Paul, 25
Satan, 55–56
satisfaction, 124–25
Schuller, Robert, 61
Schultz, Richard, 5n8, 212
Schwienhorst-Schönberger, L., 84n5
sea, 20
secret deed, 220
secular, 45
seeing, 82
self, 109n2
self-centeredness, 51
self-control, 189
self-indulgence, 51, 189

selfishness, 51–52
Self-Made Man (sculpture), 46
sensual pleasures, 65n14
Seow, Choon-Leong, 144n14, 189n12, 219n17
Sermon on the Mount, 138, 208
serpent, 55
servants, 44
seven (number), 70
sexual immorality, 49, 210
Shakespeare, William, 83, 201
shalom, 73
Shea, George Beverly, 53
sheol, 180
shepherd, 214–15, 222
silence, 114–16
similes, 5
Simpsons (TV sitcom), 50
sin, 147, 216
sinner, 149–51
slaves, 44
sloth, 98, 153, 204
Smith, Henry, 179n24
snake's bite, 184–86
solitude, 100
Solomon
    as author of Ecclesiastes, 5–6
    house of, 46n6
    wealth of, 46–48
    wisdom of, 34
song of fools, 138
Song of Songs, 179
sorrow, 38, 40
speaking, 116–19
Spektor, Regina, 135
sports, 24
stillborn child, 128
Sting (singer), 199
storms, 76–77
suffering, 37
suicide, 126
sun, 10, 20, 198. *See also* under the sun

synonymous parallelism, 5, 71, 121, 139n8, 147
synthetic parallelism, 5,v 71, 122, 139n8

table, 66–67
Talbot, Mark, 3
Tammet, Daniel, 31–32, 68
tapestry on a loom, 74
technology, 18
temple consecration, 6
thief on the cross, 28
threefold cord, 101–2
time, 23, 70, 72–73, 78, 80
Titanic (movie), 79
Tocqueville, Alexis de, 48n8
toil, 17–18, 26, 32, 72. *See also* work
Tolstoy, Leo, 24
tongue, 150, 187–88
topical sermons, 108–9
tornado, 36
trembling trust, 9, 78–79, 110, 143, 148, 217
Trueman, Carl, 135, 182
"Turn! Turn! Turn!" (song), 69–70
Twain, Mark, 145–46
Twitter, 190–91
two, 100

under the sun, 10, 17, 27, 29, 37, 82, 95, 219
unresolved seventh, 194
unrighteousness, 82–84
Updike, John, 87

vanity, 7–9, 54, 171–72, 201, 211
Vanity Fair, 50
vanity mirror, 201
"vanity of vanities", 7, 9, 18, 201, 211
vexation, removing of, 206–7
vineyards, 46, 52
Voltaire, 26
vow, 116–18
Vulgate, 6n11

Waiting for "Superman" (documentary), 144
Watson, Richard, 169–70
Watterson, Bill, 38
wealth, 123, 125
weariness, 12, 20
Webb, Barry G., 9n18
weeping and mourning, 87
Wells, David, 159
Wesley, John, 52, 206
Westminster Confession of Faith, 3n1, 76
Westminster Shorter Catechism, 51, 217
Whybray, R. N., 62, 88n14
wickedness, 82–85, 148, 150, 153
wife, 178–79
Wilberforce, William, 97
Wilson, Douglas, 74
wind, 20, 35
wine, 45, 52, 177–78
wisdom, 4, 10, 148, 159–60, 183–84
    cannot change reality, 35–37
    cannot protect from death, 58
    as elusive and incomprehensible, 151
    and folly, 137–41
    and light, 56–57

no protection from ill-deserved
    inheritors, 59–60
path of, 141
sufficiency of, 214–15
through autobiographical reflection,
    32–33
vulnerability of, 170
wisdom literature, 4–6, 12, 19
"wisdom of the wise", 40
Wolfe, Thomas, 197
Wolterstorff, Nicholas, 88
wordplays, 5
words of delight, 213
work, 10, 20, 72, 179–80. *See also* toil
    adds nothing new to this world, 18–19
    not in vain, 28–29
working hard, 202–6, 209
worldly wisdom, 59
worship, 107–8, 110
writing, 88

Yahweh, 36, 217n12
Yanagi, Yukinori, 127
Yolen, Jane, 88, 200
youth, 201–2

AVAILABLE IN THE REFORMED
EXPOSITORY COMMENTARY SERIES

1 Samuel, by Richard D. Phillips
1 Kings, by Philip Graham Ryken
Esther & Ruth, by Iain M. Duguid
Ecclesiastes, by Douglas Sean O'Donnell
Daniel, by Iain M. Duguid
Jonah & Micah, by Richard D. Phillips
Zechariah, by Richard D. Phillips
The Incarnation in the Gospels, by Daniel M. Doriani,
Philip Graham Ryken, and Richard D. Phillips
Matthew, by Daniel M. Doriani
Luke, by Philip Graham Ryken
John, by Richard D. Phillips
Acts, by Derek W. H. Thomas
Galatians, by Philip Graham Ryken
Ephesians, by Bryan Chapell
Philippians, by Dennis E. Johnson
1 Timothy, by Philip Graham Ryken
Hebrews, by Richard D. Phillips
James, by Daniel M. Doriani
1 Peter, by Daniel M. Doriani

FORTHCOMING

1–3 John, by Douglas Sean O'Donnell